IN THE SHADOW OF THE POLE

IN THE SHADOW OF THE POLE

AN EARLY HISTORY OF ARCTIC EXPEDITIONS, 1871–1912

S.L. OSBORNE

DUNDURN
TORONTO

Project editors: Cheryl Hawley and Allison Hirst
Editor: Jenny Govier
Design: Jesse Hooper
Printer: Webcom

Library and Archives Canada Cataloguing in Publication

Osborne, S. L., author
    In the shadow of the pole : an early history of Arctic expeditions, 1871-1912 / S.L. Osborne.

Includes bibliographical references and index.
Issued in print and electronic formats.
ISBN 978-1-4597-1785-5 (pbk.).--ISBN 978-1-4597-1786-2 (pdf).--ISBN 978-1-4597-1787-9 (epub)

    1. Arctic regions--Discovery and exploration--Canadian--History--19th century. 2. Arctic regions--Discovery and exploration--Canadian--History--20th century. 3. Explorers--Canada--History--19th century. 4. Explorers--Canada--History--20th century. I. Title.

G630.C3O82 2013   910.09163'2   C2013-906066-9
                                      C2013-906067-7

1 2 3 4 5   17 16 15 14 13

We acknowledge the support of the **Canada Council for the Arts** and the **Ontario Arts Council** for our publishing program. We also acknowledge the financial support of the **Government of Canada** through the **Canada Book Fund** and **Livres Canada Books,** and the **Government of Ontario** through the **Ontario Book Publishing Tax Credit** and the **Ontario Media Development Corporation.**

Care has been taken to trace the ownership of copyright material used in this book. The author and the publisher welcome any information enabling them to rectify any references or credits in subsequent editions.

J. Kirk Howard, President

The publisher is not responsible for websites or their content unless they are owned by the publisher.

Printed and bound in Canada.

VISIT US AT
Dundurn.com | @dundurnpress | Facebook.com/dundurnpress | Pinterest.com/dundurnpress

Dundurn	Gazelle Book Services Limited	Dundurn
3 Church Street, Suite 500	White Cross Mills	2250 Military Road
Toronto, Ontario, Canada	High Town, Lancaster, England	Tonawanda, NY
M5E 1M2	L41 4XS	U.S.A. 14150

Christmas 2013

Dad,

I hope there is something
that is real to you in this
book!

To my anchors,
Cathy and Janet

Love,

Kathy xo

These islands and these forbidding seas which surround them have a history....
Suffice it to say that deeds have been done here as great in valour as any that
led to the conquest of Mexico, the acquisition of Peru, or the opening up of the
better known portions of Canada; but, unlike the captains and conquerors
to the south, these explorers have come and gone, leaving behind them little
trace of their passage. They pillaged no cities, they robbed no temples, and the
only treasure that they brought back was an incomparable record of human
courage and endurance.

George P. Mackenzie, Commander
Eastern Arctic Patrols 1925–29
Address to the Canadian Club
Ottawa, November 27, 1926

TABLE OF CONTENTS

MAPS

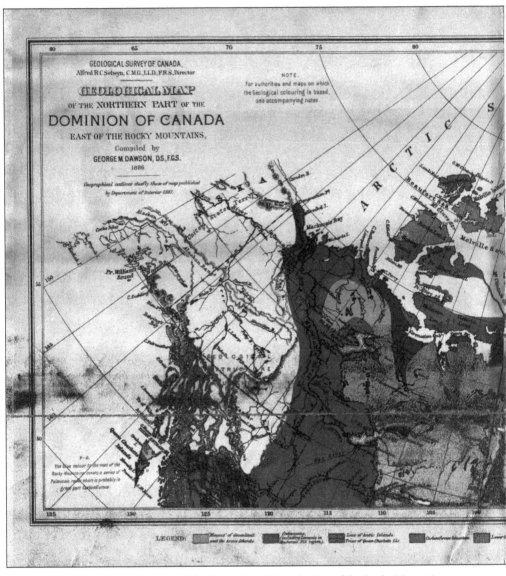

Geological Map of the Northern Part of the Dominion of Canada, East of the Rocky Mountains, Compiled by George M. Dawson, 1886.

This map shows the limited knowledge of the Arctic islands in the mid-1880s, with the majority of the archipelago not being accurately mapped. In particular, large blank areas exist where Ellesmere and other northern islands, such as Axel Heiberg, had not yet been explored.

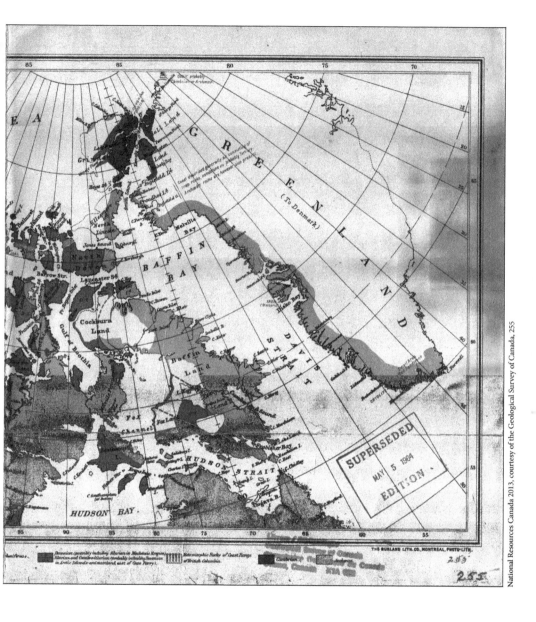

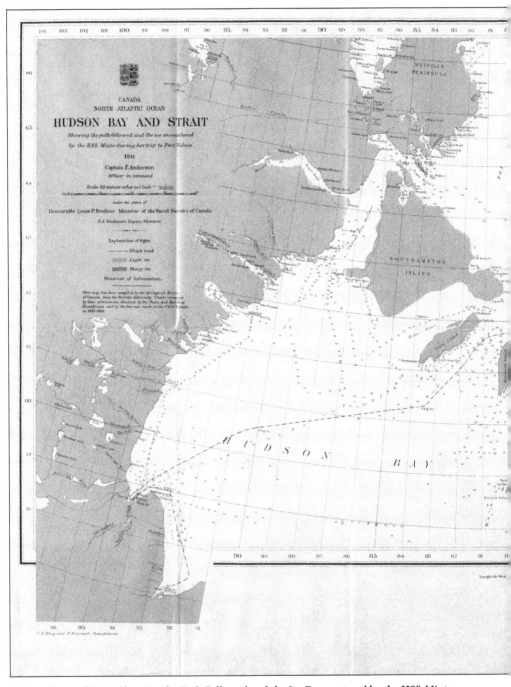

Hudson Bay and Strait Showing the Path Followed and the Ice Encountered by the HSS *Minto* During Her Trip to Port Nelson, 1911.

This map of Hudson Bay and Strait details the locations named by commanders Gordon, Wakeham, Low, and Moodie. Many of these places have since been renamed to reflect the cultures of the people who live there.

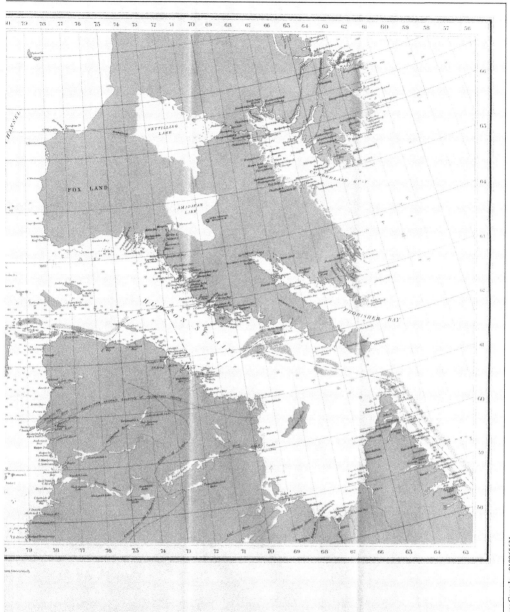

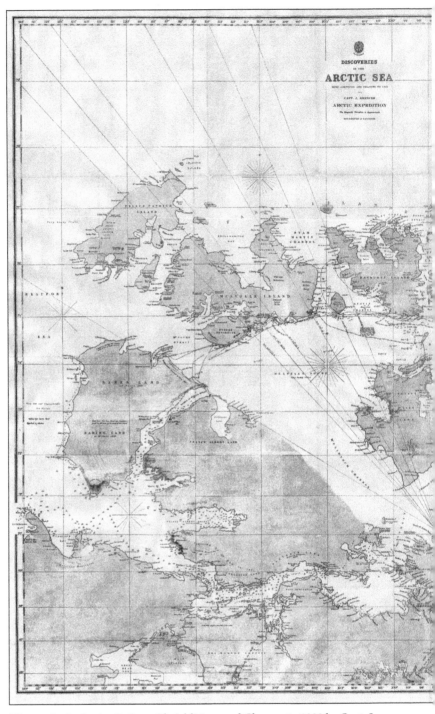

Discoveries in the Arctic Sea with Additions and Changes to 1909 by Capt. J. Bernier, Arctic Expedition.

Captain Bernier's 1906–07 and 1908–09 High Arctic expeditions are highlighted on this more detailed map. However, almost the entire west side of Baffin Island remains unsurveyed here. It was later mapped by J.T.E. Lavoie, meteorologist and surveyor on Bernier's 1910–11 expedition.

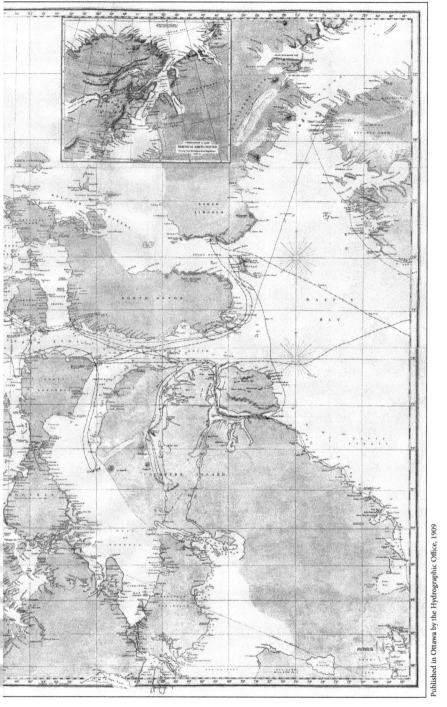

Published in Ottawa by the Hydrographic Office, 1909

INTRODUCTION

The invisible grid lines that horizontally circle the Earth are known as lines of latitude. Latitude is measured in degrees and minutes. Each degree is divided into sixty minutes, with approximately sixty-nine miles between each parallel degree. Each minute is, therefore, 1.15 miles.

This bit of information is of absolutely no interest to the general population. However, for a good part of the nineteenth century, countries such as Great Britain and the United States were preoccupied with gaining the highest degree of latitude. Each minute of latitude that an explorer attained closer to that elusive point at 90°N — the North Pole — garnered heaps of praise, incredible financial remuneration, and unbounded glory for his homeland.

Fame and glory come with a heavy price tag, though. In their bid for the Pole, countries and private individuals spent the equivalent then of what has been spent on the space program. Expeditions were outfitted and lives wagered in order to notch another degree in that country's exploration belt. The number of lives lost in striving for the prize of 90°N is both staggering and appalling.

Sir John Franklin, undoubtedly, holds the record for lives tragically lost for the sake of Arctic exploration. In 1845, the British Admiralty gave Franklin command of an expedition with two ships, the *Erebus* and the *Terror*. His orders were to find the Northwest Passage — the other coveted Arctic prize. Franklin and his 128 men sailed into Lancaster Sound, north of Baffin Island, and were never seen again by their countrymen.

Receiving no word of the expedition by 1847, the British government, and later Franklin's wife, Lady Jane, spared no expense in sending expeditions to find the missing men. They combed the Arctic, searching as many of the snow- and ice-covered islands and channels as was humanly possible for men unaccustomed to, and ill-prepared for, living in an environment where the mercury in the thermometer remains below zero degrees for the majority of the year. Finally, in 1859, Leopold M'Clintock's expedition returned to England with evidence of the death of Franklin and his crew.

In those twelve years of searching for Franklin, thirty-five ships and five overland expeditions explored the archipelago, greatly increasing the knowledge of the Arctic frontier. The irony of Franklin's disappearance is that his search parties mapped more of the Arctic than Franklin could have done in his lifetime. When the search was over, only the most northern islands remained to be explored.

For over a decade after M'Clintock's return, Britain ceased its Arctic explorations. However, American interest in the Arctic had been kindled by its participation in the search for Franklin. By 1870, exploring the High Arctic with the intent of claiming the North Pole held great appeal. The idea of an American being first to the Pole offered possibilities of glory, international fame, and recognition.

Yet Canada, the country directly south of the Arctic region, had no interest in exploring it. While the first United States North Pole Expedition was readying for departure in 1871, Canada was celebrating its fourth birthday. It was a new nation whose physical size had quadrupled the summer before when, on June 23, 1870, an imperial order-in-council transferred the two territories controlled by the Hudson's Bay Company to the Dominion of Canada for £300,000. Known as Rupert's Land and the North-Western Territory, the addition of these territories expanded the new country's boundaries to the west coast, east to Hudson Bay, and as far north as the Arctic Ocean; a significant area of 1,351,600 square miles.[1] Three weeks later, on July 15, 1870, the province of Manitoba was created from the southeastern section of Rupert's Land, and the remaining area became known as the North-West Territory. On July 20, 1871, days after the First American North Pole Expedition ship *Polaris* weighed anchor in St. John's harbour, Newfoundland, on its way north, the province of British Columbia joined Confederation.

Canada encompassed almost the entire northern section of the North American continent, stretching from sea to sea. Although its physical size was enormous, Canada was a small country, population wise. The first formal census of 1871 put the population at 3,737,257 people. Its southern neighbour, the United States of America, counted a population of over thirty-eight million souls.[2]

Despite the pledge to "assume the duties and obligations of government and legislation" for the new region under its administration, the Dominion government did little about it other than redraw the map of Canada to include the territory.[3] The fledgling country was preoccupied with governing the small and scattered population that stretched along the southern regions of Manitoba, Ontario, Quebec, Nova Scotia, and New Brunswick. The vast northern region, sparsely populated by Aboriginal people, a handful of fur traders, and Hudson's Bay Company employees, was left to thrive on its own.

However, economic considerations in the mid-1880s led to the government sending out three expeditions to the Low Arctic region of Hudson Strait and Hudson Bay.* Though the expeditions did not cross the Arctic Circle, they were the first official northern voyages after the Arctic had been transferred to Canada. The purpose of these expeditions was not to assert sovereignty in the region, but to carry out scientific studies.

At the end of the nineteenth century, two main geographical prizes had yet to be attained: the North and South Poles. It became an international race to see which country's flag would be raised first at these points. Britain and America were leaders in the race, each besting the other by a degree, sometimes merely by minutes, or a few miles.

As expeditions from other countries publicized their treks across the Arctic, it became apparent to members of Parliament that there was a possibility that one of these countries might claim more than just the North Pole. Foreign expeditions were roaming land that supposedly belonged to Canada. The government needed to assert itself in the Arctic, but a limited budget prevented this from being carried out in any overt way. The Dominion government managed to send another seven modest expeditions to the North over three decades. In all, ten government expeditions went to the Low and High Arctic between 1884 and 1912.

---

* The region defined as the Arctic in this book is made up of two areas: north of the Arctic Circle at 66°33'N, referred to as the High Arctic, and the treeless zone along the shores of Hudson Bay, Ungava, and the Labrador coast, known as the Low or Subarctic.

These expeditions were not widely publicized and are relatively unknown today. There was no glamour or glory about them. The expedition men were not dashing adventurers. They were heroes of a modest kind — scientists, geologists, policemen, and administrative officers — who carried out their civic duties quietly, asserting sovereignty in the North with flags and legislation. These men named geographic landmarks, made scientific studies, and informed the people they met in these regions that they were on Canadian soil or in Canadian waters. They established a presence in the most unobtrusive and unoffending way possible. They collected scientific data, issued whaling and hunting permits, and raised the Red Ensign from Hudson Bay to Ellesmere Island.

The expedition leaders, Lieutenant A.R. Gordon of the Meteorological Service, Dr. W. Wakeham of the Fisheries Protection Services, Major J.D. Moodie of the North West Mounted Police, A.P. Low of the Geological Survey of Canada, and Captain J.E. Bernier, carried out work in relatively unknown territory with no contact with the southern world they came from. They endured as much hardship (including scurvy) and as many incredible adventures as any of the well-known British, American, or Norwegian explorers who published their tales of exploration. Yet only snippets of these men's stories and their expeditions appear in books on the Canadian Arctic. And no one book tells how collectively these men contributed to Canadian Arctic sovereignty.

This book sets out to tell their stories. It focuses on a period of just over forty years, from 1871 to 1912, when Canada first took interest in the Arctic.

In the Shadow of the Pole examines the main expeditions to Canada's Arctic that influenced the Dominion government's awareness of it, with particular focus on those little-known expeditions organized by the government itself. It is a tribute to the intrepid men who weren't as concerned with latitude as they were with establishing Canada's presence in the North.

CHAPTER ONE

THE FIRST AMERICAN NORTH POLE EXPEDITION

The USS *Periwinkle* was used as a gunboat by the Union Navy during the Civil War. The ship did not encounter ice in its war service, nor had ice been a consideration when it was built in Philadelphia in 1864. Nonetheless, the *Periwinkle* was chosen in 1871 for the first United States North Pole Expedition.

Expedition commander Charles Francis Hall re-christened the ship *Polaris* — the North Star — a name more suited to an Arctic expedition than "Periwinkle." The ship underwent significant modifications in the Navy Yard in Washington, DC, to prepare it for its Arctic voyage. After its makeover, it was believed that the *Polaris* was better protected against the thick sea ice it would encounter than any vessel ever built.

With an unsinkable, *Titanic*-style attitude, the *Polaris* sailed for the Brooklyn Navy Yard on June 10, 1871, where it shipped its crew and received the last necessary alterations, supplies, and stores for the six-year journey. At high tide on the afternoon of June 29, 1871, the USS *Polaris* slipped her moorings, the Stars and Stripes waving from its stern flagstaff. A twenty-one-gun salute officially sent the ship on its mission. The crowd that turned out to cheer the vessel's departure was conspicuously small, though — an astonishingly poor send-off for a momentous North Pole expedition. The *Polaris* then steamed down the East River toward the Atlantic Ocean on its last voyage.

On August 30, 1871, the *Polaris* reached a latitude of 82°11'N in the strait between Greenland and Ellesmere Island. The ship had successfully attained the farthest point north of any expedition, and had explored seven hundred miles of previously unmapped coastline. Despite these accomplishments, the *Polaris* expedition retains a place in history not only for its success, but also for its abysmal failure.

However, the demise of the *Polaris* led to a series of events that changed the map of Canada. It was the catalyst for Canada becoming landlord of the entire Arctic Archipelago.

The *Polaris'* company totalled thirty-one: Commander Hall, twenty-one crew members, three scientists, two Inuit couples, and four children. Captain Sidney O. Buddington was sailing master, and Dr. Emil Bessels was surgeon and chief of the scientific corps. Both men were at odds with Hall before the ship crossed the Arctic Circle. Assistant Navigator Captain George Emery Tyson remained loyal to Hall. He also kept a journal detailing the expedition, which was later published.

When its prow hit the Atlantic waves, the *Polaris* charted a course northward, docking at St. John's, Newfoundland, on July 11. The ship continued its odyssey up the coast of Labrador, into Davis Strait, through Baffin Bay, Smith Sound, and beyond. Robeson Channel, the narrow strait between northwest Greenland and Ellesmere Island, was relatively ice-free that summer. The weather was with them. Pushing as far north as possible, it reached the highest north latitude on August 30. Ice prevented any further progress. So, on September 5, the men landed, raised the American flag, then turned back and took refuge in a harbour on northwest Greenland, which Hall named Thank God Harbour. Within weeks, the ship was frozen in for the winter.

On October 10, Hall and three others set out on a two-week sledging trip, scouting for a route north along which they could make an attempt at the Pole. Shortly upon their return to the ship, Hall became violently ill after drinking a cup of coffee. He died on November 8, 1871. Bessels, the ship's doctor, pronounced the cause of death to be "apoplexy," or a stroke. However, until his death, Hall deliriously accused various members of the expedition, including the doctor, of poisoning him.[1] His crew despondently chipped out a shallow grave in the frozen ground. A mound of stones still marks Hall's resting place on a rocky promontory.

The expedition, now leaderless and rife with discord, fell apart. When the ship was released from the ice the following August, no one was interested in making an attempt at the Pole. Instead, the *Polaris* headed south, down the coast of Greenland.

In a vicious gale on October 15, 1872, the ship appeared to be mortally struck by ice. When its sinking seemed imminent, supplies were tossed overboard onto the ice and the crew prepared to abandon ship. Nineteen of the expedition members had disembarked when the *Polaris* suddenly broke free and floated away, leaving them stranded on an ice floe about four miles in circumference.

The abandoned party included Assistant Navigator Captain Tyson; nine of the crew members and scientists; Hans Hendrik, the Inuit guide from Greenland, and his wife with their four children (the youngest had been born aboard ship only two months previous); and Hall's Baffin Island Inuit companions Ebierbing and Tookoolito and their young daughter. The ice floe broke apart and shrank to a fraction of its original size, but the nineteen managed to survive on what rations they'd tossed overboard and food hunted from the sea. This floe was not stationary, but slowly drifting south.

On April 30, 1873, the Newfoundland sealing ship *Tigress* spotted their SOS signals through the fog off the coast of Labrador. The ship's boats were lowered and the nineteen castaways were rescued from their floating frozen campsite. The party had spent 197 days on the ice and drifted fifteen hundred miles.

The sailing steamship *Tigress* was in the midst of a sealing voyage when it dropped anchor alongside the pan of ice with the *Polaris* refugees on it. Sealing ships like the *Tigress* were typically out at the floe edge hunting from March to the end of May. Picking up the *Polaris* party partway through the hunting season meant that the rescued party would have to wait until the *Tigress* had caught its quota of seals. So, although Captain Isaac Bartlett generously offered those rescued passage to St. John's, the ship did not head for shore but continued sealing.

Two weeks later, they were about one hundred and thirty miles north of St. John's. The *Polaris* crew were very ill. Tyson noted that after coming on board, all the rescued suffered "with colds, swollen feet, sore-throats, and rheumatism."[2] After their ordeal on the ice floe, the rescued party should have had immediate medical attention. But as it was now mid-May and there were seals in the hold, Captain Bartlett decided to return home.

The *Tigress* moored at the St. John's wharf on the evening of May 12. The rescue of the nineteen expedition members who had survived for so long on the drifting ice was soon front page news. There was no doubt, though, that the group survived because of the expert assistance of the two Inuit men and their families, who did the majority of hunting, cooking, and making shelter and clothing. Had the two families not abandoned ship with them, all would have perished.

The United States steamship *Frolic* picked up the entire party at St. John's on May 27, and docked at the Navy Yard in Washington on June 5. The *Polaris* party finally arrived back in the United States five weeks after they had been rescued from the ice floe, and almost two years after they had sailed north aboard the *Polaris*. It was not the glorious return any of them had imagined.

A naval inquiry into the plight of the expedition promptly took place, and was followed closely in the newspapers. A decision was made to dispatch a search vessel to find the *Polaris* and bring back the fourteen people still on board when it drifted away. While the Navy searched for an appropriate rescue ship, it sent the U.S. sloop-of-war steamship *Juniata* to drop off coal and supplies on the west coast of Greenland that would be used by the search ship. The three-masted *Juniata*, which was twice the size of the *Polaris*, was not built to handle Arctic ice packs and so was instructed to wait for the coming rescue party at Disko Island, halfway up the west coast of Greenland.[3]

In Greenland, Lieutenant George Washington DeLong, one of the officers on the *Juniata*, was given command of a thirty-two-foot steam launch, nicknamed *Little Juniata*. It would cruise the fiords and inlets along the Greenland coast for any sign of the missing ship and crew. The *Little Juniata*, with a party of nine, set out on its search on August 2. The launch was provisioned with two months of supplies. It explored some of the fiords, but met with extreme weather conditions and returned to the mother ship nine days later.

The *Juniata* set up a supply depot on Greenland as instructed, then returned to New York, arriving on November 1, 1873 — a period of little more than three months during the mild, relatively ice-free summer months.

THE RESCUE MISSION

As it turned out, the United States Navy had no available ice-worthy ship, and without the luxury of time to refit one of its existing fleet, settled for a privately owned vessel built for the icy North Atlantic waters. The Navy purchased the *Tigress* (the same ship that had rescued the party from the ice) for $60,000. It gave the owners, the prominent Newfoundland sealing and fishery business Harvey and Company, the option to buy the ship back after the rescue operations.

The three-masted sailing steamship *Tigress* was built in Quebec in 1871 for the sealing trade. The *Tigress* differed from ordinary vessels because its bow was designed at an acute angle, with a flat hull that widened gradually below the waterline. This flaring of its hull enabled the ship to rise up on the floe ice and break through the ice with its sheer weight. Modern icebreakers employ the same principle.

At 165 feet, the *Tigress* was twenty-five feet longer than the *Polaris*. The first twenty feet of the *Tigress'* bow were more than three feet thick, with the first twelve feet of that encased in half-inch-thick iron. It was fitted with two steam engines of twelve hundred horsepower. However, its boilers were designed to burn soft coal, and as the *Juniata* had only deposited hard coal at Disko for the rescue vessel, the boilers had to be replaced.

The ship was brought to the Brooklyn Navy Yard for modifications. There the boilers were changed and the ship outfitted with new rigging, sails, and topmasts. Steam pipes were added to the interior for heating in the event that the *Tigress* would be forced to overwinter in the North. As well, the cabin was enlarged, and two deckhouses were constructed to accommodate the large number of naval personnel required for the rescue mission.

Civil War veteran James A. Greer was given command of the expedition, and Captain George Tyson was named acting lieutenant and ice-master. The *Tigress* carried a complement of eleven officers and forty-two men. However, only thirteen of these men were actually seamen, who had to do all the work of the ship. One of the men who shipped as ordinary seaman was Mr. Commagere, a reporter for the *New York Herald*. He was given clerical duties. Ebierbing, Hall's faithful Inuit companion, was on board as interpreter.[4]

The publicity surrounding the rescue from the sea ice and the impending search for the remaining crew drew huge crowds to see the *Tigress* off. The turnout for the departure of the rescue mission was far bigger than that of the North Pole expedition two years earlier. The *New York Times* reported that thousands of people stood on the Brooklyn Navy Yard docks and along the riverbank to cheer as the *Tigress* cast off her lines at five o'clock on the evening of Monday, July 14, 1873. Women in bright summer dresses waved handkerchiefs while the men waved their hats. People shouted farewells and "God bless yous" to the men on board as the ship slowly steamed up the East River. Through the steamer's smoke, the crowd could make out the hats and handkerchiefs of the men on board waving back.

The crews of the ships *Vermont* and *Brooklyn* manned the yards and sent up cheer after cheer at the passing ship. The men standing in the rigging of the *Tigress* returned the cheers. Ships' whistles sounded as the *Tigress* passed in the lanes, and a parting salute was fired from the government battery. The crowds only dispersed after the vessel steamed out of sight.[5]

The ship's orders were to locate the *Polaris* and, if it was found in seaworthy condition, sail it back to Washington. On August 14, one month after leaving Brooklyn and cruising the Greenland and Baffin Island coasts, the *Tigress* approached Littleton Island off the coast of Etah, Greenland, near the scene of the abandonment in the previous October's gale. Here a dinghy was lowered. The men who went ashore found an encampment that the remaining *Polaris* crew had used as their winter campground. But the *Polaris* men were no longer there. The site was inhabited by a small group of Inughuit men from northern Greenland who explained how they had helped the *Polaris* crew survive the winter.

The *Polaris* had run aground the day after the October storm. The crew had dismantled much of it and used the timbers and canvas sails to build two boats. Then, when the ice began to break up, they sailed south. The *Polaris* sank shortly after their departure. While the *Tigress* and *Juniata* were plying the waters off Greenland and Baffin Island, the men they searched for had already managed their own rescue.[6]

Having discovered what had become of the *Polaris*, the *Tigress* turned its bow south. Arriving at Godhavn on Disko Island, Greenland, on August 25, the men learned that nine Dundee whalers had gone north.

Commander Greer figured that at least one of these ships would have met the boats carrying the *Polaris* crew and picked them up. The *Tigress* then headed west to the whaling grounds in an attempt to intercept the whalers and carry the missing crew home to America.

The likelihood that the men were safely aboard whaling ships took the urgency out of the *Tigress'* journey. This was strictly a search-and-rescue expedition and the officers were not expected to make any scientific observations. Tyson noted, however, that some of the members took the initiative to make mineralogical collections of their own at the various anchorages on Cumberland Sound.

> Mica is here in abundance, and its collection could, I believe, be made to pay. One of our company got the "stone fever" bad this morning. Taking chisel and hammer, and a good-sized canvas bag, in which to put the precious specimens, he started off to make his fortune. This evening, just at dark, he returned. The officer of the deck heard his hail, but the shore-going boat was at that time away ... so Billy had to wait until it returned. He sat himself down on a rock, which happened to be on an extensive shoal. He was on the outer edge of it looking wistfully toward the *Tigress*, and as the inside of the shoal was lower than the off shore, and the tide was setting in, he was, without knowing it, very soon surrounded by water. Suddenly discovering that he was on an improvised island of somewhat limited extent, he yelled most lustily for relief, and we finally got a boat out to him. But poor Billy was the most frightened man I have seen for many a day.[7]

Having no success locating the men at the whaling grounds, the *Tigress* made for home. Upon arriving at the Brooklyn Navy Yard on November 9, the men learned that the remaining *Polaris* crew had shipped aboard the Scottish whaler *Ravenscraig* in June 1873, three weeks before the *Tigress* had set sail to search for them. The *Ravenscraig* picked up the men as it headed west into Baffin Bay for the summer hunt. Like their compatriots on the sealer *Tigress*, the rescued men were compelled to go along on its summer whale hunt. Eventually, the men split up and took passage on three separate whaling vessels that were returning to Dundee, Scotland, before the *Ravenscraig*. From there, each of the men found their own way back to the United States, with the last man arriving in New York City on November 13, 1873.

Amazingly, with the exception of Commander Hall, the entire *Polaris* expedition returned alive. The birth on board of baby Charlie Polaris to the family from Greenland actually meant that the company's numbers had not diminished. Despite the harrowing escapade of the *Polaris* expedition, the loss of life was minimal by comparison with countless other Arctic expeditions before and after.

Captain Tyson detailed the whole misadventure in his book *Arctic Experiences: Containing Capt. George E. Tyson's Wonderful Drift on the Ice-Floe, A History of the* Polaris *Expedition, the Cruise of the* Tigress, *and Rescue of the* Polaris *Survivors. To Which Is Added A General Arctic Chronology*, published in 1874. Tyson's version was the only account of the ordeal published in English, Hall's journal being lost. Emil Bessels published his own account in German in 1879. Tyson's book was not a financial success.

The *Tigress* was promptly sold back to Harvey and Company for $40,000, $20,000 less than what the United States government had purchased it for five months previous. This was a good financial venture for the owners, especially since the *Tigress* had been outfitted with new sails, rigging, and other improvements required for the *Polaris* rescue. The *Tigress* returned to the sealing grounds with Captain Isaac Bartlett again at the helm in the spring of 1874. Sadly, it suffered a disaster more deadly than that which had befallen the men it had rescued from the ice the year before.

On April 2, one of the boilers exploded, scalding and causing the death of twenty-one of the men on board, including the captain's son, James Bartlett. Flag signals of distress were hoisted, but it wasn't until the following day that they were seen. The steamer *Brigus* then towed the powerless *Tigress* out of the ice, where it solemnly proceeded under sail to Bay Roberts, Newfoundland, bringing the bodies home to their families. The *Tigress* then sailed for St. John's to deliver the two dead men from that city, one of whom was the chief engineer who had tended the boiler at the time.

The *Bay Roberts Guardian* reported, "The *Tigress*, it will be remembered, was purchased last summer, by the U.S. Government and fitted out for an Arctic voyage in search of the missing *Polaris* crew, from whence she returned in the fall, and was subsequently sold to her former owners here. She had new boilers, furnished by a Philadelphia firm, put in at New York, previous to her departure for the Arctic seas."[8]

The implication that one of the new boilers was faulty seems an easy conclusion to draw. However, an inquiry determined that water had become low in one of the boilers, and when the feed cock was turned on, "the crown of the firebox gave way." The chief engineer, "an excellent, careful, and sober man," had been deceived by the water level shown in the gauge glass. The accident was a result of human error.

THE TRANSFER

Three months after the *Tigress* returned from its search for the *Polaris*, a Wm. A. Mintzer of the United States Navy sent a letter to Mr. George Crump, acting British consul in Philadelphia. His letter of February 10, 1874, read,

> Sir:
>
> I hereby make application to the British Government, through you, for a land grant giving me possession of a tract of land situated on what is known as the Labrador coast, on the shore of Cumberland Gulf.
>
> I apply for a tract of land twenty (20) miles square, having north latitude sixty-four degrees, fifty-six minutes (64°56') and west longitude sixty-six degrees, twenty-one minutes (66°21') as a geometrical centre.
>
> The space bounded by the limits stated above is not inhabited except by a few wandering esquimaux and does not appear to be claimed by anyone. It and the

surrounding country is wild and desolate with no vegetation but moss, and for about eight (8) months of the year is covered with ice and snow, and apparently not available for anything except mining purposes.

It contains a deposit of a useful mineral, which under the protection of a land grant a company or individual might develop with advantage.

In consideration of the above, I respectfully ask that the within application be granted that I may be enabled to investigate and develop the mineral resources of the space herementioned.

I have the honour to be, very respectfully,
your obedient servant,
Wm. A. Mintzer,
Corps of Engineers, U.S. Navy[9]

This William Mintzer obviously had firsthand knowledge of the locale referred to in his letter. Cumberland Sound is on the east side of Baffin Island, not Labrador, as Mintzer states. Whalers were generally the only non-Inuit with knowledge of that northern vicinity. Mintzer was not a whaler, though. He is listed as second assistant engineer aboard the *Tigress* on its *Polaris* rescue mission the summer before. This was the same "Billy" that Captain George E. Tyson had jested about who was stranded by the tide while collecting minerals.

Mintzer did not specify in his letter what "useful mineral" he planned to mine. Judging by Tyson's account of what the men had found on Cumberland Sound, it was likely mica that Mintzer was after. Mica is a transparent mineral found in large glass-like sheets. Its heat-resistant properties made it an ideal replacement for glass in windows for wood stoves, kerosene heaters, and furnaces. In 1874, mica would fetch $10 a pound, an equivalent of $194 today.[10] Mintzer was not just a young man with "stone fever," as Tyson had termed it. He was enterprising and had seen the potential of profitable mining operations on Cumberland Sound.

It was really only crude chance that this letter had been written at all. The likelihood of an American naval officer applying for a tract of land on eastern Baffin Island is slim. If the United States Navy had not gone in search of the missing *Polaris* crew, Lieutenant W.A. Mintzer would not have been anywhere near the Arctic. As a result of his participation in this mission, his subsequent request launched a succession of uneasy correspondence that would lead to the Arctic becoming part of the map of Canada.

Acting British Consul George Crump forwarded Mintzer's letter to the Earl Granville, British secretary of state for foreign affairs. He sent it February 20, 1874: the day the British general election was held and Benjamin Disraeli's Conservatives swept into power. Mintzer's inquiry was directed to the Earl of Derby, Granville's replacement as secretary of state.

Mintzer's letter inadvertently raised the question of whether the region had been taken possession of on behalf of the Crown. The Earl of Derby had no idea if it had or not, so he passed Mintzer's letter on to the Earl of Carnarvon, colonial secretary of state. Carnarvon had no answer either, so forwarded it on April 13 to the secretary to the Admiralty.

The British Admiralty was the institution most informed about the territory north of Canada, as its naval officers had accomplished the majority of the exploring and mapping of it. Royal Hydrographer Frederick John Evans researched the matter, and his resulting April 20, 1874, report said, "Our knowledge of the geography and resources of this region is very imperfect; according to Admiralty charts much of the area above applied for is on the sea, although, it is to be presumed from the precision with which the applicant marks out his requirements that he must have some certain local knowledge."[11]

Evans' report did not engender any confidence, and only pointed out the inaccuracy of the British Admiralty's charts. Despite the fact that Scottish whalers had been in Cumberland Sound since the 1840s, they had provided no official charts of the region.[12] What maps the Admiralty had showed water and not land at the specific coordinates Mintzer had given.

Mintzer's was not the first request the Royal Hydrographer had researched about the region, either. Only a month before Mintzer sent his letter, an A.W. Harvey had put in a request to use the region.

August William Harvey was a prominent Newfoundland businessman and politician, appointed to the Newfoundland legislature in 1870. He was the head of Harvey and Company, carrying out profitable fishing and sealing operations in Davis Inlet and Cumberland Sound. One of the vessels owned by Harvey and Co. was the sealing ship *Tigress* — the ship that had rescued the *Polaris* party from the ice, and the very ship that Mintzer had been aboard when he found mica on Baffin.

On January 3, 1874, Harvey was in London and sent a letter to the undersecretary of state for the colonies, inquiring,

> Can you inform me whether the land known as Cumberland on the West of Davis Straits belongs to Great Britain and if it does — is it under the Government of the Dominion of Canada?
>
> I wish to know as during the past two years I have had some fisheries carried on there and shall probably erect some temporary buildings during the present year and should like to know before I do what government claims it.[13]

When after two weeks Harvey had received no reply, he wrote again. He was soon leaving London and wondered who could give him information about the "Sovereignty of Cumberland on the West side of Baffins Bay."[14]

Harvey's inquiry took a different bureaucratic route to the Admiralty than Mintzer's. Assistant Undersecretary for the Colonies Henry Thurstan Holland forwarded Harvey's inquiry to Curtis Miranda Lampson, the deputy governor of the Hudson's Bay Company. Holland wanted to know if this particular locale had been part of the company's fur-trading territory. Lampson responded that it had not.[15]

Holland's January 16 reply to Harvey's letter is an honest admission of the British government's uncertainty about the ownership of the land inquired about. "I am to inform you that the land in question was not comprised in the Territories of the Hudson's Bay Company recently transferred to Canada, as it did not come within the Charter of the Hudson's Bay Company, nor does it appear to have formed a part of Canada before confederation. His Lordship would suggest that you should enquire of the Board of Admiralty as to whether the land has ever been taken possession of on behalf of the Crown."[16]

Harvey then sent his query to the Board of Admiralty in February 1874. The hydrographer refers to Harvey's request in his April 20 report: "Cumberland Gulf is occasionally visited by English & American Whaling & Sealing ships, and it is understood that summer fishing stations are established, — not very far from the locality applied for, — by mercantile enterprise from Newfoundland. On 2nd of Feb. last on the application to their Lordships for similar information by Mr. A.W. Harvey who is interested in a fishery not far from the head of Cumberland Gulf—."[17]

Harvey's request did not cause much concern. After all, as a Newfoundlander he was considered a British subject, and his letter was answered as frankly as possible. Whether Harvey and Mintzer were ever aware of their mutual applications is unknown. The synchronized timing of their requests and the closeness of the region both were applying for is curious, but perhaps just coincidence.

Mintzer's letter, on the other hand, was more alarming to the British. This was no longer a question of fishery or whaling operations, which had been carried out in the region for the past thirty years, but mining that would be more intrusive to the area. More importantly, the inquiry was from an American. America had a reputation for stretching its empirical arm, embracing western states in the early 1800s and reaching out to California by 1850.

The British were nervous about the Americans claiming land north of the Dominion of Canada. This is spelled out in an April 25 letter to Assistant Undersecretary for the Colonies Holland: "It would be desirable to ascertain the views of the Dominion Govt. I think before the FO [Foreign Office] give any answer. We must remember that if this Yankee adventurer is informed by the British FO that the place indicated is not a portion of H.M. dominions he would no doubt think himself entitled to hoist the Stars and Stripes, which might produce no end of complications."[18]

Mintzer's application made the British nervous. By admitting to Mintzer that they had minimal knowledge of the area in question, the British would concede they had little jurisdiction there. This could potentially open up title of the territory and the United States could claim it for itself. However, Britain didn't really want control or administration of the region, as it was considerably far away and had not yet proven to be of value. It was more the principle of the issue at stake.[19]

The British did not know how best to respond to Mintzer's request, so they didn't. His letter went unanswered while attempts were made to rectify the situation he had inadvertently created.

Harvey returned to Newfoundland without a definitive answer to his request either. Six months later, and well into the fishing season, Harvey was still in the dark about his right to use land on Cumberland Sound, so he applied again to the Colonial Office, asking for a square mile of land for buildings and mining, as well as fishing rights. On August 25, Undersecretary of State for the Colonies R.G.W. Herbert replied that Lord Carnarvon would consult with the governor general on the matter, but was not hopeful that his application would be granted.

There is no further correspondence, and what Harvey did is not documented. It is possible that he went ahead and erected "temporary" buildings, having a relatively clear conscience that there was no particular country he was required to lease the land from.

Canada, having recently received the greater part of the northern region, seemed the most logical choice to also govern the entire, but partially mapped, Arctic region. On April 30, the secretary of state for the colonies, Lord Carnarvon, enclosed Mintzer's application for a grant of land and the Royal Hydrographer's report in a secret dispatch to Canada's governor general, Lord Dufferin. Carnarvon wanted Dufferin to confidentially raise the question with the cabinet ministers of whether or not Canada would "desire" to have the Arctic region "formally annexed to the Dominion of Canada."[20]

Carnarvon's proposal had been forwarded to the right man. Lord Dufferin, who had become governor general in 1872, was an advocate of Canadian unity. In his six-year term, he saw Prince Edward Island admitted to Confederation and the establishment of the Supreme Court. He was very involved in Canadian politics, even installing an office in the East Block on Parliament Hill in Ottawa. Dufferin gladly brought the proposal of Canada accepting the Arctic region to Prime Minister Alexander Mackenzie and his Liberal ministers.

However, it took six months from Dufferin's presentation of the proposal for the government to agree that the Dominion of Canada would accept administration of the lands. On October 9, 1874, William Alfred Himsworth, clerk of the Queen's Privy Council for Canada, signed the memo, which said "that her Majesty's government be advised that the Government of Canada is desirous of including within the boundaries of the Dominion the Territories referred to, with the Islands adjacent."[21] Dufferin sent the memo to Carnarvon. Thus began prolonged negotiations between the British and Canadian governments over the transfer of the land.

Before passing the memo on to Her Majesty, Lord Carnarvon wanted to qualify the land that would be transferred. The Royal Hydrographer's responding two-page report was severely lacking in information.

In a secret memo dated January 6, 1875, Lord Carnarvon wrote Lord Dufferin,

> From this minute it appears that the boundaries of the Dominion towards the North, North East and North West are at present entirely undefined and that it is impossible to say what British territories on the North American Continent are not already annexed to Canada under the Order in Council of the 23rd June 1870, which incorporated the whole of the territories of the Hudson's Bay Company, as well as the North Western Territory in the Dominion.[22]

Carnarvon asked the Canadian ministers to specify the limits of the land to be annexed. He suggested that an act of British Parliament might be a suitable vehicle with which to transfer the territory. Clerk Himsworth replied that the Privy Council concurred that an act of British Parliament would be the best way to annex the northern region. Himsworth wrote to Lord Dufferin, "As, however, the acquisition of this additional territory by the Dominion of Canada will entail a charge upon the revenue of the country, it is essential that the sanction of the Canadian Parliament should be had before the passing of any Imperial Act adding the new territory to the Dominion."[23]

Unfortunately, the subject received little attention at the next session of Parliament in Ottawa, and the whole transfer process stalled and was virtually halted for two years.

CHAPTER TWO

A British Polar Expedition

As the transfer negotiations were being debated, the Lords Commissioners of the Admiralty decided that it was an ideal time to extend their activity to the High Arctic. The last official expedition that Britain had sent out in "pursuit of Arctic discovery" was the one under Franklin that had ended in tragedy.[1]

The *Polaris* expedition attained the highest latitude of 82°11'N. It was imperative that the region be properly explored by British men. Forty-four-year-old Royal Navy officer Captain George Strong Nares would lead the three-year expedition and was requested "to attain the highest northern latitude, and, if possible to reach the North Pole."[2]

On Saturday, May 29, 1875, Nares, with 120 men aboard Her Majesty's ships *Alert* and *Discovery*, sailed out of Portsmouth harbour. The ships headed north through the strait between Greenland and Ellesmere islands, now known as Nares Strait, successfully reaching 82°N. The *Discovery* wintered at Lady Jane Franklin Bay on northeast Ellesmere Island. The *Alert* wintered fifty miles farther north, on the northern tip of Ellesmere Island.[3]

In April 1876, fifty-three men and officers left the *Alert* on sledging expeditions. One party led by Senior Lieutenant Pelham Aldrich set out to explore the north coast of Ellesmere to determine how far north the land stretched. The other party, under the command of Lieutenant Albert Hastings Markham, forged northward over the polar sea. The men hauled heavy sledges and boats loaded with supplies and equipment over the rough, jagged ice. They attained 83°200'N, a degree farther than the *Polaris*, setting a new record for the highest northern latitude.

Men in both sledging parties suffered an outbreak of scurvy and returned to the ship.[4] When members of the *Discovery*'s party to the south were also found to be suffering from the illness, Nares cut the expedition short. They returned to England, arriving in November 1876.

In the eighteen months they had been away, fifty-six of the one hundred and twenty-one men had been stricken with scurvy. Four died. This was puzzling, as scurvy had been virtually non-existent in long-distance naval voyages since 1795, when the Admiralty included a daily ration of lime juice. Nares' ships had been fully stocked with enough bottles of lime juice to keep the disease at bay for the extent of the three-year voyage. However, as part of the bottling process, the juice had been boiled, destroying virtually all of the vitamin C in it.[5]

Despite this calamity, Nares was knighted for his work. Markham was given a gold medal by the Royal Geographical Society and promoted to the rank of captain by the Royal Navy.

AN AMERICAN BUSINESS VENTURE

The spirit of the British Empire thrived in Canadian hearts when Nares ventured north to Ellesmere. His accomplishment was not seen as an intrusion on Canadian territory. However, news of an American expedition to the Arctic sparked a complete opposite reaction.

On May 31, 1876, an article appeared in the *New York Times* titled, "The Schooner *Era* to Sail for the Polar Seas Next Monday — A Search for Graphite and Other Rich Materials."

> It appears that during the search of the '*Tigress*' for the ill-fated '*Polaris*,' over a year ago, rich veins of graphite were discovered in Cumberland Inlet. On the return to St. John's, Lieut. W.A. Mintzer, United States Naval Engineer, chartered a small steamer and went back and continued his mineral survey.
>
> He found large beds of graphite and mica, but owing to the lateness of the season was unable to bring any away. The topsail schooner '*Era*' has been recently

fitting at New London, and will sail next Monday under Mintzer's command, and under government auspices to get a cargo of these minerals.... She is well provided with mining tools and labourers for quarrying, and as deposits are situated some distance up the mountain side they will take 3,000 feet of tramway in order to more easily load the vessel, and a quantity of lumber to erect tool-houses and buildings for the purpose of observation ... the deposit is, though almost pure, under rock as hard as flint. Provision, therefore, is made for blasting on an extensive scale.

This was alarming news. Extensive operations were planned for erecting buildings, constructing a mining tramway, and blasting rock. Mintzer's original 1874 application had requested developing the land for mining purposes. The trouble was that he was following through with it despite not having received "permission" to do so.

According to the newspaper report, upon the *Tigress'* return to St. John's in 1873, Mintzer had gone back to Cumberland Sound to further survey the mining potential there. In fact, by the time he sent his letter to Crump in February 1874, he had gathered enough information about the vein of mica to know that it would be a profitable enterprise.

The Dominion government was only alerted to this expedition in August of 1876, when the secretary of state for Canada sent a clipping of the *Times* article to Edward Blake, the Canadian minister of justice. Blake forwarded the clipping in a letter to the Earl of Carnarvon, saying,

No doubt the territory referred to is the same which was about 1874 the subject of an application by Mintzer to Her Majesty's Government for its purchase; whence arose the negotiation with the Canadian Government for the incorporation of the Northern Territories with Canada. My colleague suggests that I should bring the extract under your Lordship's notice, assuming that no authority has been given by Her Majesty's Government for the proposed expedition.[6]

Indeed, no authority had been given by Her Majesty's government, nor had any permission been requested of the Government of Canada for this mining expedition. Mintzer, likely tired of waiting for a response from the British government, had decided to mine the land. However, the British government decided not to intervene. As Carnarvon stated in his September 13, 1876, letter, "In view of the probable annexation within a short time of this and other Northern Territories to Canada, Her Majesty's Government do not propose to take any action in reference to this expedition unless expressly asked to do so by the Dominion Government."

Carnarvon supposed the annexation process would soon be wrapped up. It would then become Canada's problem to deal with. Yet the Dominion government did not ask the British government to intervene, either. However, the annexation still had not taken place before a second *New York Times* article on October 27, 1876, announced the successful return of Mintzer's six-week expedition to mine mica.

The article said, "Altogether about 15 tons were excavated, which exhausted three veins. Six weeks were thus spent. Three days were spent in further prospecting, after which 'Era' sailed for home. The sailors named their diminutive village of three wooden structures 'Mintzerville' in honour of their commander."

The Americans had freely exploited what was supposedly soon to be Canadian territory. At ten dollars a pound, Mintzer's profit from his mining expedition totalled over $300,000, a worthwhile enterprise that today would net close to six million dollars.[7] Mintzer and his backers gained a substantial amount of wealth from an expedition that was virtually ignored by both Britain and Canada. Also, by creating "Mintzerville," they had made unofficial claims to land with no reaction from either the British or Canadian governments.

The matter was not of immediate import to the Dominion government, though, so was virtually ignored. Even if it had decided to intervene in Mintzer's project, it had no real means of doing so, other than hiring a sealing or whaling vessel to investigate the matter.

In 1877, Lord Carnarvon urged action "to place the title of Canada to these territories upon a clear and unmistakable footing." The Canadian government's delay was perhaps indication of its lack of interest in these lands, but the transfer was perceived as an action on the part of Britain "to prevent the United States from claiming them and not from their likelihood of their proving of any value to Canada," said Edward Blake in a report to the Colonial Office.[8]

Blake had called it correctly. News of a request for funding for an expedition to Lady Franklin Bay on Ellesmere Island before Congress in Washington had spurred the British to once again press Canada about the transfer process. Captain Henry Howgate, chief disbursing officer for the United States Army Signal Corps and an exploration enthusiast with no Arctic experience, had presented a plan to establish a colony at Lady Franklin Bay, Nares' ship *Discovery*'s overwintering spot. Here, scientific studies and exploration would be carried out for three years, as well as an attempt on the North Pole.

Howgate hired Captain George E. Tyson to make an advance expedition to Baffin Island.

In August 1877, Tyson led the Howgate Preliminary Arctic Expedition aboard the *Florence*. Tyson spent the winter locked in the ice close to the head of Cumberland Sound. He collected skins for clothing, recruited ten Inuit, and picked up thirty sled dogs. In July 1878, Tyson sailed the *Florence* to Disko, Greenland, where he was to rendezvous with the American ship heading north to Lady Franklin Bay. When he arrived, the local agent informed him that he had read in a Danish newspaper that the expedition had been postponed. Howgate had not raised enough money for the project. Tyson discharged his recruits and headed back to America.[9]

In the meantime, in Ottawa on May 3, 1878, a week before Parliament was dissolved for the general election, Minister of the Interior David Mills recommended that the transfer proposal be accepted. Discussion about it in the House was lengthy. Mills suggested that the boundaries include all the islands between the waters west of Greenland and the 141st meridian, and that the territory should come under the full and regular administration of Canada. He stressed that American speculators were interested in the mineral potential of the region — likely a reference to Mintzer's mining venture.

Peter Mitchell, Independent Conservative MP from New Brunswick, was against the transfer. He objected to the government asking "us to assume the responsibility of governing one-fourth of the whole continent of North America without a single reason being alleged that in its results it would benefit the Dominion."[10]

However, the MP was alone in his objections. The official Opposition leader Sir John A. Macdonald approved Canada's acceptance of the territory. He believed the region would incur minimal costs to administer and would eventually produce revenue to offset its expenses. Macdonald's view won out and a draft of an address to Her Majesty was sent to the Senate. Included in this was the note that an act of British Parliament for the transfer had been approved by the Canadian government.

Sir Michael Hicks-Beach, who had replaced Lord Carnarvon as colonial secretary in February 1878, replied to Dufferin on July 17 that he had consulted with the law officers of the Crown, the Queen's chief legal advisers. They felt that an imperial order-in-council would be sufficient for Her Majesty to annex the territory to Canada, but any future division of the territory into provinces would require an imperial act.

Minister of Justice Rodolphe LaFlamme responded that they had requested an imperial act for the transfer because that was what had been recommended to them by Hicks-Beach's predecessor. As far as creating provinces, the *British North America Act* of 1871 had included an addendum to the *BNA Act* of 1867 giving provision to the Canadian Parliament to administer the new territory and create new provinces from it without permission from Her Majesty.

Hicks-Beach answered LaFlamme's letter on April 3, 1879, admitting negligence in not drawing the law officers' attention to the *BNA Act* of 1871. However, they stood by their earlier opinion that Her Majesty could annex the lands to Canada by an order-in-council. An imperial act introduced into British Parliament would be published in the press and potentially draw unwanted attention from the United States. This would then leave the transfer open to challenge, especially as the British were uncertain about the limits of the lands they were transferring.

So, negotiations between the Dominion and British governments slowed again, mainly because the two countries could not agree on the method of transfer.[11] The Dominion government finally acquiesced. On November 4, 1879, the House of Commons approved a memorandum by Prime Minister John A. Macdonald stating that the Dominion government now requested an order-in-council of Her Majesty's government for the annexation of the Arctic to Canada.

The Second American North Pole Expedition

In July of 1879, while ministers in the House of Commons were still debating the means of transferring the Arctic, another American expedition was preparing to depart in search of the North Pole. This time the approach to the Pole would be from the west. The *Jeannette* would leave San Francisco and steam northward up the coast, around Alaska and into the Arctic Archipelago.

American Navy lieutenant George W. DeLong, a serious, studious-looking man with droopy mustachios and round spectacles, was in command of the expedition. In the summer of 1873, DeLong had been part of the *Juniata* expedition to Greenland to drop off supplies for the *Polaris* rescue mission. He had commanded the thirty-two-foot steam launch on its nine-day search, cruising the waters of Davis Strait at the end of August and barely venturing above the Arctic Circle at 66°33'N. Still, the experience convinced him of the value of Arctic exploration. DeLong returned to the United States consumed with Arctic fever.

Whalers hunting in the Bering Strait region had reported that when they were beset by ice, their ship drifted with it in a northerly direction. There was also a popular theory that a Japanese current running north through Bering Strait kept the channel open for navigation. DeLong felt that the combination of this drift and the current could be used to reach the Pole.

Almost thirty years earlier, in late July 1850, while searching for the missing Franklin expedition, Robert M'Clure, commander of the British Naval ship *Investigator*, encountered an impermeable polar ice pack north of Point Barrow, Alaska. Later that fall, his ship became frozen in the ice in Prince of Wales Strait. In 1851, M'Clure discovered and identified the channel of water between Banks and Melville Islands as the channel linking the Atlantic to the Pacific Ocean — the coveted Northwest Passage. This strait was later named after him. However, a wall of ice blocked any access to it. The *Investigator* became permanently trapped in the ice a second year, this time at Mercy Bay on northern Banks Island. The ship never escaped the ice's grip. M'Clure and his starving men were eventually rescued and returned to England in 1854 with Sir Edward Belcher's expedition.[12] And all this had occurred in waters at a more southerly latitude than that which DeLong proposed to take.

Nonetheless, DeLong was determined that Bering Strait — west of M'Clure Strait — would be an open passage to the North. DeLong convinced James Gordon Bennett Jr., the wealthy *New York Herald* newspaper publisher, to finance his expedition. Bennett purchased the three-masted British steam barkentine *Pandora* in 1878, renaming it *Jeannette* after his sister. The U.S. Navy agreed to man and operate the ship.

The *Jeannette* sailed from San Francisco on July 8, 1879. However, there was no open passage north. By September 6, the ship was beset southeast of Wrangel Island, north of the Siberian coast. Caught in the moving ice, the ship drifted in a west-northwesterly direction for twenty-one months before being crushed by the ice in June 1881. The men abandoned ship with supplies and three lifeboats only hours before the *Jeannette* sank. DeLong and his thirty-three crew members headed for Siberia.[13]

It was a tortuous three-month journey, with the men dragging lifeboats and stores over the ice pack. One of the boats with eight men aboard it was lost in a storm. The other two boats landed at separate points on the Lena River Delta in Siberia. DeLong and his thirteen companions struggled southwards to find a settlement of some sort. The men were weakened by severe frostbite and hunger. The two strongest men, Noros and Nindemann, went to seek help. They made it to civilization, but could not get back in time to help the others. DeLong and the eleven remaining men died between October and November 1881.

The third boat, with eleven men aboard, landed safely about 125 miles away. George Melville, who had also been chief engineer on the *Tigress'* rescue mission, led the boat party to safety in the Lena River Delta. He also headed the search that found the frozen bodies of Lieutenant DeLong and his men in March 1882. Melville returned to the United States with the expedition journals and records.[14] DeLong's detailed journal was later published by his young widow.

Only thirteen of the thirty-three expedition members survived. The expedition had succeeded in discovering three new islands in the East Siberian Sea, one of which DeLong named "Bennett" after his benefactor.[15] The ill-fated *Jeannette* expedition, like the *Polaris* before it, contributed valuable geographic information, but the tragic loss of lives overshadowed its success.

THE ADJACENT TERRITORIES ORDER

The *Jeannette* expedition was not viewed as the same sort of threat to Canada's Arctic ownership as Mintzer's mining expedition had been three years earlier. But even that venture, perceived threat and all, had not succeeded in speeding up the transfer process. When DeLong sailed, the Arctic islands had still not been transferred to Canada.

An order-in-council was drafted on February 6, 1880, and sent to the law officers of the Crown for their legal opinion. The law officers endorsed the draft, and on July 24 it was passed on to Prime Minister Macdonald, then visiting England. Three days later, on July 31, 1880, the order-in-council was presented to sixty-one-year-old Queen Victoria, who was staying in her summer residence on the Isle of Wight. Present at this auspicious occasion were Lord President, Lord Steward, and Lord Chamberlain of the Privy Council. The Lord President read aloud,

> Whereas it is expedient that all British Territories and Possessions in North America, and the islands adjacent to such Territories and Possessions which are not already included in the Dominion of Canada, should (with the exception of the Colony of Newfoundland and its dependencies) be annexed to and form part of the said Dominion.
>
> And whereas, the Senate and Commons of Canada in Parliament assembled, have in and by an Address, dated the 3rd day of May, 1878, represented to Her Majesty "That it is desirable that the Parliament of Canada, on the transfer of the before-mentioned Territories being completed, should have authority to legislate for their future welfare and good government, and the power to make all needful rules and regulations respecting them, the same as in the case of the other territories (of the Dominion); and that the Parliament of Canada expressed its Willingness to assume the duties and obligations consequent thereon:"
>
> And whereas, Her Majesty is graciously pleased to accede to the desire expressed in and by the said Address: Now, therefore, it is hereby ordered and declared by Her

Majesty, by and with the advice of Her Most Honourable Privy Council, as follows:—

From and after the first day of September 1880, all British Territories and Possessions in North America, not already included within the Dominion of Canada and all Islands adjacent to any of such Territories or Possessions, shall (with the exception of the colony of Newfoundland and its dependencies) become and be annexed to and form part of the said Dominion of Canada; and become and be subject to the laws for the time being in force in the said Dominion, in so far as such laws may be applicable thereto.[16]

Her Majesty gave her royal assent to the transfer and the order was signed by Sir Charles Lennox Peel, clerk of the Privy Council. At last, the Arctic islands were officially transferred to Canada. With the transfer, the country increased by an impressive 1.5 million square miles in size. Within thirteen years of Confederation, the Dominion government had become the proprietors and administrators of half the North American continent.

The order-in-council's legalese does not disguise the vagueness of the wording of the transfer. Conspicuously absent from the document are latitude and longitude coordinates or points of the compass. Nothing on paper would indicate that "all British territories and possessions in North America" were even north of the present boundaries of the Dominion of Canada.

A 1921 report on Canada's title to the Arctic islands spelled it out. "The Imperial government did not know what they were transferring and on the other hand the Canadian government had no idea what they were receiving.... They could not define, that which in their own minds was indefinite, and hence the language and order-in-council was indefinite."[17] Most probably, though, the British were nervous about drawing international attention to the fact that their claim to the Arctic region was tentative. This could open up the possibility of foreign claims in a region that they felt was rightfully theirs and so should belong to Canada.

The imperial order-in-council, named the *Adjacent Territories Order 1880*, was dispatched to Governor General Lorne on August 16, and published in the *Canada Gazette* on October 9, 1880. The publishing of the order signified that the Arctic islands had officially been transferred to Canada. The snail-paced transfer process had taken six years.

THE FIRST INTERNATIONAL POLAR YEAR

The first International Polar Year was inspired by the Austrian naval officer Lieutenant Karl Weyprecht, scientist and co-commander of the Austro-Hungarian Polar Expedition of 1872–74. He felt that valuable meteorological and geophysical information could be gleaned from the earth's polar regions, but studying the geophysical phenomena of these regions would be difficult for one country to undertake. He envisioned a multinational series of coordinated scientific observations and studies performed during the same time period. He felt that if nations put aside their competition for geographical discovery and focused instead on coordinated scientific research, it would be of greater importance to mankind in general.

Weyprecht succeeded in convincing other European countries, and plans got underway for an international common program to study the top of the world for an entire year, from one summer to the next. Unfortunately, Weyprecht died of tuberculosis in 1881, before his dream of countries uniting for scientific research was realized.

The International Polar Year (IPY), planned from August 1, 1882, to September 1, 1883, was a remarkable, ambitious scientific operation. Eleven countries established fourteen principal research stations across the polar regions, twelve in the Arctic and two in the Antarctic region. Research stations were set up to take observations of meteorology, geomagnetism, auroral phenomena, ocean currents, tides, formation of ice, and atmospheric electricity. In all, seven hundred men participated, conducting elaborate environmental and geophysical studies.

Three of the Arctic research stations were established in the Canadian North: a German station at Kingua Fiord on southeastern Baffin Island, with auxiliary observatories at the six Moravian missions in Labrador; a British station at Fort Rae on Great Slave Lake; and an American station at Fort Conger, Lady Franklin Bay, on the northeast coast of Ellesmere Island.

The Canadian and British governments agreed to subsidize the British expedition, which was organized by the Royal Geographical Society of London. Although no Canadians were involved in the field research, the Canadian Meteorological Office in Toronto played a support role in the organization of the station, and the Toronto Observatory carried out the same observations as the Arctic observatories. In September 1883, Charles Carpmael, the superintendent of the Meteorological Office, was invited to become a member of the International Polar Commission.

The British expedition was led by Captain Henry P. Dawson of the Royal Artillery. The three soldiers who accompanied him were also artillery men. Fort Rae on Great Slave Lake was chosen for the observatory location because, at 62°39'N, it was close to the north magnetic pole. It was also the site of a Hudson's Bay Company post.

Travelling to Fort Rae was a long and arduous journey. Dawson and his men left Liverpool the second week of May, arriving in Winnipeg in July. They travelled north along various river systems and overland by steamer, ox-cart, and canoe. Their boat voyage across Great Slave Lake in stormy weather was such a treacherous crossing that it took eight days. Their boat was eventually stove in and sank, but they made it to shore with most of their supplies and instruments. The four men finally arrived at Fort Rae on August 30, 1882.

A partly finished cabin became their observatory. As with the other IPY observatories, all iron nails were removed from the buildings and replaced with copper or wooden pegs that would not influence the magnetic measurements. Inside, the instruments were placed on wooden pillars. Dawson and his men constructed a second magnetic observatory with shutters in the roof that could be opened for astronomical readings. Unlike at other sites, though, they were forced to erect a fence around it to keep out the wolves.[18] At year's end, the group made the long trek back to England, where their copious notes and data were analyzed at the Kew Observatory and the British Meteorological Office. The expedition cost £12,500 — about £925,000 today, or $1,655,750 Canadian.[19]

The most ambitious of the IPY expeditions was an American one. Since the IPY focused on meteorology, Weyprecht had approached the U.S. Army Signal Corps, which operated the Weather Bureau. He made the suggestion that the Signal Corps set up a station at Point Barrow, Alaska.

Congress agreed, but organized two IPY parties. One would operate out of a station at Point Barrow. A second would establish operations as far north as possible.

On March 3, 1881, the United States Congress authorized the establishment of a research station at Lady Franklin Bay, the location that Howgate had previously suggested for a polar research station.[20] It would last two years instead of just one. Despite Weyprecht's insistence that the countries involved put aside goals of geographic pursuit for purely scientific research, the proposed American expedition's main function was to reach the North Pole. Any other scientific observations would be secondary to this purpose.[21]

Henry Howgate would not lead this expedition, however. In December of 1880, he had resigned. He was arrested the following August for embezzlement of Signal Corps funds.

Thirty-six-year-old signal service officer Major Adolphus Washington Greely was chosen to command the expedition, although he had no previous Arctic experience. Greely had enlisted with the Union Army before he was eighteen. He was specifically interested in telegraphic signalling and the use of meteorological reports sent via telegraph to predict weather changes, and became a signal service officer. Howgate's idea of studying the physical conditions of the Far North, as well as conducting signalling experiments under the Arctic's severe weather conditions, appealed to Greely.

Greely's Lady Franklin Bay Expedition of twenty-five men left St. John's, Newfoundland, aboard the SS *Proteus* the first week of July 1881. They arrived at their destination on Ellesmere Island, at latitude 81°44'N, on August 26. The men constructed buildings from wood carried on the ship, and called their post Fort Conger in honour of Senator Omar D. Conger, who had recommended the $25,000 to fund the expedition. The men carried out their studies of weather and tides, making magnetic and astronomical observations and collecting plant, animal, and mineral specimens. As well, they explored the interior of Ellesmere and the west coast of Greenland in expeditions that totalled twenty-five hundred miles. One party succeeded in reaching and planting the American flag at 83°24'N, besting Nares' record for the highest northern latitude by just over four miles.

The following summer of 1882, the supply ship *Neptune*, scheduled to arrive with fresh supplies, was thwarted from reaching Lady Franklin

Bay by ice in the channel. It turned back, leaving only a small ration of supplies at Littleton Island and Cape Sabine. It returned to port with the majority of the expedition stores in its hold. When the ship didn't arrive, Greely began rationing supplies. They managed for the second year, but the relief ship that was supposed to pick them up in 1883 failed to arrive as well, starting a chain of events that doomed the party.

In the summer of 1883, two United States Army relief ships were to proceed to Littleton Island, construct a storehouse, and stock it with supplies for Greely's party. The first ship, *Proteus*, was then to proceed to Lady Franklin Bay. No effort was to be spared to reach Greely and his men. Taking advantage of the good weather, the commander of the *Proteus* decided to head directly to Lady Franklin Bay without first stopping to leave stores on Littleton. The *Proteus* ran into heavy ice several days later and was crushed. When the men abandoned ship, they only cached ten days of supplies at Cape Sabine, though they had enough time to land the rest of the large supply of food intended for Greely.

The second relief vessel, *Yantic*, a Civil War gunboat, went in pursuit of the shipwrecked men without also leaving any stores on Littleton Island for the expedition it had headed north to re-supply. By the time the *Yantic*, with the *Proteus* crew safely on board, returned to St. John's, it was too late in the year to send another relief ship for the Greely party.[22]

Greely's instructions were to retreat south by September 1, 1883, should a ship fail to arrive. On August 9, they abandoned Fort Conger and began the arduous two-hundred-mile journey south in three boats. By the time they realized that they were sailing into worse conditions than they had left behind, it was too late to turn back. They made it to the appointed meeting point at Cape Sabine, set up a makeshift camp, and lived on a meagre supply of rations.[23]

In 1884, realizing that without supplies for two years, Greely's expedition would be in dire straits, the United States Navy rallied a relief expedition of three ships: the *Thetis*, the *Bear*, and Nares' ice-strengthened ship the *Alert*, seconded from the British for the rescue operations. Neither the *Bear* nor the *Alert* reached Greely and his men. The *Thetis* did.

By the time the *Thetis* arrived in June 1884, only Greely and six others were found alive. Weakened by hunger, Greely and four barely living skeletons had to be carried aboard on stretchers. One man died on the rescue ship's homeward voyage. Only six of the twenty-five men survived the ordeal.[24]

After the Fort Conger disaster, the third ill-fated American North Pole expedition, the United States Congress ceased sponsoring expeditions to the Arctic. American explorers then turned to scientific societies and private individuals for funding for their northern exploration.[25]

Of the seven hundred who participated in the field during the International Polar Year, Greely's men and one Russian seaman were the only deaths. [26] Overall, the first International Polar Year was a success. However, each participating nation published their observations independently, and so, in the end, the concept of coordinated research was not carried through. Nonetheless, the IPY set a precedent for international scientific co-operation. The information, data, and images acquired from the first International Polar Year offer a view of the circumpolar environment in the late nineteenth century.[27]

CHAPTER THREE

An Arctic Shipping Route

While countries were establishing scientific stations to study the world's polar regions, western Canadian farmers were making their own plans for using the Low Arctic.

To turn the once fur-trading West into an agriculture-based colony, the Canadian government had passed the *Dominion Land Act* in 1872 to tempt settlers west by offering one hundred and sixty acres of free land. Manitoba's population jumped from twenty-five thousand in 1871 to sixty-six thousand by the time the International Polar Year was organized in 1881.

The Prairies proved to be rich, arable land for growing grain, with wheat as the main crop. In 1879, the federal government introduced its National Policy to create a continent-wide economy, which included building a publicly supported transcontinental railway. Grain produced on the Prairies could be shipped east to Montreal, where it would be exported to Europe.

To support this plan, the Canadian Pacific Railway (CPR) was given a guaranteed monopoly for twenty years to its mainline through the Prairies. This monopoly meant that its freight rates were the only rates available, and the CPR could charge whatever exorbitant prices it wanted. Farmers began to look at alternative shipping routes to get their grain to foreign markets. The shortest possible route from Manitoba and the North-West Territory (Saskatchewan) to Europe was by ship through Hudson Bay and Hudson Strait to the Atlantic Ocean. However, this would require a railway to a port on western Hudson Bay.[1]

Exporting via Hudson Bay would cut off about 365 miles. But more importantly, it would eliminate railway transportation controlled by the CPR. Western farmers calculated that this would amount to savings of between fifteen and twenty cents a bushel.[2] Farmers shipped over ten million bushels of grain annually, so this would mean significant savings. As Prairie wheat production increased, so did the enthusiasm for such a shipping route.

On Wednesday, January 2, 1884, the *Winnipeg Daily Times* reported on a meeting of farmers who had put forth a motion, "That the farmers of this Province are in absolute want of better railway facilities for exporting their grain, and propose that steps should at once be taken to obtain a way of shipping grain via Hudson Bay."

One of the farmers' biggest allies was Joseph Royal, member of Parliament for Provencher, Manitoba. Royal envisioned Manitoba as a maritime province, with its northern frontier bordering the great saltwater Hudson Bay. He raised the issue of the Hudson Bay route in the House of Commons on February 11, 1884. Several other MPs followed Royal's impassioned speech with their own, making a case for the shipping route.

Finally, Prime Minister Macdonald addressed the House: "The importance of opening up a trade there, I think, cannot be exaggerated with respect to the future of the North-West. Not only will it be the means of access to Europe for the general products of the North-West, but it will be exceedingly valuable on account of the known mineral wealth and the wealth of the fisheries that have been alluded to."[3]

By the end of the prolonged discussion, parliamentarians were convinced of the merits of a Hudson Bay route for shipping purposes. Two weeks later, a fifteen-man committee of members from both sides of the House convened to investigate the navigability of the Hudson Bay route. It would examine Hudson's Bay Company journals, which documented the annual voyages of company ships. It would also interview eleven experts on Hudson Bay.

One of the key people interviewed was Dr. Robert Bell, the senior assistant director of the Geological Survey of Canada. Bell was a geologist who had carried out extensive travels in the James Bay area and visited Hudson Bay and its adjoining regions between 1875 and 1881. Bell told the committee it was "Essential to successful farming in our North-West that we should have an easy and cheap route to the markets of the world; and also for carrying heavy freights from Europe to the North East, such as iron and heavy goods generally, it is very desirable to have as short a land carriage as possible." He added, "It would afford a cheap and direct way of bringing immigrants to the North-West."[4]

On February 26, the committee examined Captain J.G. Boulton, Esq., staff commander in the British Navy and hydrographical surveyor for the Dominion government. Boulton laid out a well-formed plan for how the government should proceed. He suggested that it procure a Newfoundland steamer, hire a sailing captain experienced in ice navigation, and, with a surveyor from the British Admiralty on board, land six or seven small parties at various points along the straits that would be left all winter and picked up in the spring. This would give them the opportunity to take observations of the daily weather, the conditions of the ice, and the velocity of currents.

Records claimed that a total of eight hundred vessels had traversed Hudson Bay, including British troop ships, emigrant ships, and exploration vessels, as well as whalers. Hudson's Bay Company records alone revealed that during the 223 years the company had sailed the bay and strait, it had sent out an average of two to four sailing vessels a year to retrieve and carry furs to Europe. Only two ships had been lost in all that time.

The *Report of the Committee of the House of Commons to Enquire into the Question of the Navigation of Hudson's Bay* was released on April 8, 1884.[5] It said,

> For more than 250 years, sailors have counted upon having an uninterrupted navigation of from two months to three months and this without marine charts, without an accurate knowledge of these waters, without light-houses, without a system of telegraphic communication, and without the aid of steam. It is not, then, an unwarranted belief, that with all the appliances now at the disposal of nautical science, this navigation will be prolonged for some weeks.[6]

On paper, a Hudson Bay route seemed to be a relatively safe one. However, the committee realized the importance of physically testing the route. It put forth Boulton's recommendation to send a vessel north to Hudson Strait to make a firsthand assessment of the route. The committee felt that one year's voyage would not give a fair example of annual navigability of the bay and strait, and advised taking observations over a period of at least three years. This would entail manning a number of temporary observatories on the shores of Hudson Strait, and on particular spots along the Hudson Bay coast.

In the end, it was decided that the first of three expeditions should be sent out immediately. The Dominion government voted to spend $70,000 to outfit a steamship and set up six observation posts along the Hudson Strait. The expeditions would also assess whether the most suitable port on Hudson Bay for a railway to be built to would be the mouth of the Nelson or Churchill River.

Although Canada had been in possession of its Arctic for four years, this would be the first official government expedition to the region.

THE HUDSON BAY AND STRAIT EXPEDITION OF 1884

The Marine and Fisheries Department, overseeing the Hudson Bay project, chose its lead meteorologist as the able commander of the mission. Thirty-three-year-old Lieutenant Andrew Robertson Gordon would command all three government expeditions to Hudson Bay.

Born in Aberdeen, Scotland, in February 1851, Gordon joined the Royal Navy at the age of twelve, and specialized in navigation. In 1871, he was specially promoted to rank of lieutenant for meritorious examination. He retired from Her Majesty's service in October 1873 at the age of twenty-two. He then immigrated to Canada and settled in the village of Cooksville (now Mississauga, Ontario), an important stagecoach stop on the road from Toronto.

Gordon's naval experience held him in good stead, and he became an officer in the Department of Marine and Fisheries. In 1880, Gordon became deputy superintendent of the Meteorological Service within the department at its central office in Toronto. He increasingly saw the importance of creating a national weather service and visited weather observation stations in Quebec and around the Gulf of St. Lawrence. He also travelled west to Manitoba to assess the possibility of extending the service's activities across the country.

The dark-haired, stocky Gordon, with his experience in "weather gauging," was an ideal choice to head the expeditions to Hudson Bay. His extensive hydrographic and meteorological expertise was critical to the nature of the expeditions, which would ascertain the length of time when ice conditions would permit the navigability of Hudson Bay and Hudson Strait as a shipping route.

For the 1884 expedition, the department chartered the Newfoundland sealing ship the SS *Neptune* from Job Bros. & Co. for the sum of $16,500.[7] The St. John's century-old company, Job Brothers, was in the business of outfitting vessels for the annual seal hunt.

Thomas E. Appleton Collection, Library and Archives Canada, e010691139

Lieutenant Andrew Robertson Gordon commanded the Hudson Bay and Strait Expeditions in 1884, 1885, and 1886.

The *Neptune* was considered to be the Newfoundland sealing fleet's largest and most powerful vessel. In fact, when the *Neptune* sailed into the port of St. John's on April 3, 1884, it carried the largest seal catch ever recorded, with 41,500 prime harp seals in its hold. The seals were "taken" in twelve days by three hundred men. The cargo weighed in at over eight hundred tons and was valued at $125,000. This impressive news made the front page of the *New York Times*. The *Neptune* proved to be a lucrative vessel that year for the Job Brothers, with its profitable catch and subsequent lease to the Canadian government for the summer expedition to Hudson Bay.

Built in 1873 in Dundee, Scotland, the barque-rigged sailing steamship was constructed of British oak, sheathed with "iron-bar," and covered with greenheart, a dark-green, strong, dense wood. The wooden screw steamer was 109.6 feet long and 29.8 feet beam, and had a depth of hold of 18.4 feet. It could carry over eight hundred tons of coal and cargo. Because the schooner's three masts were low, it had little sail power, but its steam engines could achieve one hundred and ten horsepower, which could propel the loaded ship along at about eight knots an hour — just over nine miles per hour on land or the speed of a horse's trot.[8] The *Neptune* also had some High Arctic ice experience as one of the ships used in the 1882 Greely Relief Expedition, coming to within thirty miles of 80°N.

On July 2, 1884, Gordon received his instructions as expedition commander and proceeded by train to Halifax to oversee preparations and the loading of supplies on board. The ship's decks were piled with lumber and sections of the prefabricated buildings constructed in Dartmouth, Nova Scotia, that would be used for the observation stations. As well as carrying the coal necessary for powering the ship, one hundred and eighty sacks of hard coal equalling twenty tons were stowed on board for use in the observation stations' stoves. Barrels of salt pork, beef, sugar, oatmeal, flour, soap, bagged bread, canned mutton, root vegetables, apples, and butter; kegs of vinegar, coffee, lime juice, beans, canned fruit, and currants; and boxes of cocoa were earmarked for the stations. In short, everything the men would need to live for up to eighteen months — everything, that is, but fresh meat and vegetables. Upon leaving Halifax, the *Neptune* carried 833 tons of freight.

In a March 1885 article published in *Science* magazine, Colonel William P. Anderson, a hydrographic surveyor with the Department of Marine and Fisheries, described the station buildings erected along the Hudson Strait in 1884. He noted that each "hut" was sixteen feet by twenty feet and divided into three rooms with a porch. The buildings "had double walls of board, with an outer and inner air-space formed by a sheathing of tarred paper."[9] It was recommended after construction that the men should set to work collecting sod to cover the house "to further protect it from cold," and to pack snow over the whole thing for extra insulation.[10] This was sage advice, except that most of the ground the buildings were erected on was rocky, with no insulating sod to be found within a hundred miles.

At two o'clock on Tuesday, July 22, all was in readiness. The expedition members boarded the ship. The Honourable A.W. McLellan, minister of Marine and Fisheries, along with a group of Halifax citizens, all wished the expedition Godspeed. An hour later, the *Neptune* pulled away from the marine wharf to the hearty cheers of those on the dock. The men on board returned the cheers and sang a rousing rendition of "Auld Lang Syne." The ship slowly steamed out of the harbour, and was saluted by numerous flags being dipped on the marine dock buildings and on a German man-of-war at anchor near the shore. The ship nosed its way into the swells of the Atlantic and was welcomed to the ocean by "a stiff breeze and showers of rain."[11]

In all, fifty-five men were on board. The ship's sailing master was Captain William Sopp, of St. John's, Newfoundland. The crew was made up of a first and second mate, two stewards, two enginemen, two cooks, one oiler, three firemen, one blacksmith, two trimmers, and twelve able-bodied seamen. Three carpenters were enlisted for the voyage to help erect the buildings that would be home to nineteen observers for the next two winters and three summers. The expedition staff included Robert Bell, of the Geological Survey of Canada, as the medical officer and geologist; the six young men who would be the stations' observers — R.F. Stupart of Toronto; W.A. Ashe of Quebec City; C.V. De Boucherville; A.N. Laperrière of Ottawa; W. Skynner of Springfield; H.M. Burwell of London, Ontario; and the journalist C.R. Tuttle of Winnipeg, who, as well as acting as the expedition's historian, would be the observer taking meteorological measurements at Churchill.

Thirteen other men, listed as part of the expedition, would be the station men. Two men would stay with each head observer for the winter. These men were all under thirty and unmarried. They had signed up for a year of adventure in the name of science. The men were engaged at a rate of thirty-five dollars per month, with an additional four dollars per week as board money during the voyage.

The instructions for the officers in charge of the stations were as follows: "As the primary object of the whole expedition is to ascertain for what period of the year the Straits are navigable, all attention is to be paid to the formation, breaking up and movements of the ice."[12] Each station was provided with a sundial and timepiece, and the clock was to be tested at noon each day when there was sunshine. Daily temperature, barometric pressure, tidal observations, and weather conditions were all to be noted in detail. Also, remarks about wildlife, the movements of birds and fish, and grasses and other flora were to be recorded.

The men were instructed to take every precaution against fire: "Two buckets full of water are always to be kept ready for instant use."[13] Each station was equipped with a boat with the understanding that no one was to travel farther from the station than they could return from in the same day.

Instructions on health were also given. "As the successful carrying out of the observations will, in a great measure, depend on the health of the party, the need of exercise is strongly insisted on during the winter months, and also that each member of the party shall partake freely of the lime juice supplied."[14] The hazards of living in the North during the dark winter months had long been recognized by Arctic adventurers, and the Dominion government was taking every precaution to ensure the welfare of its men.

NORTH TO HUDSON STRAIT

The *Neptune* made its way up the coast of Nova Scotia and through the Strait of Belle Isle, between Newfoundland and the mainland. Here, it encountered the first icebergs, which studded the strait like small white islands. The icebergs ranged in size from one hundred feet to a quarter of a mile long and an impressive two hundred to three hundred feet high.[15]

The *Neptune* gave these imposing monoliths of ice a wide berth by as much as a quarter of a mile. An iceberg overturning or collapsing in close proximity to a vessel would have calamitous consequences.

Commander Gordon showed his leadership colours in the first few weeks of the expedition. He was quiet and unassuming. He had a constant interest in the movements of the ship and had his own compass erected on the roof of his charthouse. He was able to tell the location of the ship at any time within a mile or so. He was "moderately companionable to his men, solicitous for their good health and general welfare, but sufficiently reserved to ensure respect to his orders."[16] Gordon was of high moral character and conducted church services, Anglican style, for his men every Sunday morning. All on board had great respect for him and were confident that he was the right man to lead the expedition.

During that first week of the voyage, the men were treated to a lecture by Dr. Bell on the contents of their medicine cabinets and a variety of injuries they might have to treat, including severed arteries. The men most in need of this instruction were those who would soon be living isolated existences at the stations.

Robert Bell was a geologist who had worked with the Geological Survey since he was a teenager. In 1857, at the age of sixteen, he had accompanied Sir William Logan, the survey's director, on fieldwork in Quebec's Saguenay region. Bell gained a lot of prestige and respect in geological circles, carrying out explorations of the northern sections of Quebec, Ontario, and Manitoba, mapping rivers between Hudson Bay and Lake Superior, and travelling extensively in the James Bay region. Bell became assistant director of the Geological Survey in 1877. In 1878, he obtained a medical degree from McGill University in order to be prepared for any mishap in the field.

A week after departing, the steamer anchored near the Nain Mission House, halfway up the east coast of Labrador. At the time, the Moravian missionaries had six posts along the Labrador coast. The German missionaries not only imparted their Protestant Christian beliefs to the Inuit, but also made a good living trading with them for furs. Expedition historian Charles Tuttle noted that the Moravian brethren claimed that the income from their trade barely paid one half of the expenses of maintaining the mission. Tuttle concluded, though, that the missionaries had made a miscalculation, and that their trade business was a thriving one. He questioned whether their mandate of Christianizing the locals was actually secondary to that of trading with them.

In his official report, Gordon only briefly notes their stop in Nain. He had hoped to purchase some fur clothing for the station men who would be wintering along the coast, as well as hire Inuit interpreters. He had no success in procuring either.

The *Neptune* cast off from Nain at 4:30 on the morning of July 31. As the men headed north, the scenery became more grand and pictur-esque, with the coastline rising in a jagged wall of rock, towering two thousand feet above them. The little ship entered an inlet surrounded by craggy precipices and glorious snow-covered summits. It steamed twenty miles down the winding channel to where the Hudson's Bay Company post was nestled at its end at Nachvak Bay, dropping anchor at 4:00 p.m. on August 1.

Nachvak Fiord, at latitude 59°10'N, 63°30'W, stretches through a gla-cial trough of the rugged Torngat Mountains for twenty-eight miles to where the river widens at its head. For eight thousand years the Inuit spent summers there because of the ideal fishing grounds and the presence of caribou. The Hudson's Bay Company established a post on the fiord in 1828, because of its access to both marine traffic and the native people. Gordon had success procuring skin clothing from George Ford, the com-pany agent, and hiring James Lane, an Inuit-Scot, as interpreter.

On the second of August, the *Neptune* continued northward up the coast to Hudson Strait. The ship met with dense fog that compelled it to "stand off to sea and lie to." By August 5, the weather had cleared, and the ship steamed into Hudson Strait via Gray Strait, between Cape Chidley at the tip of Labrador and the Button Islands to the north. The expedition entered the strait at the same time of year that the Hudson's Bay Company ships usually did.

After rounding the tip of Labrador, Gordon chose a small sheltered bay on the southwestern shore of Cape Chidley for the first observation station. This station, at the southern entrance to Hudson Strait, seemed an ideal harbour, well-protected from the northwest winds. Being almost landlocked, it provided vessels the safety of riding out the worst storm. Shortly after dropping anchor, Gordon announced, "This place shall be called Port Burwell, in honour of Mr. Burwell, the observer who is to take charge here."[17] Herbert Mahlon Burwell was only twenty-one years old. He had a year of immense responsibility ahead of him, and a geographical place name.

The stores were landed and the station building erected in three days. By August 8, all was in readiness, and the *Neptune* ventured out into the strait. Here, Hudson Strait, between the Button Islands on the south and Resolution Island to the north, is forty-five miles wide. This is the main entrance to Hudson Strait from Davis Strait, with the waters as much as three hundred fathoms deep.[18]

Gordon intended to cross to the north side to establish the second station on Resolution Island. However, the island was unapproachable. The weather turned nasty in the early afternoon, throwing up a heavy snowstorm that forced the *Neptune* to retreat. The next morning, as they steamed westward along the strait's north shore, they saw a snow-white streak on the horizon extending across the strait as far as they could see. It was field ice: quite literally, a field of floating ice.

The ship charged through the ice, crashing, tearing, and mulching it to pieces under its solid prow, "something after the fashion of a Grand Trunk snow plough in a Canadian snow-drift," wrote Tuttle.[19] The *Neptune* was able to do this because of its steam power. A sailing ship would have foundered and been jammed in the icy midst. At one point, the ship was halted by the ice, but it backed up about a hundred yards and charged, cleaving a passage through. The ship shuddered and groaned, and got stuck half a dozen times before pushing out to open water near the east coast of Big Island on the north side of the strait.

Here they dropped anchor and found a suitable site to erect a station. Gordon called it Ashe Inlet after William Austin Ashe, the main observer in charge of the station. However, bad weather and field ice followed them into the harbour, "interfering," as Gordon says, "with the work of landing lumber and supplies."[20]

They met a number of Inuit there who came aboard with gifts of two stag hearts, which the ship's company thankfully ate for breakfast the next morning. The Inuit also informed them of the American Captain Spicer's trading post on the mainland thirty miles away. Gordon encouraged the people not to deal with Spicer, but to trade only with the "Canadians."

Some sort of political message was given about the "great and good mother, Queen Victoria and of her noble Governor-General Lord Lansdowne."[21] The Inuit responded with smiles, but likely didn't understand the gibberish the southerners told them.

The station was constructed in a few days. Mr. Skynner and Messrs. Jordan and Rainsford, who were originally supposed to remain at the station on Resolution Island, would spend the summer here. The ship would collect them on its way back through the strait and set up a station as intended on Resolution Island. The three left the *Neptune* in their boat and rowed ashore to join the three others who were unpacking and settling into their roles as the station men at Ashe Inlet for a year.

The *Neptune* weighed anchor and headed across the strait to Prince of Wales Sound, to select a location for a third station. The ship forced its way through field ice to the south shore, a distance of between sixty and seventy miles. The next afternoon, the *Neptune* moored in a safe harbour surrounded by majestic mountains. Lumber and supplies were loaded onto a smaller boat that was rowed ashore and unloaded. It took four days to construct the three buildings: one for living quarters, and two others that were specifically designed to house the instruments that the men would use to carry out complex magnetic observations. These instruments, borrowed from the British government, had been used by Captain Dawson in Fort Rae as part of the International Polar Year three years earlier.

The new station was named Stupart Bay after its head observer, Robert Frederic Stupart. Stupart had joined the Meteorological Service in 1872 at the age of fifteen. He was twenty-seven when he signed on to overwinter as an observer in the Hudson Strait. Stupart had several years of magnetical work experience, and so was specifically put in charge of this station. Because of the additional magnetical observations to be carried out at the post, Stupart was provided with an assistant, Harry T. Bennet, along with the usual two station men. This was the only station with four men.

Gordon notes in his report that a number of Inuit greeted them upon their arrival and seemed pleased that a station would be established there. However, Gordon did not consult them when he named Stupart Bay, a name that would grace maps for decades.

Robert Bell, Library and Archives Canada, C-086377

Station men and locals at the newly erected observation station at Stupart Bay on the south side of Hudson Strait, August 17, 1884. Seventeen Inuit starved to death the winter of 1884–85.

Robert Bell, Library and Archives Canada, C-086362

Port De Boucherville Observation Station on rocky Nottingham Island, at the north entrance to Hudson Bay on the western end of the strait, August 24, 1884.

On the evening of August 22, the *Neptune* proceeded west to Nottingham Island, close to the entrance to Hudson Bay. As it approached the western end of the strait, it encountered a seemingly endless pack of heavy ice that stretched for twenty miles and filled the strait as far as the eye could see. The ice measured forty feet thick in places. One of the propeller blades sheared off while pushing through the ice. It took three days to replace it with the new propeller they had brought along for just such an event. The quiet, reserved Captain Sopp was quite upset about the incident, being "out of temper to the extent of using unparliamentary language."[22]

The scenic scapes of towering fiords had been reduced to low, rocky ground. Nottingham Island was an inhospitable place with nothing more than sparse inch-high vegetation. Here, they built the fourth station and named it Port De Boucherville. C.V. De Boucherville apparently looked at the location of his home for the next year with such distaste that Tuttle thought it would have been more appropriate to name it "De Boucherville's Disgust." Tuttle noted, "It required lively exercise of all his [De Boucherville's] nerve power, of which he possesses a liberal store, to reconcile himself to this voluntary exile."[23]

After settling the observer and his two companions in their new homestead, the expedition headed toward Mansfield Island, the island inside the southern entrance to Hudson Bay.[24] After cruising the eastern side of Mansfield for an adequate harbour and finding none, Gordon decided to set up the fifth station on nearby Digges Island on the return journey. The *Neptune* steamed into Hudson Bay and headed for Marble Island on the west side, which was known as a site frequented by American whalers.

To Hudson Bay and Back

At Marble Island, the *Neptune* dropped anchor and the company went ashore. They found whalers' graves, but were disappointed not to meet any living souls. Gordon also found a letter in a bottle from one of the whaling captains.

This habit of leaving notes about where a ship was headed in bottles and cairns of piled stones was one of the few means of letting other ships know of an expedition's activities. If an expedition did not return, a note left on their last stopping place with details about where they were headed would make a search for them easier.

The *Neptune* men surveyed the harbour, then Gordon charted a southward course for Churchill on Hudson Bay's west coast. The ship arrived on September 3. The harbour at the mouth of the Churchill River is about a mile and a half wide, two and a half miles in length, and from five to twenty fathoms deep: ideal for large ships' anchorage. However, the village of Churchill, where the Hudson's Bay Company had operated a fur-trading post since 1717, was upriver and could only be reached by small boats.

The ship's company was invited to the village (population: forty) for Sunday church service. For several months the men had not worn shirt collars or even shaved, but with the prospect of attending church, razors were stropped and faces shaved. Rumpled shirts, dress coats, vests, and pants were pressed, and squashed-up hats patted back into their original shapes. By nine o'clock that morning, the crew was transformed, and the men barely recognizable to each other in their clean and washed state.

The ship's boats were lowered; ten men to a boat, with four oarsmen. It took less than an hour to row the three miles upriver. They then hiked the last mile overland to the village of Churchill. W.W. Fox, the ship's photographer, lugged his camera, his wooden tripod, and a package of prepared photographic plates along, and photographed the whole congregation outside the little church.[25]

Thirty-six-year-old Charles Tuttle, who was supposed to winter at Churchill to take weather observations, resigned, owing to ill health. Gordon then arranged for the Hudson's Bay Company agent to take the required meteorological readings instead. Chief Factor Spencer accepted a salary of $120 per year for the added duties. An anemometer to measure the force of the wind was erected on one of the company buildings, a thermometer set up, and a barometer hung in a suitable place.

With the steamer's load of lumber, building materials, and supplies having been offloaded at various points along the strait, the ship was now riding high in the water. Ballast was required to maintain the correct trim to keep the ship sailing properly, and the men took on water for ballast.

The *Neptune* departed on August 9, with an additional stock of fur clothing for the station men, and made for York Factory at the mouth of the Hayes River, sixty miles south of Churchill and just south of the mouth of the Nelson River. York Factory was a much larger and more imposing post than the one at Churchill. It even had two small churches: one inside the Hudson's Bay Company stockade and the other outside the post, built by the missionaries for the local Cree people.

At York Factory, Gordon met Mr. Wood, the storekeeper, who had carried out meteorological observations for several years. Gordon checked his instruments and records and found all "well done." After some discussion with the Hudson's Bay Company men, it was apparent that they were against a port being at York Factory. Whereas the folks at Churchill welcomed the idea, the "Factory" men were concerned that such a route would cut into their trade and export enterprise. The acting chief officer, Mr. Matheson, even outright ridiculed the whole project.[26]

On September 12, the *Neptune* shaped a course across Hudson Bay for Digges Island. The crew found a good harbour on the southwestern side of the island and built the fifth observation station, with Arthur Laperrière in charge. Laperrière Harbour was an appropriate companion station to Port De Boucherville, as Digges Island was forty-five miles south of Nottingham Island. The islands lie on either side of the entrance into Hudson Bay.

Laperrière Observation Station on Digges Island south of Nottingham at the entrance to Hudson Bay, August 29, 1884. The Neptune *is anchored in the background to the left.*

Some of the men explored the island while the carpenters raised the frame of the observatory. One man rushed back to the ship with news of having seen five polar bears. A bear hunt ensued with fifteen men, nine with rifles. Three of the great white bears were shot, and the men debated who should get custody of the skins. Dr. Bell, who hadn't even been on the hunt, won one of the skins under the auspices of science.

On the morning of September 20, the *Neptune* departed, heading east through Hudson Strait. It stopped in at the other stations on its way to drop off furs and bid a final farewell before leaving the men until the following summer. At Ashe Inlet, the men intended for the Resolution Island station, Messrs. Skynner, Rainsford, and Jordon, re-boarded the *Neptune*, leaving Ashe and the two others to enjoy a little more space.

At five o'clock that evening, the *Neptune*, escorted from the bay by six Inuit men in kayaks, made for Resolution Island. The ship spent three days steaming along sixty miles of the island's coastline. With no signs of a harbour, a gale threatening, and considering the ship had twice been damaged from hitting rock bottom, Captain Sopp advised abandonment of a station on Resolution. The *Neptune* made for Port Burwell without haste, stopping briefly before heading south.

Robert Bell, Library and Archives Canada, C-086357

Skynner's Cove, the last observation station, was established September 30, 1884. But because it was located at Nachvak Bay in northern Labrador and not on Hudson Strait, it was abandoned at the end of the summer of 1885.

At noon on September 30, after steaming south along the Labrador coast for a day, they anchored in a cove on the north side of Nachvak Bay. Gordon decided on this as the site for the final station. They erected the house and landed stores. Gordon named it Skynner's Cove after lead observer William Skynner.

On Monday, October 6, the ship weighed anchor and charted a course for St. John's. The expedition arrived on Saturday morning and the ship was delivered to its owner, Job Bros. & Co. Gordon and the majority of the men took passage on the steamship *City of Mexico* for Halifax. From there they returned by train to their respective residences in Quebec and Ontario.

The first Dominion government expedition to the Low Arctic was successfully completed. Six research stations had been established and men left there to carry out scientific observations and collect data.

GORDON'S 1884 HUDSON BAY AND STRAIT EXPEDITION REPORT

The *Neptune's* Captain Sopp gave the 1884 voyage a very favourable appraisal when he remarked, "I would sooner navigate Hudson's Strait than the English Channel."[27]

In 1885, Charles R. Tuttle published a 589-page book about the Hudson Bay and Strait, titled *Our North Land*. He suggested in it that Hudson Strait was easily navigable for a longer period than just the summer months. He wrote: "There are certain months of winter when the temperature in that region is probably too low for nautical operations, but there will be found to be not less than eight months navigation of the Hudson's Bay route, navigation free from all kinds of danger and far superior in every way to that of the St. Lawrence."[28]

Gordon was not quite as enthusiastic or naive in his appraisal of the route. He also refrained from commenting on the navigation period until all three summer expeditions could offer more conclusive results. Gordon's official *Report of the Hudson Bay Expedition under the Command of Lieut., A.R. Gordon, R.N., 1884* is a concise forty-two pages. He recommended closing the station at Nachvak Bay on the Labrador coast, as Newfoundland fishermen often visit that locale, offering enough information about the conditions there. It was never part of the plan to establish a station at Nachvak anyhow. Gordon doesn't suggest any further attempts to set up a post on Resolution Island.

Gordon noted the exceptional amount of ice that summer. The Inuit they met informed them of this, as well as the factors at the Hudson's Bay Company posts they stopped at. Figuring that the ice would not be as heavy the following summer, Gordon recommended that the following year's expedition leave Halifax by May 15 to determine the earliest that ships could pass through the strait.

A great part of his report examines the resources of the region. Gordon refers to the whaling carried out by the Americans. The chief whaling grounds were in Roes Welcome Sound, "a vast basin in the north-western portion of Hudson's Bay" between the mainland and Southhampton Island.[29] Gordon reported that whalers from Massachusetts and Connecticut had been carrying out a profitable industry at "the Welcome" for a quarter of a century.

Gordon referred to the 1875–76 report by the United States Commissioners of the Fish and Fisheries, which stated that in the eleven years preceding 1874, fifty voyages had been made to Hudson Bay by New England whalers, with their returns of $27,420 per voyage, amounting to a total of $1,371,000. Gordon calculated that an average of three vessels per year since that date would mean returns of $822,600 in the last decade, making a combined total of $2,193,600 since Americans had begun whaling in the bay.

This added up to a significant amount of revenue in tariffs and fishing licences that the Canadian government had missed out on. Interestingly, although this was readily available information, none of it was included in the report compiled by the committee inquiring into the navigability of Hudson Bay and Strait submitted the previous April. That report had been concerned mainly with navigability, and not with the economic usage of the bay.

Gordon also detailed the Hudson's Bay Company fishing operations, which included extensive beluga fisheries in both Ungava and Churchill, where beluga whale and walrus blubber were rendered to oil in blubber refineries and then sent in casks back to England. Gordon considered these fisheries to be solid industries that could be developed by Canadian fishing companies. He noted that the Hudson's Bay Company paid something for the privilege of fishing in the bay, but that the Americans did not. Gordon writes, "If American whalers are to be permitted to continue to fish in those waters, arrangements should be made by which Canada would receive substantial equivalent for the privilege."[30]

Unfortunately, there is no evidence that Gordon's advice was heeded. The Canadian government did not, subsequent to his report, issue whaling licences or collect tariffs on any of the American whaling fleet. It would be close to twenty years before the government sent a patrol ship to Hudson Bay, in the meantime losing thousands of dollars in revenue.

Gordon also mentions that a trading post, established by the American Captain Spicer on the north shore of the strait, was inhabited year-round by a trader and that about fifty Inuit families traded with him. If they killed a whale, Captain Spicer would pay them for it in "spirits." Gordon wrote, "The evil effects of such payment are too well known to need comment."[31] Until the six new observation stations were established, Captain Spicer's station was the only non-native settlement on the strait and northern Hudson Bay.

Gordon suggests that the 1885 expedition ship should stop in at Captain Spicer's trading station, the Hudson's Bay Company post at Ungava Bay, and Roes Welcome Sound, as well as the Churchill whale oil rendering factory, for firsthand experience of activities. He advised erecting beacons on Mansfield and Southampton Islands, as the low-lying islands spread their treacherous shoal fingers out under the water, making them difficult to see at night and thus dangerous to ships. Gordon also recommended carrying out detailed surveys of the strait's coasts.

BELL'S REPORT OF THE EXPEDITION

Dr. Robert Bell's report of his findings was included in Gordon's report as Appendix A. It is twenty pages in length, as long as Gordon's own.

Although Bell was along on the expedition in the capacity of ship's doctor, he makes no mention in his report of the medical condition of the men on board ship. This is surprising, especially as Gordon comments on several of the men being unfit to remain at the stations for the winter.

Tuttle mentions that any medicines that Bell had brought with him were "stowed away under the hatch, where they could not readily be had."[32] Bell was first and foremost a geologist. Fortunately, for the most part the health of the men on board was exceptionally good.

Bell prefaced his report with a letter from the Department of Marine and Fisheries that stated, "Nothing beyond board and berth accommodation can be given to Dr. Bell, the vessel being chartered to the Department, and no special accommodation being guaranteed, but space will doubtless be provided sufficient for the storage of any specimens, & c., which Dr. Bell may collect."[33] It also stated that Dr. Bell could not be provided with a special boat and crew, but could easily land at every place the vessel anchored to "carry out his work."

On the 1884 voyage, Bell only managed to make brief geological excursions. When the stations were being built or the crew was taking on ballast, Bell hitched a ride and went ashore with his notebooks, camera, and collection boxes. He took copious notes, interviewing the native people he met about the mineralogy of the area. Bell collected over fifty specimens of insects, animals, and birds, and fish, as well as molluscs dredged from the bottom of the bay. In his report, he comments scientifically on everything he discovered at each station, including the vegetables grown in gardens in Nain.

Bell was also a fine photographer, and took sixty-five black and white photos. He photographed people, the places the expedition stopped at, and subjects pertinent to the geology of the region. Gordon makes no comment in his official report of the stunning scenery and landscape they travelled through. Much of Hudson Strait runs through some of the most spectacular and wildest coastlines in the world. The stations farther west along the strait and near the entrance to Hudson Bay were situated on low-lying rocky terrain, which offered more sweeping horizons but, perhaps, bleaker vistas than the eastern stations. The diversity of landscape is artfully captured on Bell's plate glass negatives.

In all, it was a successful expedition that accomplished what it set out to do. It established six meteorological stations, and put men on the ground who would monitor the weather and ice conditions in the strait. The expedition's officers noted the strait's troubled or dangerous spots where shipping vessels could run into problems. The expedition also established that there was a need for some kind of government surveillance of foreign vessels in the region. Moreover, the 1884 report justified the need for two consecutive expeditions, and the Department of Marine and Fisheries began planning for the 1885 summer expedition.

CHAPTER FOUR

The Hudson Bay Expedition of 1885

On Wednesday, May 27, 1885, the *Halifax Herald* announced, "The Arctic steamer *Alert* will sail at daylight for Hudson's Bay."

However, it was noon before the *Alert* steamed out of Halifax harbour, heading out on the second government expedition to Hudson Bay and Strait. The ship was departing almost two months earlier than the previous summer's expedition to determine the earliest the strait could be entered.

Although the sailing-steamer *Neptune* had been built to withstand ice, it was not an icebreaker that could punch through it. Having encountered so much ice the previous year, Commander Gordon felt that the *Neptune* might not measure up to the task of navigating the strait earlier in the season. As well, the *Neptune* had been built for the sealing trade, and so its large cargo hold meant that room for crew and expedition members was limited and not as comfortable as desired.

In 1904, after spending fourteen months aboard the *Neptune* on a later government expedition, Dr. Lorris Borden noted in his diary that the men were anxious to have a "hot bath and shave, etc." as the ship's seal oil smell "saturated everything and we were not very comfortable company until that smell had been eliminated."[1]

No doubt, this odour was part of the olfactory comfort that Gordon felt was lacking on the first voyage. So, for the subsequent 1885 and 1886 summer expeditions, the British Navy loaned the Dominion government the HMS *Alert*. The *Alert* had never seen service on the seal or whale hunt, so did not carry the pungent musk of seal carcasses in its wooden pores.

The *Alert* was launched in 1856 as a barque-rigged sloop, designed as a fighting ship. It was a mighty vessel of 1,340 tons. Larger than the *Neptune*, it was one hundred and sixty feet in length and had a thirty-two-foot beam with a fifteen-foot draught. The steamship was fitted with a full sailing ship rig and constructed with a strong wooden hull that was sheathed in copper. In 1874, when it was refitted for Arctic service for Sir George Nares' North Pole expedition, its hull was ice-strengthened with felt-covered iron and then sheathed with teak, Canadian elm, and pitch pine below water.

In May 1884, the American government seconded the *Alert* to aid the rescue operations of the Greely expedition from Cape Sabine. The following spring, when Gordon was searching for a replacement for the *Neptune*, the ice-worthy *Alert* was available. The *Alert*, which was still on the United States Navy's books, was returned to the British Admiralty on April 28 in a brief ceremony in Halifax. The senior British naval officer then handed the ship over to the agent of the Department of Marine. On May 4, Gordon took command of the ship, and it was provisioned for the second Hudson Bay expedition, scheduled to leave mid-May. Readying the ship for the voyage took longer than originally anticipated, and the ship was not ready by May 12 as planned, but two weeks later.

The expedition was made up of fifty-two men. Dr. Robert Bell again joined the expedition in the same capacity as the summer previous. This year, his position as official geologist had been given more importance and he brought along an assistant, James MacNaughton. Frank Payne, James W. Tyrrell, John McKenzie, Percy Woodworth, and Gilbert Shaw were the new observers. They, and ten other men aboard, would replace the men at the meteorological stations. As well, Mr. D.J. Beaton, editor of the *Winnipeg Daily Times*, accompanied the expedition as a representative of the Winnipeg and Hudson Bay Railway.

The ink was barely dry on the *Winnipeg and Hudson's Bay Railway and Steamship Company Act*, having received assent from the Legislative Assembly of Manitoba on May 2, 1885. The act approved the construction of the railway line from Winnipeg to "some port on the Hudson's Bay and connect with the main line of the Canadian Pacific Railway within the Province of Manitoba."[2] Construction of the railway was to commence within two years from the passing of the act and be completed within five years. It was, therefore, in the company's best interest to have a representative on the expedition to ensure a proper assessment of whichever port would prove most suitable for the railway's destination. The Canadian Pacific Railway, now nearing completion, stretched from one side of the country to the other. A railway to Hudson Bay would extend Canada's dominion northward to its third coast.

A crowd gathered on the Halifax wharf to wave farewell, and after an official send-off, with handshakes and ceremonial speeches from the minister and deputy minister of Marine and Fisheries, the *Alert* headed north. On May 30, the ship passed out of the Strait of Belle Isle and encountered the first ice. The entire coast of Labrador appeared to be sheathed with a belt of tight, heavy ice almost fifty miles wide. The ship veered around this frozen belt. It wended its way circuitously northward, skirting seemingly boundless fields of ice. Despite the captain's careful attempt to avoid the ice, by June 16 it had engulfed them, and the *Alert* was forced to drift, frozen in the pack, for the next three weeks.

Unfortunately, the iron stem plate and some of the stern's sheathing was broken and torn off by the ice. This damage was serious and required repairs before the ship could attempt Hudson Strait. The expedition lost another week travelling south to St. John's in dense fog. Twelve days later, repairs had been made and the ship, with fresh provisions and a replenished stock of coal, headed north again to Hudson Strait. By the time the *Alert* left St. John's, they had lost a month of their navigation period. It was July 27. Ice still clogged some of their passageway and icebergs flowed by the ship on southward journeys. The fact that the expedition was still encountering heavy ice at that time of year confirmed that making the strait before July was virtually impossible.

Unfortunately, though, Gordon was heavily criticized for his decision to return to St. John's. Even supposed experts in Arctic marine travel blamed him for allowing the ship to get stuck in the ice in the first place.

The first port of call was the station at Skynner's Cove near Nachvak Inlet on the Labrador coast. They found all three men in good health, having "passed a very pleasant winter."[3] The lead observer, William Skynner, came on board for the journey through the strait, but the two station hands were left at the station to continue taking measurements for the remainder of the summer.

Continuing on its northward trek, the ship encountered mostly ice and fog, entering the strait on August 4. Just inside the entrance to the strait, the *Alert* steamed past a couple of Hudson's Bay Company sailing ships that were heading west to the Churchill post. Manoeuvring through the thick ice into the harbour at Port Burwell proved difficult. The ice closed in so tightly around them after they anchored that Gordon was

HMS Alert *in dry dock for repairs in St. John's, Newfoundland, in July 1885, after being damaged by ice attempting passage of Hudson Strait.*

able to walk from the ship to the shore. He found Mr. Burwell and his two companions in good spirits. They had also passed a comfortable winter in their cabin. The ice was rough and hummocky in the harbour, which would make landing supplies problematic. Gordon decided that on their return trip in early fall, the ice would be out of the bay and they would land the stores then.

The three new station men bade the ship farewell and joined the occupants of Port Burwell who would remain for the summer. The *Alert* weighed anchor and headed across the strait to Ashe Inlet, on Big Island. Gordon noted that the ice was still heavy, even on the north side, which had been relatively ice-free the year before. For the next week and a half, they struggled against the ice in the strait. They spotted the two Hudson's Bay Company ships again, which hadn't progressed far. Being dependent on wind power, these sailing ships were at a significant disadvantage in the ice-congested strait.

When the *Alert* was within twelve miles of the entrance to Ashe Inlet, Gordon decided to force the ship in. About two miles from shore, one of the propeller blades broke. The screw was hauled up on deck, but by the time a new blade had been attached the ship was beset in ice. It was another five days before they could inch the ship closer to shore. On August 17, they succeeded in getting only to within a half mile of the entrance to the harbour. The two assistants, alerted by the ship's whistle, trekked out to the ship over the ice with news that Mr. Ashe was ill, after having sprained his wrist. The ice prevented the ship getting any nearer the station and soon closed around the *Alert*, pushing it helplessly for forty miles to the west of the inlet.

At this point, Gordon discarded the plan to visit the station until the return trip and set a course for Stupart Bay on the strait's south side, anchoring there on August 22. When they went ashore, they were surprised to find the station had been abandoned. Robert Stupart had left letters stating he and his men had anticipated that the ship would arrive a month earlier. As the four men were all in excellent health, they had decided to head out in their boat for Fort Chimo in Ungava Bay. The letter was dated August 21. The *Alert* had missed them by one day.

The winter of 1884–85 at Stupart Bay, or Aniuvarjuaq to the local people, was severe and the hunting poor. Stupart's logs reported that the

January mean temperature was 23°F below zero, with -35°F as the coldest temperature. The local people were starving. The station men gave the Inuit what they could, but their own provisions were limited. Stupart later told the *New York Times* that his station had not been provided with more provisions than the other three-man stations, despite having a fourth man living there. Sadly, eighteen local Inuit died of starvation that winter.

Considering how close to the station the people had settled, it would have been horrendous to know of their plight and be unable to offer assistance. Tuttle had noted that when the station had first been established, the Inuit had looked curiously through the windows at the men in their cabin. One can imagine how it would have filled Stupart and his companions with guilt to have these starving people watching through the window as they ate their government rations. No wonder when the ship was late arriving, Stupart realized they would have no better luck living off the land if the ship failed to arrive at all, and decided to set out for Fort Chimo.

Chimo Bay was three hundred miles distant. Stupart and his men rowed and sailed through gales and rough weather in an open whaleboat, amazingly making the journey relatively unscathed in fourteen days. Their adventure did not end there, though. At Chimo the men took passage aboard the Hudson's Bay Company steamer *Labrador*, headed for Rigolet on the north coast of Labrador. The ship ran aground on some rocks en route. Fortunately, though, it was freed within a few nail-biting hours. At Rigolet the men borrowed a sailboat and headed to Indian Harbour, where they caught a lift on the mail steamer *Hercules* to Grady, and there boarded a whaling ship bound for Harbour Grace, Newfoundland. Stupart and his men finally reached Halifax on November 1, 1885. It was not the trip the men had envisioned when they cast off from Stupart Bay in late August.

Gordon and those on the *Alert* never imagined the journey Stupart's group would endure. Bell was accustomed to travelling the land alone, so he, no doubt, thought a boat with four men would manage satisfactorily. Bell's experienced opinion likely swayed Gordon. The expedition had already undergone more setbacks than necessary, and chasing after Stupart's boat could only delay them further. After the three replacement men and supplies were landed at Stupart Bay, the *Alert* weighed anchor and headed for the next station on Nottingham Island at the mouth of Hudson Bay. It made Port De Boucherville on Monday, August 24.

Sadly, the men found that one of the station hands, Andrew Inglis of Halifax, had died on June 3. Had they been able to make passage of the strait when they had left in May, the ship would still not have reached Inglis before he succumbed to his illness. With no means of communicating with the southern world, no one in Ottawa or on board ship could have known how any of the station men were faring. Even if they had known, there was no means of getting aid to them until the ice had sufficiently receded from the strait in mid-summer.

Both Dr. Bell and Lieutenant Gordon interviewed C.V. De Boucherville and W.F. Esdaile separately in the commander's cabin about Inglis. From De Boucherville and Esdaile's accounts, Inglis had spent the majority of the winter lying in his bed. He had refused to exercise or eat the food recommended by the doctor and did not drink his lime juice. Bell concluded that the man had died of scurvy. Depression, or melancholia, as it was termed then, wasn't mentioned in the report, but Inglis seems to have suffered from melancholia, which was manifested in his apathy to take the prescribed actions to prevent scurvy.

The two men from the station came aboard, exchanging places with the observer, Mr. McKenzie, and two others who would take up their meteorological tasks for the next year. How these three felt being left on the isolated island where a man had so recently passed away is not recorded. The *Alert* continued on its westbound trek and stopped at the final station at the entrance to Hudson Bay, Port Laperrière on Digges Island. Here, officers and crew were relieved to find all three men in excellent health and good spirits, having passed a pleasant winter.

The crew shifted the coal and took on ballast before heading across the bay to Churchill. Arriving on August 31, they found that the *Cam Owen*, one of the Hudson's Bay Company sailing ships they had seen in the strait, had beat them to the port by two days. A gale blew up while they lay at anchor and the poor weather forced them to remain at Churchill until September 7. When the *Alert* left the harbour, it was towing the *Cam Owen*, which was unable to get to sea in the stormy weather under its own sail power. As it was, it took another fourteen days for the *Cam Owen* to reach Fort York in the stormy weather; a distance of less than two hundred miles.

Originally, Bell and his assistant James MacNaughton planned to be dropped off at one of the major rivers on the west coast of Hudson Bay. They would canoe southward, taking a survey of the land along the way. After leaving Churchill, Bell decided that the best route for them to start their canoe journey was the Severn River. The Severn originates in northwestern Ontario and empties into Hudson Bay south of both the Churchill and Nelson Rivers. Unfortunately, the coast there offers only shallow water and the foul weather made it too dangerous for the *Alert* to put into the mouth of the river. Bell's plan was abandoned.

The *Alert* instead crossed Hudson Bay to examine two sets of islands just west of the Ungava Peninsula known as the Sleepers. After surveying the northern group, Bell and Gordon agreed to rename them the Ottawa Islands. They named the main islands after wealthy Ottawa lumbermen: Booth, Gilmour, Eddy, Bronson, and Perley. The islands boast spectacular mountainous terrain, with cliffs rising a thousand feet above the sea. Gilmour Island has the highest elevation at eighteen hundred feet.

The *Alert* carried on up the east coast of Hudson Bay to Port Laperrière to check in with the men so recently ensconced in their station. It then continued through the strait, stopping at each station to visit the new station men and drop off additional supplies. This was the last contact with southerners these men would have for a full year.

Men aboard the Alert *on the 1885 Hudson Bay expedition. Lieutenant Gordon is seated centre. A bearded Robert Bell is seated to the left of Gordon.*

This time the ship was able to anchor in Ashe Inlet, which had been jammed with ice a month earlier. Here they discovered that William Ashe was suffering not from a sprained wrist, but from scurvy. His illness had reached an advanced stage where he couldn't even walk. Once he was brought on board and received medical attention from Dr. Bell, though, he improved rapidly. He had apparently neglected to take his daily ration of lime juice.

Finally, James W. Tyrrell and his assistants were landed at Ashe Inlet along with their supplies. The twenty-two-year-old Tyrrell was the younger brother of Joseph Burr Tyrrell, who had discovered dinosaur bones in Alberta's badlands the year before. James Tyrrell would become one of Canada's foremost Subarctic explorers, canoeing with his brother from Lake Athabasca to Hudson Bay in 1893. He may have acquired a taste for exploring during his stint as station observer.

The ship paused only long enough to unload the men and necessary supplies before carrying on to Stupart Bay. It then stopped in at Port Burwell to pick up Burwell and his two companions before heading south along the Labrador coast. At Nachvak, Messrs. Jordan and Rainsford, the station men at Skynner's Cove, came aboard with their instruments and unused provisions. Gordon was also handed letters from Mr. Stupart about his safe arrival at Fort Chimo and taking passage aboard the steamer *Labrador*. Unbeknownst to Gordon, the rest of Stupart's harrowing journey was still unfolding.

The expedition then headed south along the Labrador coast, arriving in St. John's harbour on October 13. The ship was re-supplied with coal and water and sailed for Halifax, anchoring on October 18, at 3:00 a.m. After daylight, it steamed up to the Department of Marine wharf. Gordon then discharged the ship's company and the fourteen men who had been station hands for 1884–85.

THE 1885 EXPEDITION REPORT

In his report, Gordon included the 1884–85 ice records made by the station men along the strait, as well as relevant information from his interview with Captain Hawes of the *Cam Owen*, who had made fourteen voyages through the Hudson Strait and Hudson Bay. Gordon says, "Capt. Hawes places the probable period of navigation for steam vessels properly fitted for ice work as seldom exceeding three months, 15th July to 15th October."[4] This was certainly a far cry from the Nelson River Railway Company's 1881 prediction that steamship service would be practicable by the Hudson Bay route from May to December.[5] Experience proved otherwise.

An editorial in the *Montreal Gazette* on October 23, 1885, suggested that this period of navigation rendered the use of the route too costly:

> The risks attendant on the navigation of Hudson's Bay would make insurance rates on vessel and cargo extremely high, a special class of steamers would be required to cope with the floating ice, the danger of being frozen in and compelled to await another season for release would be an ever-present one, freight because of these risks and to compensate for them would be made unusually dear; in a word, there would be such a combination of adverse circumstances as to render the advance of shorter distance of little consequence.

The risks of such a route looked like they outweighed the benefits. This was not the sort of commentary that would've sat well with those in the West who were counting on a favourable assessment. So far, the experience of the two expeditions didn't support an overwhelming endorsement of a longer navigation season, which was needed for the Hudson waterway to be lucrative for shipping.

Gordon's report drew no conclusions about the length of time the strait could be navigable for shipping, though. He would wait for the final expedition to make a more informed decision. However, he wrote, the sea ice "conditions observed in Hudson's Straits this year are exactly the reverse of those found, in 1884, on the voyage made in the *Neptune*. In 1884, the ice met with was heaviest on the south shore and in the west end of the Straits. In 1885 all the ice was on the north shore and the east end of the Straits."[6] The inconsistency of weather and ice conditions only supported the need for a third year's assessment of the strait.

Due to the delays from the ice, the expedition had not called in at Spicer's trading post or at Roes Welcome, where the American whalers operated. But Gordon editorialized again about the whaling and fishing habits of foreigners in the bay and was adamant that the government should regulate for this.

The 1885 report also included two appendices. One was Bell's fifteen-page analysis of the geology of Hudson Bay and Strait. The other was Superintendent of the Meteorological Service and Director of the Magnetic Observatory Charles Carpmael's report on the magnetic work and findings made by each station.

In the *Summary Report of the Operations of the Geological Survey of Canada* submitted December 31, 1885, as part of the *Annual Report of the Department of the Interior of 1885*, Robert Bell included a summary of his excursion to "Hudson's Bay and Straits" that summer. Bell managed a number of successful forays during the expedition to various spots along the coast, making geological examinations and surveys. He again collected a multitude of rocks, as well as flora and fauna, to take back to the Geological Survey. He acknowledged that, during the previous year, the men at the various stations had all collected a number of species of birds and plants, some of which were new to the survey's collection. Bell listed the cost of the season's exploration at $859.47.[7]

Bell was again denied the tools and resources needed to carry out the task he had been appointed to do. The expedition was controlled and operated by the Department of Marine and Fisheries and the needs of the Geological Survey were not tantamount to its own. The irritation that Bell felt at not being able to fully do his job as geologist lies between the lines of his report.

Gordon's official report on the 1885 expedition to Hudson Bay was released to Parliament in the spring of 1886, as plans were being made to send out the third and last expedition to make a final assessment of conditions in the strait. A second expedition to Hudson Strait had been accomplished, but with difficulty. The hope was that the final expedition of 1886 would put Gordon in a position to make a more informed decision on the length of time the route would be navigable.

THE HUDSON BAY EXPEDITION OF 1886

On March 22, 1886, a question was raised in the House of Commons on whether a request for mercy had been made prior to the execution of Louis Riel six months earlier. Riel's death was a contentious issue and a cloud over the Conservative government. A less controversial topic that day, but one of equal importance to western Canadians, was the Hudson Bay route.

The Honourable Arthur W. Ross, Liberal-Conservative MP for Lisgar, Manitoba, asked "Whether it is the intention of the Government to again send out to Hudson's Bay, during the coming season a sailing vessel with weak auxiliary power as last season, or a strong steam vessel."[8]

The Honourable George E. Foster, minister of Marine and Fisheries, answered that the government was sending a third expedition that summer aboard the steamer *Alert*, "the same that was sent out last year, which is considered one of the best vessels for that purpose in the United States, Great Britain or Canada."[9] He confirmed that the expedition would gather as much knowledge of the region's geography and resources as possible.

Three months to the day later, Gordon received orders from Foster regarding this final expedition to Hudson Bay. It would proceed through Hudson Strait, without stopping at any of the observation stations, to the western coast of Hudson Bay to examine the harbours at Churchill and the mouth of the Nelson River and assess the suitability for future shipping ports. The expedition would delay its homeward voyage to the latest possible period of navigation as was safely possible. On the return trip through the strait, "the observers, houses, and all portable and valuable articles at the stations" would be taken on board the *Alert* and returned to Halifax.[10]

The *Alert* cast off from the Halifax wharf at 3:00 p.m. on June 24, 1886, with forty-three men on board, including Robert Bell once again as medical officer and geologist.

Forty-five-year-old Captain Albert Hastings Markham, R.N., of the famed Nares Expedition, was the celebrity member of the ship's company. Markham was the representative of the Winnipeg and Hudson Bay Railway Company. He had been planning a holiday to Hudson Bay when he was offered passage on the *Alert* by an MP involved with the railway, on condition that he submit a report to the railway company that would "demonstrate the feasibility of the proposed route."[11] Markham was not paid for his efforts but, like Beaton the previous year, he was along to ensure the railway company's interests were being met. His appearance on board a few days before the expedition's departure was the first that Commander Gordon knew of him accompanying the expedition, though a room was quickly made available for the esteemed guest.

However, later, in an address to the Royal Geographical Society on June 11, 1888, Markham talked about accompanying the 1886 expedition but made no mention of being invited on behalf of the railway. He elaborated, though, on the *Alert* being caught in ice in 1885:

> Through some mismanagement, or want of experience in ice navigation on the part of those who were occasionally entrusted with the charge of the ship, she was allowed to be beset by the ice. No advantage appears to have been taken of her steam power to extricate her. In fact, the reverse seems to have been the case, for in the official report of this voyage we read that, instead of utilizing the power that was at their disposal to release her from her imprisonment, they "banked the fires and left the ship to pull under foretopsail and foretopmast staysail."
>
> The "pull," however, does not appear to have been in the desired direction or if so it was misapplied; for we learn that shortly afterwards the stern of the ship was so seriously injured that it was considered not only desirable, but necessary to return to the southward, and they put into St. John's (Newfoundland) in order to effect the necessary repairs.[12]

Markham blamed the *Alert* getting caught in the ice on "some mismanagement," implying that as the commander is ultimately responsible for the ship, Gordon was the one who mismanaged the situation. One wonders if alarm bells rang at the Royal Navy when it discovered in 1885 that its ship had been damaged en route to Hudson Bay, when a decade earlier the ship had survived a full eighteen months at a latitude twenty degrees farther north. Markham's "invitation" to participate in the third expedition may have also been a means of protecting its interests: the *Alert*. However it was arranged, Markham joined the 1886 expedition.

Regardless of Markham's perception of how things were handled, the second year's expedition would succeed in pointing out that consistent ice and weather conditions could not be relied on. Hudson Strait was a temperamental passage.

The last week of June 1886, the *Alert* followed the route up the coast taken on the two previous voyages. It encountered rough conditions almost the entire way: snow, sleet, fog, icebergs, and pans of ice measuring twelve feet in thickness. On July 9, the steamer entered the Hudson Strait north of the Button Islands, and not via Gray Strait, between the "Buttons" and Cape Chidley.

Despite orders not to visit the stations, Gordon called in at Ashe Inlet to take James Tyrrell on board as his survey assistant. The other two remained to continue making observations for the duration of the summer. The men had fared well, having been supplied with fresh meat by the locals through-out the winter.

The *Alert* continued through the strait but came up short against a massive field of ice that loomed for two hundred miles ahead of them. The ice was between fifteen and twenty feet thick. While the ship was trying to ram through it, a propeller blade was broken and had to be replaced with a new one. Broken propellers were now typical of each voyage. By July 14, Gordon decided, "The ice met with tonight, in my opinion, settles the question of the practicability of the navigation of the Straits; up to this date, at any rate, the Straits are not navigable for this season, because no ordinary ship that could be used as a freight carrier, even if strengthened to meet the ice, could have stood the pounding which this ship has had this afternoon."[13]

The ship pushed through the ice and arrived at Port Laperrière at the entrance to Hudson Bay on July 20. It was able to steam into the harbour, though the ice up to the shore was thick enough that observer Percy Woodworth and his two assistants, Bissett and Bowditch, walked out to the ship. They had passed a "comfortable winter," and Woodworth reported that the ice had only broken up in the harbour a few days before the *Alert*'s arrival.

Five days later, after making engine repairs, the expedition bid farewell and headed to Hudson Bay. The ship headed into broad streams of tightly packed ice. After thirty hours spent battling ice, the ship was finally clear, but it had progressed only nine miles. Gordon planned to venture to the north of the bay to meet the American whalers, but decided instead to head directly to Churchill and York Factory. Gordon's orders hadn't included intercepting whalers. It was his own mandate to seek them out.

The expedition arrived at Churchill on July 29, having encountered no other serious ice in Hudson Bay. It had made the journey in forty-six hours. The men spent the next four days surveying Churchill Harbour. Gordon concluded that "this harbour is admirably suited for a railroad terminus. The necessary docks could be easily and cheaply built, and the deep water basin enlarged at small cost."[14]

Markham concurred with Gordon, noting later in an article on his trip, "It is certainly a most excellent anchorage, completely land-locked, and well sheltered from all winds. There is but little doubt in my mind that Churchill harbour will, if the railway from Winnipeg to Hudson's Bay is ever constructed, be the terminus of the road, as it surely ought to be."[15]

On August 4, they weighed anchor and headed for York Factory, arriving two days later in the Nelson River. Owing to the shallowness of the water there, the *Alert* was forced to anchor twelve miles from shore. Markham wrote, "It is this absence of any harbour, and the long distance at which a ship has to anchor from the shore, that renders the situation of York Factory undesirable for the terminus of the proposed railroad."[16]

Markham disembarked at York Factory for his "holiday" canoe trip along the Hayes River to Winnipeg. Markham hired a birchbark canoe, provisions, and two men for the first part of the journey west from the Hudson's Bay Company post.

Gordon and his men then spent several days surveying the harbour. Gordon did not give Port Nelson a favourable review either. The channel in the Nelson River was narrow, requiring a great deal of dredging to make it and the basin capable of accommodating freight-carrying vessels. As well, the low surrounding land wouldn't provide adequate shelter to vessels, and through the summer months, fog hung closely over the water, making it treacherous for navigation.

Gordon wrote, "The cost of the construction and maintenance of a harbour at this place together with the inevitable risks of navigation in approaching it, even after all had been done that could possibly be done, to render it safe and accessible, would, in my opinion, far outweigh the construction of the necessary additional mileage of railway required to reach the port of Churchill."[17] Gordon even went so far as to say that he considered the estuary of the Nelson River to be one of the most "dangerous places in the world for shipping to go to."

By August 14, the survey of Port Nelson was completed, and the *Alert* headed north. It had consumed a great deal of coal on the outward voyage, and taking on ballast was necessary. On the twentieth, the ship stopped at Marble Island, where its rocky terrain supplied plenty of ballast. The men took on board eighty tons of rock.

They began to have trouble with the compasses on the way north to the island. The U.S. Navy spirit compass was useless and the Sir William Thomson standard was erratically swinging to south-southwest when they headed north. After leaving Marble Island, they encountered a heavy sea. Because of this, along with the problem of poorly operating compasses and the end of August fast approaching, Gordon decided to give up his plans to visit whalers in Roes Welcome. Instead, the ship bore up for the entrance to Hudson Strait.

The *Alert* arrived safely at Digges Island, anchoring at Port Laperrière at 6:40 p.m. on August 30. Over the next few days Observation Station Number Six was dismantled and all remaining supplies brought on board. While the men were busy with this project, Messrs. Tyrrell and Skynner (who had been observer in 1884) were sent to the mainland to complete a survey of the coastline. On September 7, with all evidence of the station removed from the rocky island, the expedition steamed across the strait to Nottingham Island.

When the *Alert* dropped anchor in the little harbour at Port De Boucherville, the station men were busy collecting and drying turf to burn for fuel for the coming winter in the event that the *Alert* failed to arrive. Station observer McKenzie and his men had proven to be good hunters and would likely have passed another year comfortably enough had the ship not arrived. All hands were immediately put to work dismantling the house and loading it and the remaining supplies on board.

The task was completed in under ten hours. Gordon notes that they brought enough supplies and sacks of coal on board from Observation Station Number Five to last another winter. McKenzie said that the temperature of the station house was kept at between 50°F and 60°F even when the outside temperature was forty-five degrees below zero.

From Nottingham Island, the *Alert* continued on an eastward course to Ashe Inlet through a gale and snow showers. At Ashe Inlet, Gordon had a large beacon erected on a high bluff close to the shore and christened it Tyrrell's Bluff and Beacon after the station observer and invaluable surveyor. All hands were employed in the work of getting the remaining supplies and equipment on board, but the building was not dismantled. They left Ashe Inlet at 5:00 a.m. on September 9, and arrived at Stupart's Bay across the strait at 3:00 p.m. that afternoon.

Fortunately, the winter of 1885 was not as difficult as the previous one. No Inuit had starved to death. Game had been plentiful; so much so that the station men had hardly touched their supply of salt pork. Mr. Payne, the observer, had recently shot seventy geese in one day, and the ship's company enjoyed the change to their diet. The weather turned nasty again, and a gale delayed the departure for Port Burwell until September 25. En route they made a running survey of the coast. As a result, Gordon discovered that the true position of the coastline east of Prince of Wales Sound was farther south than marked on the Admiralty charts. Gordon also ascertained that Green Island, as laid down by Sir William Edward Parry on the charts, did not exist.

At Port Burwell, the observer Gilbert Shaw was suffering acutely from scurvy. He could not sit up for more than three minutes without passing out. For some time before the arrival of the ship, Shaw had been so incapacitated that his assistants, brothers Telesphore and Jean Mercier, had carried out his observations for him. Fortunately, the man quickly regained his health after he was moved on board the *Alert* and eating proper food. After the two cases of scurvy in 1885, it is most disturbing that there would be a third case the following year.

The house was dismantled on the twenty-seventh, but the ship's departure was delayed until the weather improved two days later. On September 30, the *Alert* pulled into Nachvak Inlet. At the Hudson's Bay Company post, Gordon arranged for Mr. Ford, the agent, to purchase the house at Skynner's Cove. They spent that night at the abandoned post, then had a "fine run down the Labrador Coast."[18] Gordon was aware of the necessity of getting Shaw some proper medical attention, so didn't bother with the surveying he had intended to do.

The *Alert* arrived at the departmental wharf at 4:00 p.m. on Sunday, October 10, 1886, completing the three-year study of Hudson Bay and Hudson Strait. All hands were discharged at once, except for the men who were re-engaged at port wages to carry out the work required to get the ship ready to return to Britain's Royal Navy.

THE 1886 EXPEDITION REPORT AND RESPONSE TO IT

On September 20, 1886, the *New York Times* ran an article titled, "The Hudson's Bay Route, An Official Report Regarding Its Navigability for Steamers." The news piece announced Captain A. Markham of the Royal Navy had just passed through Minneapolis on his way from Winnipeg to Montreal, after completing "an official inspection of Hudson's Bay, with a view to ascertaining the facts in relation to the navigability of the bay."

It is unclear why Markham went to Montreal via Minneapolis; however, he told the press there that he was "satisfied that the bay is navigable for at least four months of the year." No mention was made of the continuing expedition of the *Alert* or of Commander Gordon. The reader of the article was in no doubt that Markham held the position of utmost authority on the expedition. However, it was not Markham's opinion but Gordon's that the Canadian government was most concerned with, and it waited for his official report to draw conclusions about the Hudson Bay route.

Upon his return on October 10, Gordon told the newspapers that he believed the strait was navigable four months of the year. This opinion was in apparent agreement with Markham, but it was hardly news. Gordon had drawn the same conclusion the year before.

The *Globe* reported, "He regards the straits as navigable under certain risks early in the season, from the beginning of July to the end of October, and the period might be extended half a month more."[19]

On July 22, 1887, just prior to the report's release, William Austin Ashe, the 1884 observer, published an article in *Science* magazine in response to a previous enthusiastic commentary in the magazine about the Hudson Bay route. Ashe says,

> The special objection I would point out as to this route, apart from the ice-question, is the difficulty of the passage itself: an unknown, an unlighted coast-line, with very few harbors of refuge, or none at all, and very little room to ride out a gale; extreme depths of water, one hundred fathoms being often found right up to the shore, with generally very foul holding-ground where the depths are more moderate. In foul weather, no sounding being possible that would be of value, a vessel would receive no warning of her proximity to the coast until the information would be of little or no avail.[20]

Ashe's short piece takes the wind out of the sails of the author who advocated Hudson Bay as an ideal passageway.

Gordon's long awaited *Report on the Hudson's Bay Expedition of 1886* corroborated Ashe's opinions. It was presented to the Dominion government the first week of August 1887. The substantial 125-page report was eagerly pored over by those with an interest in seeing a Hudson Bay shipping route proceed. It left many Hudson Bay railway advocates dissatisfied, though.

Like the two previous reports, it contained the commander's daily summary of the expedition and a compilation of the data from each of the stations for 1885–86, and included information on ice conditions and meteorological conditions, as well as the flora, fauna, and geology of the region. Gordon again went into detail about the economic resources of the region, with emphasis on the American whaling activities in Hudson Bay. He strongly recommended that a government vessel visit and patrol the area annually in order to regulate the fisheries there.

Gordon's task was to determine the duration of time when the passage could be safely traversed by commercial freighters. He suggested that a vessel of two thousand tons gross strengthened against the ice should be the optimum used. Any larger and the ship would be too unwieldy in the unpredictable ice of the strait. Based on his three-year experience, Gordon deemed navigation in Hudson Straits to be "more than ordinarily difficult."[21] In his estimation, between the first and tenth of July to the first week in October was the optimal travel time, and the limit of the shipping season through Hudson Bay and Strait.

The most serious difficulty that Gordon foresaw with the route was the problem with the working of the compasses. Gordon observed that the compass no longer operated properly once the ship arrived at the western end of Hudson Strait. This was due to a combination of the high latitude and changing magnetic conditions with the proximity to the north magnetic pole. He predicted that the compass problem would be compounded in iron ships, which most likely would be the kind used for freight.

The report, to the disappointment of many, was not a resounding endorsement of a Hudson Bay route. Those who had invested in the Hudson Bay railway venture refused to accept Gordon's assessment. One individual who strongly opposed Gordon's opinion was D.J. Beaton, who had accompanied the *Alert* in 1885 as a railway board member. He was one of those determined to get the railway through to Hudson Bay, but the project was largely dependent on Gordon's favourable assessment of the navigability of the route. For, ultimately, his report would be the position adopted by the federal government. Gordon was a cautious man and his experience of the strait made him cautious about advocating the route itself.

Beaton's fury over Gordon's report is apparent in his caustic letter to the *Montreal Herald* on September 10, 1887, a month after Gordon's final report was released. In it he says, "The selection of the *Alert* as the expedition ship was an injudicious one and I cannot but think but that a second and graver error was in the selection of its commander. Lt. Gordon had no previous knowledge of ice. His ideas are limited to the narrow circle of his early training, and he is much too self sufficient and stubborn to be taught either by his own experience or that of others."

Despite the personal attack on Gordon's abilities, he had proven a competent commander. He was hired to assess the passage of the strait over three years and had done so. Unfortunately, Gordon's final expedition did little to dispel doubts that the Hudson Bay route would ever be a feasible one. His report fell far short of an endorsement of it and settled the question for the government about continuing sponsorship of the project.

At the same time, wheat prices were declining in the Prairies. This, in addition to Gordon's moderate assessment of the Hudson Strait, was one too many strikes against the project. Government enthusiasm for a Hudson Bay railway fizzled. Gordon's three annual reports were virtually shelved for the next decade, and little was done to implement any of his recommendations.

The following year, in 1887, Lieutenant Andrew Gordon became a fisheries officer. He was promoted to nautical adviser and commander of the Fishery Protection Fleet in October 1891. Sadly, Gordon held this post for less than two years. He died in 1893 of tuberculosis. He was forty-two years old.[22]

CHAPTER FIVE

NANSEN'S POLAR DRIFT

In 1884, a pair of oilskin trousers labelled with Louis Noros' name was discovered frozen in ice on the southwest coast of Greenland. Noros was one of the *Jeannette*'s crew, and one of the two men in DeLong's boat who went for help. Amazingly, two other articles rescued from the ice with Noros' trousers were pieces of paper: a list of provisions and a list of the *Jeannette*'s boats.

These remnants of the 1879 *Jeannette* expedition had been caught in the ice floe when the ship was crushed near Siberia and carried north by currents, drifting eastward with the ice. The ice was carried down the east coast of Greenland, and around its southern point to where they were discovered. These relics had drifted 2,900 miles.

Pieces of driftwood had long been collected off both the east and west coasts of Greenland. As no trees grow in Greenland, it was assumed that the driftwood originated in Siberia and was carried to Greenland by Arctic sea currents. The Norwegian zoologist Fridtjof Nansen was captivated by the idea of this polar current. He eventually formulated a plan to use this current to reach the North Pole.

Nansen was a remarkable man of diverse interests with a string of accomplishments to his name. He was an athlete, scientist, Arctic explorer, author, statesman, and laureate of the Nobel Peace Prize. Though he was most interested in physics and mathematics, he loved the outdoors, and decided to pursue a doctorate in zoology so that the majority of his work would be outside. Nansen's scientific mind, in combination with his insatiable curiosity, single-minded determination, and attention to detail, contributed to the success of any project he undertook.

In 1882, the six-foot blond shipped aboard a sealing vessel headed to the Arctic Ocean, where he glimpsed the uninhabited eastern coast of Greenland. No European had explored it. Only Inuit had left footprints on this side of the island. Nansen decided to ski across it.

In July 1888, twenty-seven-year-old Nansen led an extraordinary six-man skiing expedition across Greenland, starting on the uninhabited east side so that his team would be able to take passage on a ship when they reached the west coast. If they started on the west side they would have to retrace their steps across Greenland in order to catch a ship home. However, departing on the trek across the ice cap from the east side meant they had no option to retreat should they run into trouble. Their gruelling trip took two months. Despite the thermometer dipping below -50°F, the team studied and recorded meteorological conditions along the way. They reached the west coast without mishap, becoming the first Europeans to cross Greenland.

Nansen then turned his attention to the theory of polar drift and formulated a plan to attain the Pole by using this drift. Nansen theorized that if he purposely allowed his ship to become frozen in the pack ice of the western Arctic Ocean, the wind and polar currents would carry it to the warmer Atlantic. Nansen, therefore, had a ship built that would specifically withstand being frozen in the ice.

The massive curved hull was designed like a coconut, so that pressure from ice on its sides would not compress it but force the ship to rise up out of the ice. Its keel extended only two and a half inches below the hull, so that the ice could not grip it.[1] Nansen's wife, Eva, christened the ship Fram — meaning forward. Nansen and his scientific crew of eleven men departed on June 26, 1893, from Tromsø, Norway. The Fram was beset and frozen in on September 22, 1893, at 78°43'N latitude. For the next year and a half it moved west with the drifting ice. By March 1895, the Fram had reached 84°4'N. When it looked like the ship would drift no closer to the Pole, Nansen and crew member Hjalmar Johansen left the ship to make an over-ice sledging attempt on the Pole. It was forty-five degrees below zero when the two men strapped on skis and left, hauling three sledges with 1,400 pounds of supplies and equipment. After fifteen weeks,

Nansen and Johansen reached 86°15'N and got within two hundred and forty miles of the Pole. Ahead of them was nothing but a jumble of ice hummocks and boulders. They turned back and headed to Franz Josef Land, the archipelago north of Russia.

Here, they spent nine months in a rough hut they assembled out of stones, skins, and moss. The following May, they began their trek towards Spitsbergen and by happy coincidence met up with the British Jackson-Harmsworth Polar Expedition (1894–97), which was carrying out scientific studies there. The two men took passage aboard the expedition's supply ship, and were taken to Vardö Haven, Norway. They were welcomed home as national heroes.

Meanwhile, the *Fram* had continued on its odyssey, drifting north over the top of the world and then southward, emerging in August 1896 in open water north of Spitsbergen. It had reached a latitude of 85°57'N; the highest any ship had navigated. Nansen's mission was a scientific success. He became one of the first scientists to suggest that there was no land at the Pole, but a polar sea — and a frozen one at that.

YUKON AND THE WESTERN ARCTIC

While the *Fram* was drifting across the top of the world, events were unfolding far to the south in Canada's Yukon.

Since the Hudson's Bay Company lands were transferred to Canada in 1870, the remote region had virtually been left to operate on its own. Its physical distance from Parliament in Ottawa, and its sparse population, meant that it received almost none of the government's attention. The Dominion government concentrated on administering more settled areas of the country along the Canada-United States border. However, when foreign gold miners began arriving in the Yukon, the Dominion government began to notice.

Part of the lure of the Yukon was its wildness and remoteness, which attracted men who lived outside the social norm or sought a reclusive life, away from society. The prospectors were mostly Americans who had tried their luck panhandling in the California Gold Rush. These miners lived a rather anarchistic existence. Their methods for preserving law and order were based on American mining traditions. In the form of a crude democracy called the miners' meeting, often held at the local saloon, a miner could air his grievance in front of an assembly of fellow miners, who then made a decision on it. The miners' meeting had the power to impose fines, banish or imprison a man, or hang him for murder. This self-governing community conducted its affairs as it saw fit without following Canadian-British law.[2]

In 1893, Bishop William Carpenter Bompas, of the Selkirk Diocese, wrote a letter to Ottawa, citing the demoralizing effects the miners were having on the First Nations people.[3] He encouraged the government to send in the Mounties. In August 1894, two policemen arrived. Inspector Charles Constantine and Staff Sergeant Charles Brown of the North West Mounted Police (NWMP) assessed the situation and abolished the miners' meeting in short order. Constantine returned south, but headed back a year later with a detachment of nineteen men and a government surveyor, William Ogilvie, who would deal with mining claims. They constructed a police post, and modestly named it Fort Constantine. Law and order had come to the Yukon.[4]

In July 1897, two ships carrying Yukon prospectors with sacks and suitcases bursting with gold arrived at ports in San Francisco and Seattle. When newspapers publicized this news, it caused a veritable "gold rush." For three years after, an estimated one hundred thousand fortune seekers headed to the Yukon. Thirty thousand completed the trip.[5]

The main access to the Yukon was through the long series of islands running alongside the coast of British Columbia known as the Panhandle, claimed by the United States as part of Alaska. This route to the Yukon was easier than an overland route through the interior of British Columbia. So, prospectors and fortune seekers took steamers to the Alaskan towns of Skagway and Dyea at the Lynn Canal just south of the Yukon. From there, they travelled mostly on foot, hauling their own gear and a year-worth of supplies over the mountainous, thirty-three-mile Chilkoot Trail or through the lower-altitude White Pass. Twenty-two thousand men trekked through Chilkoot Pass, struggling under enormous backpacks. Then they boarded boats or made rafts, and paddled, rowed, or steamed the five hundred miles down the Yukon River to Dawson City and the gold fields.[6]

The borderline between Yukon and Alaska had gone unresolved for decades. The United States secretary of state, William Seward, had signed the papers to purchase Alaska from Russia for $7.2 million (about two cents an acre) on March 30, 1867, the day after Queen Victoria signed the *British North America Act* creating the Dominion of Canada.[7] Originally, the boundary between Alaska and Canada had been drafted in a treaty between Russia and Britain in 1825. This treaty was what both the United States and Canada used to try to establish boundaries. The eastern boundary of Alaska had been fixed at the 141st meridian, but the southern boundary was difficult to establish because it ran through mountainous and uncharted terrain along the coast with its many islands and inlets. The boundary was supposed to be drawn parallel to the coast, but the land was never accurately surveyed, leaving the 1825 treaty open to interpretation. A number of efforts were made, but the two countries could not agree on splitting the costs, so the land was never officially surveyed.[8]

The American government assumed control in this disputed southern region, claiming the land that was shown on the Russian maps.[9] This gave them control of access to all routes via the coast and from there to the Yukon. Canada unsuccessfully attempted to curb this by putting tariffs on goods crossing the border, but ever-resourceful Americans countered by imposing custom duties on Canadians using Alaskan routes.

By the end of 1899, thirty-three police posts had been set up, with 254 men stationed in the Yukon and adjacent parts of British Columbia. The steady stream of people coming over the Chilkoot Trail was the "flotsam of society." It was a rougher community than southern society, and the police adapted to it. Gamblers and prostitutes were not treated as criminals. As long as people were discreet about their activities, the police did not interfere. However, when formal government did come to the Yukon, the Americans were not allowed a voice in it.[10]

ANOTHER EXPEDITION TO HUDSON BAY AND STRAIT

Ten years after Lieutenant Gordon's last expedition, no port had been built on Hudson Bay and not one freighter had steamed across it with a load of grain.

By 1896, the campaign to develop a route through Hudson Bay had been waged for fifteen years. Despite the fact that westerners still clamoured for a railroad to Hudson Bay and public interest in the project never abated, construction of the railway failed to advance due to a number of financial and political obstacles. Only some of the line had been laid in the 1880s to Shoal Lake northwest of Winnipeg — a distance of about one hundred and eighty miles.

In 1896, Wilfrid Laurier's newly elected Liberal government was a strong nationalistic force in Parliament. Concerned with uniting Canada, the Liberals saw the importance of strengthening Dominion administration over the Yukon and North-West territories, and making its presence felt in the Arctic. A port on Hudson Bay's west side was again viewed as another means of linking the country together. In the fall of 1896, the government decided to revisit the idea of determining if a shipping route through Hudson Bay and Strait was feasible.

The government voted to spend $35,000 on an expedition to Hudson waters for the summer of 1897. Like the expeditions of the 1880s, the Department of Marine and Fisheries was in charge. Minister Sir Louis Henry Davies appointed fifty-three-year-old Dr. William Wakeham to command the expedition. Wakeham was the fisheries protection officer, and had been involved in the administration of the fisheries off the Gaspé Peninsula. He was a hardy outdoorsman with excellent interpersonal skills, and an ideal leader.

Wakeham was born in Quebec City in 1844. He received a dègree in medicine at McGill College in Montreal in 1866 and moved to the Gaspé to set up a medical practice. He closed his practice ten years later and moved back to Quebec City to become medical director of Belmont Retreat, a private asylum that treated mental diseases. However, Wakeham returned to the Gaspé three years later and began a second career. He became a civil servant in the Department of Marine and Fisheries. In 1879, the federal government appointed him inspector of Canadian fisheries on the East Coast. He was authorized to enforce Canada's maritime laws and issue fishing permits, so was given command of the steamer *La Canadienne* to patrol the East Coast. As part of his patrol, Wakeham visited the many tiny isolated outposts along the coast and was able to bring the people living there much-needed medical expertise.[11]

In 1893, Wakeham co-chaired a study of the Atlantic and Pacific fishing grounds. He and his American counterpart analyzed boundary waters in the interior of the continent in order to help the two countries resolve disputes over any of the waters. Their three-year study served as the basis for a future international fishing agreement and the Boundary Waters Treaty.[12]

William James Topley, Library and Archives Canada, C-75709

Dr. William Wakeham in 1898, after commanding the expedition to Hudson Bay and Strait aboard the Diana *in 1897.*

Wakeham's experience in the fisheries and his impeccable handling of this important international issue led to his appointment as commander of the Hudson Bay expedition. His key mission was to investigate Hudson Strait to see if the shipping season could be extended beyond the length of time recommended by Gordon.

This expedition would not involve scientific studies. The data collected by the meteorological stations during Gordon's expeditions a decade earlier had provided sufficient information in that regard. However, the Geological Survey of Canada would carry out geological and geographical research along the shores of the strait as part of the expedition.

Focusing on the practical navigability of Hudson Strait, the expedition would depart the end of May and make several passes through the strait to assess it at that early time of year. Then it would spend the summer months cruising Hudson Bay to ascertain "its capability for fishing purposes."[13] Wakeham would resume passage of the strait in the autumn to determine for how long it would be open and traversable. As this had been the mandate of Lieutenant Gordon's three voyages a decade earlier, many critics wondered if the 1897 mission wasn't redundant.

The expedition was the subject of a heated debate in the House of Commons on May 6, 1897. In defence of the project, Sir Louis Davies expounded on how the expedition would also address other concerns. He said,

> It has been reported to me that some American whalers have for a series of years visited Cumberland Sound, north of Hudson's Bay Straits and have acted as if they owned the country; and my instructions to Commander Wakeham were to proceed up the Sound to take as formal possession of the country as possible, to plant the flag there as notice that the country is ours, and take all necessary precautions to inform natives and foreigners that the laws must be observed and particularly the customs laws of Canada.[14]

However, the majority of whalers in Cumberland Sound were Scottish and not American. If Davies had read Gordon's reports, he would have realized that the Americans had been profiting from whaling and trading activities in Hudson Bay unimpeded by Canadian authorities for several decades. Thus, Wakeham was not advised to visit any whaling stations in Hudson Bay, only directed to "proclaim and uphold" Canada's sovereignty over the Arctic at the whaling stations on Cumberland Sound.

In Wakeham's orders, Davies said, "You will specially bear in your mind the necessity of being able to enforce Dominion jurisdiction. I assume, therefore, you will deem it necessary to take proper fire-arms and ammunition, and I would suggest a suitable small cannon of the most modern and improved kind."[15]

Despite the suggestion that aggressive tactics might be necessary to deal with the foreigners, a cannon is not listed in the fitting up of the ship, and no mention is made of one in Wakeham's published report of the expedition. Implicit in Davies' orders is the message that this was more than just an expedition to test the navigability of Hudson Strait. It would also be a sovereignty exercise.

In December of 1896, Davies received a letter from Rear Admiral A.H. Markham expressing interest in accompanying the voyage to Hudson Bay. The high-profile Arctic explorer was now chief promoter of the Hudson Bay and Pacific Railway, and so had a personal interest in the expedition. His expertise on the voyage was welcomed, but in the end, Markham was unable to go.

Markham had suggested a whaling or sealing ship for the expedition, but the government had already come to the same conclusion and chosen the sailing steamship *Diana*, which was one of the sealing vessels belonging to the Job Brothers of St. John's. It had been used until 1888 by the Hudson's Bay Company as a transport ship, so had already felt the icy Hudson waters on its keel. The *Diana* was further recommended by Captain Robert (Bob) Bartlett, who had great experience in Arctic waters as captain of Lieutenant Robert Peary's expeditions farther north.

The *Diana* was built by Scottish shipbuilders in 1870. The wooden screw steamer was 151 feet long and seventeen feet wide, with a sixteen-foot draft. It weighed 473 tons gross and 275 tons net. With its two low-pressure cylinder steam engines, it was capable of seventy horsepower, consuming ten tons of coal per day. It had the reputation of being one of the fastest Dundee ships.

The *Diana* was rebuilt in 1891 by its original builders, and reinforced with beams and braces throughout its hold to cope with the ice floes it would encounter in Arctic regions. Its hull was sheathed with a skin of greenheart or ironwood planking and its stem shod with bands of iron, "enabling her to force her way through the ice masses, where the strongest ironclad would be crushed like a nut."[16] Only Nansen's *Fram* was said to be more ice-worthy than the *Diana*.

An article in the *Globe*'s news section on January 29, 1897, announced the Hudson Bay expedition would start the beginning of May, aboard the steamer *Diana*, which had been secured for the upcoming expedition. However, four months later, Davies came under fire for his choice of expedition vessel. During debates in the House of Commons in May, the Opposition inquired why the department had not hired a ship that would give a true indication of how Hudson Bay would be navigated by a commercial vessel.

The Honourable Nicholas Davin of Assiniboia (North-West Territories) said, "It is not the navigability of Hudson's Bay by a sealer that is to be solved, but it is the navigability of Hudson's Bay by a commercial vessel."[17]

Davies defended the choice of vessel, but considering that the ship's details had been publicized the end of January, Davin's criticism was rather pointless. By the time Davin attacked Davies about the choice of ship, the entire crew had been hired and supplies purchased for the expedition. The 1897 expedition to Hudson Bay and Strait was a *fait accompli*. The *Diana* was being prepared to leave within weeks for another Dominion government cruise in northern Canadian waters.

WAKEHAM'S 1897 EXPEDITION

The 1897 expedition was originally scheduled to leave Halifax on May 20, but the *Diana* did not return from the sealing grounds until May 14. Its hold was full of seals, so six days was not enough time to empty the hold, clean the ship, and ready it for the voyage.

But time was of the essence, and within two weeks the ship was loaded with supplies and coal, and the passengers' cabins fitted up. Though the expedition was not expected to exceed five months' duration, the steamer was chartered for seven months (at $1,400 a month) and preparations were made in the event that it became trapped in the ice and forced to overwinter in Hudson waters. The ship was therefore provisioned with enough supplies to sustain fifty men for eighteen months.

The *Diana* set sail on the third of June. An enthusiastic crowd gathered on the dock to cheer it out of the harbour. Its departure was like that of the previous government expeditions with the minister of Marine and Fisheries, along with other officials, making speeches and ships anchored in the harbour saluting and sounding their whistles as the expedition steamed past.

The 1897 Hudson Bay expedition consisted of forty-three men. William Wakeham was commanding officer. The sailing master was thirty-five-year-old Captain William Henry Whiteley, a very experienced and capable ice navigator, famous for his invention of the cod trap. The expedition party was made up of three members of the Geological Survey of Canada, Dr. Robert Bell, Albert Peter Low, and George Albert Young; Dr. McDonald, ship's physician and meteorological officer; and Graham Drinkwater, secretary and official photographer. James Fisher,

William Wakeham Expedition Collection, Library and Archives Canada, PA-103463

The SS Diana *with the expedition company, leaving Halifax on the way to Hudson Bay and Strait, June 1897.*

a member of the Manitoba Legislative Assembly, was along as representative of both Manitoba and the North-West Territories. As a staunch supporter of a Hudson Bay railway and shipping route, he also had an interest in the conclusion of the expedition.[18]

Natural Resources Canada, courtesy of the Geological Survey of Canada, KGS-2369BB

Dr. Robert Bell accompanied the first four expeditions to Hudson Bay and Strait. He carried out duties as geologist on all four, and was also ship's medical officer on the first three.

The crew members, made up of nine able seamen, a quartermaster, an oiler, and three firemen, all received a salary of $30 a month. The two cooks were paid $22 a month each; the two engineers were paid $80; Alfred King, the boatswain, received $37; and first mate Captain Joy's monthly salary was $50. Dr. McDonald's salary was $100 per month, and Drinkwater's was $75. The crew was promised an additional half month's salary due two months after sailing.

All members of the crew had Arctic experience, working aboard whalers or in the cod and seal fishery. A few had accompanied Lieutenant Gordon on his voyages to Hudson Bay aboard the *Neptune* and *Alert*. Several had been with Robert Peary aboard the *Hope*. Only the second mate, John Ernest Stewart, had served under Wakeham on *La Canadienne*. Two brothers, Thomas and Moses Crossman, were the Newfoundlander engineers, known as "two of the best on the island."[19] Thomas himself had superintended the rebuilding of the *Diana's* engines in Glasgow six years prior. Wakeham was confident that both the ship and crew were well-versed in the sailing conditions particular to Arctic waters.

This time, the Geological Survey of Canada would carry out research as an integral and valuable part of the expedition. Robert Bell, now fifty-six, returned for his fourth Hudson Bay expedition, this time in the capacity of geologist only, not doctor. Bell and four other men would explore the Baffin Island side of Hudson Strait. His fellow geologist, thirty-six-year-old Albert Peter Low, Low's assistant and nephew, George A. Young, and three others would explore the Labrador side of the strait, between Cape Wolstenholme and Fort Chimo at Ungava Bay. Low, an extraordinary mapmaker, had spent the past thirteen summers exploring northern Quebec, the Ungava region, and the Labrador Peninsula, and welcomed this opportunity to further investigate the north coast of Ungava.

On the ship's deck were two thirty-five-foot, seven-ton yachts, which had cabins and bunks for an extended cruise. These boats would be used by the Geological Survey teams. Each yacht also carried a smaller boat aboard to enable the men to get from the yacht to the land. The Geological Survey had received little assistance on Gordon's three expeditions, with Bell only having access to whatever boat was not being used by someone else. Having two teams with their own boats was a minor triumph for the survey and a huge asset to the geologists on board.

As the expedition's main mission was to assess Hudson Strait, the first order of business was to make passage of it to Hudson Bay. The two survey teams would be dropped off at their designated locations on the *Diana's* first trip back through the strait. It took the ship three weeks to reach the entrance to Hudson Strait. Their progress was frequently halted by ice. Had the expedition left as originally planned on May 20, it would not have arrived at the strait any earlier — a fact that Gordon had noted as well. By June 14, "ice [was] closely packed around the ship" and the engines stopped. Wakeham wrote, "The ice is in large pans; it is old heavy ice of great thickness, much of it floating six or eight feet above water."[20] Fortunately, the ship was able to get up enough steam to work its way free three days later.

On Monday, June 22, the *Diana* steamed into the mouth of Hudson Strait. The Strait appeared to be so free of ice that the men imagined a swift passage through to Hudson Bay. However, the next afternoon they came up against a solid pan of ice that extended as far as they could see. They proceeded carefully, picking leads, or lanes of open water, to steam through.

Four days later, progress was halted by an impassable barrier of ice with no sign of open water ahead. The ship was soon entirely surrounded by a massive sheet of dense, shifting, moving ice. To protect the rudder, the crew set dynamite charges to blast away the ten- to fifteen-foot-thick ice

The Diana *in ice in Hudson Strait, July 1897.*

surrounding them. A few days later, two impenetrable pans of ice rafted together, which forced one pan under the ship's port quarter. The ship strained and groaned loudly, unnerving the men on board.

The next day, July 1, the men and boats were ready to abandon ship. Suddenly the ice began moving. The ship was carried along with it, then abruptly "lifted bodily about four feet out of the water."[21] When it settled back in the sea, the rudder was twisted and broken. The ordeal didn't end there. The ship endured an even worse nipping three days later, when ice squeezed around it and hove up the between and main decks. The wooden ship groaned miserably. The rigging hung slack. The pressure of the ice kept up for two hours. Then, as if in a scene out of a movie, the ice suddenly reared up on the port side, level with the rail. With a loud crack, the ice on the starboard side broke away and passed under the ship, shoving it five feet out of the water. This effectively relieved the pressure of the ice on the hull, but held the *Diana* in a precarious and dangerous position.

All hands again stood anxiously by, ready to abandon ship. The men spent a nerve-racking, sleepless night wondering if the next movement of ice would shipwreck them. The ice finally eased its grip and slackened the next morning. The *Diana* was again waterborne. Still, all that could be seen from the crow's nest was ice; not a sign of water anywhere.

The ship continued ramming the ice in an attempt to move forward. But it was July 12 when it finally made the western end of the strait. The ice was now looser, more scattered and water-soaked, and the ship was able to make progress. They had pushed through ice their entire journey through Hudson Strait, and it had taken three weeks instead of a few days. This experience shored up support for Gordon's earlier assessment that no passage of the strait to Hudson Bay was possible until mid-July. Wakeham wrote that the *Diana* received blows from the thick ice pans that no commercial freight carrier could have withstood. This was reminiscent of Gordon's experience in the strait twelve years earlier. It appears that his critics, Markham among them, were unfairly hard on Gordon.

Bell planned to be dropped off at King Charles Cape on the Foxe Peninsula of southwestern Baffin Island. As the ship headed to Salisbury Island, southeast of the Foxe Peninsula, fog descended and it encountered exceedingly heavy ice flowing down from the Foxe Channel. It was dense, old, and soiled ice, sometimes with dark bits of algae on it. After three hours, the *Diana* had progressed no more than one hundred yards. Concerned that the ship would end up locked in the ice again, Wakeham decided to head to the south side of the strait and drop Low off first.

By Friday, July 16, the ship had arrived at King George's Sound, halfway between Digges Island and the Ungava Peninsula. Here, the *Diana* spent the weekend in a spectacular harbour walled in by breathtaking, steep double fiords. Wakeham named the spot Douglas Harbour.

They met three Inuit families there hunting beluga, seal, and walrus. Low's supplies were moved ashore, and his party boarded their yacht on Sunday morning, anxious to begin their explorations and research. After parting company with Low, the *Diana* weighed anchor and headed northeast across the strait for Ashe Inlet on Big Island, where Bell decided his team would disembark.

The Ashe observation station still stood. Wakeham and his men inspected the house where the station men had lived from 1884 to 1886. It was in fine condition, with its flagstaff still standing. The group found a notice tacked to the wall stating that Lieutenant Robert Peary had stopped there with five men on his expedition aboard the *Hope* the year before.

Graham Drinkwater, Library and Archives Canada, C-084677

The observation station building at Ashe Inlet was not dismantled when the others were in 1886. It was still standing when Wakeham visited in 1897.

Bell's supplies were landed, then he and his four men boarded the yacht, ready to explore the southern Baffin coastline. Bell, Low, and their parties would be picked up in mid-September when the *Diana* passed through on one of its last voyages east. The *Diana* carried on eastward towards the Button Islands, north of Port Burwell. A narrow belt of ice clung to the coastline, but the middle of the strait was clear. Wakeham now wanted to see the state of the ice drifting down from Foxe Channel, and they swung about to head west.

The ship rounded Digges Island after midnight on Saturday, July 24. Pans of ice five- to ten-feet thick and several miles in circumference blocked any progress northward into Foxe Channel. The *Diana* then headed east in the strait, but kept a southward course to avoid ice to the north. It ran out of the ice around Big Island and had easy sailing for the rest of the way to the Button Islands.

The *Diana* was scheduled to meet a coal supply vessel on August 1 in Nachvak Bay, and so headed south. Fog obscured their destination and they could see only the mountain peaks above the heavy mist. The coal ship, *Maggie*, failed to arrive on the first, and the *Diana* settled in the harbour to wait. The crew passed the time repairing the ship and repainting its sides, which were battle-scarred after being smashed about in the ice. The men finally spotted the sails of the *Maggie* on August 6. The sailing ship had been detained at the mouth of the bay for five days, unable to move in the windless calm and fog.

It took nearly a week for the crews to transfer the three hundred and twenty tons of coal to the *Diana*. They spent a good deal of time cleaning up, as shifting coal from one ship to another was a dirty job. All aboard were happy to receive the mail and issues of the *Globe, Mail & Empire, Gazette, Herald, La Minerve, Journal,* and *Citizen* that the *Maggie* had carried up for them.

On August 13, the *Diana* weighed anchor and headed north to Cumberland Sound. It was time to carry out administrative duties. On the sixteenth, the *Diana* anchored at Kekerten Island, where the Scottish whaling station had been established in 1857. Between the time the whalers had first entered the Eastern Arctic in the 1820s until Wakeham's visit in 1897, eighteen thousand Greenland bowhead whales had been caught in the region; thirteen thousand of these had been slaughtered in the first twenty years. By the 1890s the number of bow-head captured had dwindled to 140 per year.[22] As many as thirty ships visited the station in the 1850s and 1860s, with a dozen ships overwintering there, frozen in the bay.

Kekerten was one of the last surviving whaling stations in Cumberland Sound. Arctic weather and the hazards of the job took its toll on the whalers. The graveyard on the eastern end of the island was testament to this. At Kekerten, Wakeham and his men went ashore to inspect the station and collect pertinent information about the whaling done there. They found 140 Inuit men, women, and children living at and employed by the station.

The Inuit were invaluable employees. Their skills were used for hunting the bowhead along the floe edge with harpoons. The men also carved up the mammoth whale carcasses into manageable pieces, rendered the blubber, and were crews on the whaleboats.[23] The women worked at the whaling stations, processing the whale meat and rendering the blubber into oil. Their skill as tanners was in high demand. And, typical of the plight of women everywhere, their cooking and sewing talents were taken advantage of by the men, both Inuit and Qallunaat.[24] In exchange for their services, the whaling station offered the Inuit biscuits, tea, and tobacco. Every August, the supply ship would come in with provisions and trade articles and leave with a full hold of sealskin, furs, oil, and baleen.[25]

The relationship between the whalers and local people was also a cultural exchange. The whalers and Inuit enjoyed and learned each other's games, music, and dances. The downside of living side by side was that the Inuit were also introduced to new illnesses and diseases they had no immunity from. With the introduction of foreign diseases such as tuberculosis and influenza, their population plummeted from one thousand in the 1850s to three hundred and fifty by the 1870s.[26]

The Marine and Fisheries minister's instructions to Wakeham were "to enquire into the extent to which trade was carried on in the territories North of Hudson Straits by aliens and others, and to firmly and openly proclaim our right to jurisdiction in all these British Territories."[27] So on August 17, the day after anchoring at Kekerten, Wakeham and his men returned to the whaling station to carry out a formal ceremony.

There on a rocky outcrop overlooking the bay, they built a rough cairn to hold a flag pole. Then, in front of the station master and a number of the whalers and Inuit, they raised the Union Jack on behalf of the Dominion of Canada, "formally declaring in their presence that the flag was hoisted as an evidence that Baffin's Land with all the territories, islands and dependencies adjacent to it were now, as they always had been since their first discovery and occupation, under the exclusive sovereignty of Great Britain."[28] The reaction of the Scottish whalers and Inuit to the ceremony is not noted. It would have no effect on their operations anyhow, as no other Dominion government ship would visit the area for six years.

From Kekerten, the expedition moved on to the Scottish whaling station at Blacklead Island. The locals had named it Uumanaqjuaq, "like a big sea mammal's heart," as the formation of the distant hills resembled a heart. Like Kekerten, the Inuit population on Blacklead was about one hundred and forty souls. Another one hundred and twenty people had recently arrived from New Gummiute, where a third whaling station operated by New England whalers had been abandoned.

Graham Drinkwater, Library and Archives Canada, C-084686

Wakeham and his men making the first proclamation on behalf of the Dominion government, claiming the Arctic for Canada at the whaling station on Kekerten Island, August 1897. Wakeham is second from the right.

Wakeham makes no mention of having another formal ceremony like the one at Kekerten, but he informed the whalers of the Dominion government's jurisdiction in the region. With the mission of sovereignty accomplished, the *Diana* headed south on August 19 to commence another voyage west through Hudson Strait. This time the crew met less ice, but plenty of fog. In fact, conditions were so improved that they passed through the strait in three days. They witnessed a wall of ice still coming down Foxe Channel northeast of Salisbury Island, but were in no danger of encountering it.

On August 25, they shaped their course for Churchill on the west side of Hudson Bay, dropping anchor there on the thirtieth. However, when the tide went out after midnight, the ship was grounded. At high tide, when the ship was floated again, rowboats towed the *Diana* three miles up the harbour to the Hudson's Bay Company post. Wakeham's instructions had included assessing the fishing opportunities in Hudson Bay, so on September 2 they weighed anchors, headed across the bay, and set a net for trawling. They didn't catch anything, and halted the project when they encountered a "short angry sea."

Inuit on board the Diana *at Blacklead Island, 1897.*

They cruised through the strait, making Big Island after midnight on September 10 on schedule to pick up Bell and his party. But the weather turned miserable, blowing a snow squall that prevented them from landing or anchoring. They decided to head across the strait to Douglas Harbour, where they would have shelter. The following day the storm abated, leaving the deck icy and covered in snow. The hills about them were also draped in white. When the weather lifted in late afternoon, they headed back to Ashe Inlet, arriving twelve hours later. Bell and his party were waiting, despite the early hour of 5:00 a.m. They came aboard with their belongings and collections. The *Diana* set sail that morning, towing Bell's yacht.

In Ungava Bay, Wakeham set out to confirm or dispute the existence of Green Island. This was the island that Gordon hadn't been able to properly locate on his earlier voyages, and so had wiped from the map in 1886. Gordon's decision in doing so was called into question by southern authorities, and Wakeham was charged with confirming whether or not Green Island existed. They sighted the cliffs in the direction where Green Island had been placed on the Admiralty charts. As they steamed close to it they met Inuit hunters who told them it was Akpatok Island and that there was no Green Island. Gordon had acted correctly. Akpatok Island had also been wrongly placed on the charts. Wakeham corrected the errors.

At the mouth of the Ungava River, a pilot came out to meet them. At high tide, they proceeded upriver through a thick snowstorm and anchored at the Hudson's Bay Company post at Fort Chimo (now Kuujjuaq). Low and his men were waiting there, and reported all well. Here, they stowed Bell's yacht, which he planned to use on future explorations of the area. Low's yacht had already been shipped south aboard the *Erik* on September 8.[29]

Davies' original orders stated that Wakeham would pick up the Geological Survey parties and return to Halifax once he had satisfied himself of the lateness of the navigability of Hudson Strait. However, in mid-May, Dr. George Dawson, director of the Geological Survey, forwarded a letter to the minister of Marine and Fisheries from Robert Bell. Bell was concerned that no contingency had been made in the event of accident to either of the survey parties or the *Diana*.

He recommended that the *Diana* be scheduled to call in at St. John's at the beginning of October, so that any failure to arrive would allow for prompt action on the part of the government to "dispatch a relief steamer."[30] The ship would then also be able to refuel, and any men finished with their duties could be discharged. Bell's common sense suggestion was taken, and the *Diana* headed for port with the intention of returning to the strait for the final passages.

Several feet of snow began piling up on shore, and snow followed them as they ran through Gray Strait and south along the Labrador coast. They made St. John's, Newfoundland, on Saturday, September 25, at 2:30 a.m.

They stayed over a week, making repairs to the engines and screw propeller and taking on fresh provisions and coal. Mr. Job, owner of the *Diana*, picked up the mail to be posted and handed the men the letters received for them. Bell, Low, and the scientific parties disembarked to make their way back to Ottawa. Their fieldwork was completed and they would spend the winter analyzing the specimens they had collected.

On Wednesday, October 6, at 6:45 a.m., the *Diana* weighed anchor, heading northward to make its final passage through Hudson Strait. Snow and poor weather accompanied them the entire trip up the coast of Labrador. A vicious gale blowing from the northwest turned into a heavy snowstorm, forcing them to drop both anchors in Snug Harbour. By October 16, the *Diana* was once again at the mouth of Hudson Strait. A strong, vicious wind and snow squall prevented it entering the strait. On a second attempt, the ship forged through the mid-channel course between the Buttons and Cape Chidley, through a "considerable sea and heavy tide rips, with snow squalls at intervals."[31] The ship came through with its bow, top gallant forecastle, and fore-rigging heavily iced up.

The ship steamed along the south side of the strait. Ice was forming thickly along the shores. On October 18, it anchored in Douglas Harbour, just over halfway through the strait. Some of the crew went ashore in search of fresh water, with no success. The lake and rivers were frozen over with five-inch-thick ice, enough to walk on. The following day, the men found a lake half a mile inland where they could get water. The crew lugged water in buckets from the lake to the boats on the beach. They then hauled it out to the ship's water tanks, successfully transporting five hundred gallons of water this way. It was a merciless way of refilling the tanks, though, as water froze in the buckets and boats, and on the men.

On Friday, October 22, they left their anchorage and headed back out into the strait to continue to Hudson Bay. They met with fine, light snow. The snow stopped as they neared the end of the strait, and they deduced that this was the effect of warmer water coming out of the bay.

The next day snow again obscured their vision. Their plan was to anchor at Port Laperrière at Digges Island, but the snow made it impossible to see where they were. They kept the lead going, but "laid the ship to head to the wind for the night."[32] By Sunday, October 24, the ship had made Cape Wolstenhome at the southwest corner of Hudson Strait. By two o'clock in the afternoon, the sea was the heaviest Wakeham had seen it. The mercury was falling in the thermometer and dry snow hung in the air like fog, preventing them from seeing any distance. The men kept taking the lead but had no bottom at 120 fathoms. With no place to anchor they turned back to Douglas Harbour. The weather in the strait was nasty, with heavy, blowing snow. Yet the weather in the sheltered harbour was fine, with a clear, sunny sky.

Wakeham and officers in caribou clothing aboard the Diana, *1897. Wakeham is second from the right.*

Five days later, the ship put back out into the strait in another attempt to make Hudson Bay. Again, they encountered a constant falling snow that obscured their vision. Wakeham wrote that it wasn't the ice and cold that bothered them but the wind and blinding snow, which blew incessantly and from a variety of directions. They made little progress steaming into a forty-mile-an-hour headwind. The ship's speed was little more than three knots and was icing up with the frozen spray. Wakeham decided to "give it up and run out of the strait."[33] Abandoning their plan to enter Hudson Bay, they shaped their course for Labrador. It was October 29.

The following morning, spray was freezing as it fell upon the deck. The ship's deck was so iced up it had to be rigged with life lines, so that the crew could move about. With a strong northwest wind, the ship made nine and a half knots heading south along the Labrador coast. The crew worked hard breaking ice off the rigging and hull. The ship's company was thoroughly relieved when the *Diana* steamed into Port Hawkesbury, Nova Scotia, on Sunday, November 7.

Wakeham immediately sent off telegrams of the expedition's safe passage and arrival to politicians in Ottawa. He intended to sail on to Halifax, but upon leaving the harbour, the gale they encountered was so fierce they turned back into port. The following morning, Wakeham caught a train to Halifax.

It had not been smooth sailing for the expedition of 1897. The *Diana* had passed through Hudson Strait six times. None of the trips had been particularly easy. Despite the severe nipping the *Diana* experienced in Hudson Strait, the inspection by the Lloyd's agent after it was returned to its owners at St. John's pronounced it hardly damaged.

WAKEHAM'S REPORT

On April 23, 1898, exactly one year after issuing orders for the expedition, Sir Louis Davies laid Wakeham's official report on the table in the House of Commons. The *Report of the Expedition to Hudson Bay and Cumberland Gulf in the Steamship Diana Under the Command of William Wakeham* was quickly picked up and its summary published in the papers.

Wakeham's verdict on the date of navigation appeared in the late edition of that day's *Globe*. He is quoted saying, "The risks of navigation were so great that I have no hesitation whatever in saying that after the last date which I have given above it would likely be folly to think of carrying on any commercial traffic through the Strait. I would, therefore, fix the 20th of October as the extreme limit of safe navigation in the fall."[34]

Gordon's assessment had put a closing date at the first week of October. In his summary of the voyage, however, Wakeham wholeheartedly agrees with Lieutenant Gordon in putting the date for entrance into the strait for commercial vessels between the first and tenth of July. He didn't think any passage could safely be made before that time.

Wakeham's report included his daily observations, as well as the information he received from the whaling stations and the Hudson's Bay Company posts. As well, the report included Wakeham's interviews with three American whaling captains about their experience with ice conditions going through Hudson Strait and across Hudson Bay.

He says, "In Cumberland Sound there are no longer any whaling stations owned by aliens."[35] The Scottish stations at Kekerten and Blacklead were owned by British subjects, so not considered foreigners. Wakeham admits that none of the whalers paid any duties to the Canadian government on the operations they carried out. However, he dismissed this, surmising that the amount of duty on the goods would be quite small.

The final paragraph of Wakeham's conclusion says,

> To such brave and experienced mariners as those who accused Capt. Gordon of timidity because he refused to force the "*Alert*" through the ice of Hudson Strait in June, after she had lost her stem plate, or who have dubbed the hardy men from Newfoundland who manned and sailed the "*Diana*," as feather bed sailors", because we left the strait with the end of October, these conditions are frivolous and will have no influence, but to the ordinary sailor and ship owner, I flatter myself sir, they will be plain and sufficient.[36]

Sadly, Gordon never knew he had been vindicated.

An editorial in Toronto's *Evening Star* on December 17, 1898, summed up a widely held view that the route was a waste of money. "The Dominion has spent so much money in the St. Lawrence, Welland and Soo canals, and so much has been invested in the Canadian Pacific, that it is hard to see how the people could afford to invest more funds in developing a rival route via Hudson Bay, even if it were possible to navigate those almost Arctic waters."

The Hudson Bay route was a hard sell after Wakeham's report proved that the period when commercial vessels could safely navigate Hudson Strait was just as Gordon had claimed a decade earlier — only four months.

CHAPTER SIX

A Canadian Bid for the Pole

Thousands of miles southeast of Hudson Bay and Strait, in the prison in Quebec City, a convict was sketching a map of the Arctic. The prisoner was doing time for forgery, and his artistic skills interested the governor of the prison.

This was no ordinary prison governor and no ordinary map. Joseph-Elzéar Bernier was a veteran sea captain who was taking a leave of absence from his life before the mast to be the prison's governor. It was also an opportunity for him to study the Arctic. The map he commissioned was enormous, almost twelve feet square. It showed the polar region as if the viewer was looking down on the top of the world, with all the circumpolar countries ringed around the centre. Bernier had the map drawn for his lectures on his intended expedition to the North Pole.

Bernier was born on New Year's Day 1852, in L'Islet-sur-Mer, a small village on the south shore of the St. Lawrence River, east of Quebec City. He made his first ocean voyage at age two, and was "apprenticed to the sea" at fourteen as cabin boy on his father's vessel. By age seventeen, Bernier was promoted to captain of his own ship, the youngest sea captain in the British Empire.[1]

On November 8, 1870, when Bernier was eighteen, he married fifteen-year-old Rose Caron, his childhood sweetheart. But a sailor is first married to the sea, and a week after their wedding, Bernier returned to his ship with a promise to rendezvous with his bride at the first convenient port. In mid-April 1871, the young sea captain arrived at Georgetown, near Washington, with a cargo of salt in his ship's hold. The captain arranged for Rose to meet him in the American capital for their belated honeymoon.

For a mariner, it was an exciting time to be in Washington. The newspapers and talk among maritime circles was about the sailing steamship that had spent the winter on blocks in the Navy Yard while being partially fitted for an Arctic expedition. Bernier wandered down to the docks to see for himself this much talked about *Polaris*.

He inspected the hull of the schooner-rigged screw tug with a practised eye. Bernier had built ships with his father that were designed to navigate the ice-choked St. Lawrence River and North Atlantic. This, coupled with his first-hand knowledge of the ice in the Gulf of St. Lawrence, led him to believe that the *Polaris* was not ice-worthy.[2] Despite the efforts to strengthen the ship, Bernier felt that its hull wasn't shaped to properly penetrate the Arctic ice.

Richard Finnie Collection, Library and Archives Canada, PA-207173

Captain Joseph-Elzéar Bernier petitioned for a North Pole expedition from 1898 to 1905. He captained the Arctic on the Hudson Bay expedition in 1904–05, then went on to command his own government expeditions to the Arctic Archipelago in 1906–07, 1908–09, and 1910–11.

Bernier's assessment of the vessel was proven right when, in May 1873, reports of the ship's demise and the nineteen survivors plucked from the ice floe made headlines. This disaster led Bernier to study Arctic navigation. His interest in the North was ignited. For him, the *Polaris* was the beginning of a lifelong passion for the Arctic.

He read everything he could, from explorers' published journals to scientific reports. In his memoirs, *Master Mariner and Arctic Explorer: A Narrative of Sixty Years at Sea from the Logs and Yarns of Captain J.E. Bernier,* he wrote that from 1872 on, his cabin library was stocked mainly with books written by or about Arctic explorers and their expeditions. Bernier was a toddler when British and American expeditions, backed by the British navy, Lady Franklin, and geographical societies, were searching the Arctic wasteland for Franklin and his crew. Reading these English explorers' accounts was an accomplishment for a francophone with a grade six education.

After Bernier's visit to the *Polaris* in 1871, he continued his life on the sea, becoming a competent ship's captain and obtaining his master mariner's ticket. Bernier knew how to give orders and was accustomed to having them obeyed; such talents were valued in a prison warden. In February 1895, Bernier accepted the position of governor of the Quebec prison, welcoming the opportunity to rest his sea legs and pursue his passion — the Arctic.

At forty-three, Bernier's dark hair had receded to a horseshoe ring around his head. He was below medium height with a robust build that "made up in sturdiness of build the inches for what he lacked in height."[3] He had a massive neck and muscular arms and shoulders from a life of hauling ships' rigging and sails. He stood straight-backed with his stomach out in front, like a salt pork barrel, and his feet planted widely apart as if always steadying himself against the roll of the ship.

Bernier made good use of his time as governor of the prison. He spent hours in his office, studying every Arctic-related book and chart of Arctic waters that he could get his hands on. He focused particularly on information about currents and the drift of ice across the Pole.[4] One of the books that he used extensively for his research was Fridtjof Nansen's *Farthest North.* Nansen's 1897 published record of his polar trek and the information about the polar drift fuelled and supported Bernier's plan to make his own voyage to the North Pole. Bernier firmly believed that the prize of the North Pole belonged to Canada. He felt that attaining the Pole would, in the eyes of the rest of the world, secure all the land between that point at 90 degrees and the rest of the mainland for Canada.

Bernier was so confident in his ability to reach the Pole that in 1898 he had calling cards printed depicting two eagles, American and Scandinavian, hovering threateningly over a wooden pole, with a Russian bear approaching from the left on the ice below, while a beaver sits gnawing at the pole. These animals symbolized the three international threats to the North Pole. However, on Bernier's card, the Canadian beaver, industriously chewing away at the base of the Pole, is undoubtedly the successful conqueror of it. "J.E. Bernier, attacking the Pole" is printed at the bottom of the card.

When he was convinced that he had a solid plan, Bernier accepted an invitation to lecture before the Quebec Geographical Society. One Saturday night in December 1897, Bernier presented his plan for a polar expedition and used his impressive new wall-sized map to demonstrate his proposed route. He gained the unanimous support of the society. Its president, Major Nazaire Levasseur, became his champion.

The 1898 calling card Bernier handed out when he was raising funds for his polar expedition, depicting three nations vying for the North Pole — Norway, America, and Russia. The Canadian beaver is busily chewing away at the Pole.

125

Levasseur had important connections and used them to help Bernier. He sent letters to people well-connected in Quebec society and politics, petitioning money for Bernier's project. On Bernier's behalf, Levasseur wrote a letter of introduction to Prime Minister Laurier on February 7, 1898. Bernier followed it with a letter to Laurier on March 5, 1898, laying out his plan for a North Pole expedition in a twenty-page report neatly handwritten, oddly enough, in English.

In his report, Bernier cited the voyage of the *Jeannette* as proof of a polar current. Like Nansen, he would use the ice drifting northward with this current to advance toward the Pole. He proposed two itineraries for attaining 90 degrees north. Both involved leading an over-ice approach, but from different points in Siberia. In either case, he and seven men would strike out northward across the drifting ice, using dogs, sleds, reindeer, kayaks, and enough provisions to last two years. Bernier's letter detailed how he had more accurately calculated the longitudinal location to make an over-ice attack on the North Pole and would thus succeed where Nansen hadn't.

He wrote, "If most of the expeditions undertaken up to the present have miscarried it is because they were directed in seas where the current ran towards the south.... At a cost of terrible hardships, they march towards the north and during this time, the slow current drives towards the south the ice-floe on which they thought they were advancing."[5] Bernier anticipated making about four miles per day, and would thus reach the Pole in 180 days.

Bernier received a polite thank-you note from Laurier, suggesting he seek other financial support before approaching the government.[6] A reply from the prime minister was encouragement enough, and he embarked on an extensive lecture tour.

In the late fall of 1900, Bernier addressed both the prestigious Royal Colonial Institute and the Royal Geographical Society in London, England. Seated in the audience at these lectures were distinguished explorers, including men who had searched for Franklin. One of these, Sir Clements Markham, was the geographical society's president at the time. Bernier had charisma, was a captivating orator, and was a persuasive enough visionary to convince these old veterans of Arctic exploration of the veracity and soundness of his plan. Both royal societies verbally endorsed his project.

One can imagine Bernier confidently handing out his calling card with the beaver chewing away at the North Pole, symbolizing the colonial Canadian's impending success.

Back in Canada, Bernier's public campaign for a polar expedition was gaining support. By February 1901, the Ontario Land Surveyors Association forwarded a letter to Laurier stating that the association supported Bernier's expedition and "would respectfully urge upon the Dominion government the desirability of bearing all expense in connection with fitting out the expedition and equipping the same."[7]

Bernier realized the value of publicity and eagerly gave interviews. On February 26, 1901, a *Toronto Daily Star* reporter wrote, "Undaunted by the fact that the way to the Pole is, since 1596, strewn with crushed hopes, bones and vessels, Captain Bernier said: 'I have been around the earth, I will go to the top of it.'"

If nothing else, Bernier can be credited with indefatigable tenacity.

On March 20, Bernier sent a letter detailing his project to Governor General Lord Minto. He was informed by Minto's secretary, "His Excellency has much pleasure in giving you permission to make public the fact that he has become the patron of your exploration."[8] This was the best sort of endorsement a Canadian could have.

The next day, Bernier gave a full statement of his proposed expedition in Room Sixteen on Parliament Hill that was attended by "fully 60 per cent of the members of the House and from fifteen to twenty senators, as well as a number of citizens. In fact, the room was filled to overflowing." William Edwards reported on the meeting to Laurier in a March 22 memo. "At the close of the meeting a motion was moved by Mr. Monk, MP, and seconded by Mr. Wallace, MP, thanking Captain Bernier for his address, and recommending to Parliament his scheme, and also recommending to the Government that Parliament should contribute the necessary funds for the carrying out of same. This motion was unanimously carried. Every opportunity was given but not one dissenting voice was heard."[9]

A week later, on March 29, 1901, Frederick D. Monk, Conservative MP for Jacques Cartier, Quebec, introduced the subject of Bernier's North Pole expedition in the House of Commons. Monk asked the prime minister if the government had plans to "equip a vessel for a polar expedition under the conduct of Captain Bernier."[10]

Laurier answered, "It is a matter which the government has had under consideration, but I am not prepared to say that we have reached any conclusion yet."[11]

Bernier had calculated that the cost of the five-year expedition would be about $130,000. He had succeeded in raising only $20,000 from private sources. This included $5,000 from Lord Minto, $1,000 from Manitoba's premier Rodmond Roblin, and similar donations from the mayors of Victoria, Halifax, and Ottawa. The only way he could hope to finance an expedition of this magnitude was to receive a grant from the federal government. Despite growing enthusiasm for Bernier's plan, the government did not reach a "conclusion" at all in 1901.

The idea of the North Pole being reached by a Canadian held great appeal. Still, no benefactor came forward with enough money to fund it. A year later, Bernier was still appealing to those with power and money to press the government to support his venture. On April 12, 1902, Bernier forwarded a petition to the prime minister, which included six pages of signatures, tallying 113 members of Parliament and senators in favour of his polar project.[12] The government again deferred his request.

The prime minister was concerned, more practically, with an east-west expansion rather than a northern one. Canada was thirty-six years old with a population of just over seven million people. The boundaries of the country were still amorphous. Alberta and Saskatchewan were not yet considered provinces, and the issues in the Yukon were of greater concern to Laurier and Minister of the Interior Clifford Sifton than reaching the Earth's nebulous northern axis.

However, the idea of a Canadian reaching the Pole outweighed more practical considerations for most MPs. On May 1, 1902, a long, protracted discussion about the search for the North Pole took place in the House of Commons. Liberal MP John Charlton, whose name appears on Bernier's petition, delivered a long, well-constructed speech in support of Bernier's North Pole expedition. He suggested that the expedition "would establish our right to all the territories and islands and seas that might lie between our present northern boundary and the North Pole itself — all that vast region between the 141st parallel of longitude on the west, and Baffin's Bay and Grantland [northern Ellesmere Island] on the east."[13]

Charlton described a pie-shaped section of territory that follows the longitudes from the mainland of Canada between the Yukon's 141st parallel in the west, and Ellesmere Island at the 60th parallel in the east, up to the North Pole. This became known as the sector principle, used to describe the territory within Canada's jurisdiction. Only two members of Parliament objected to the project, saying the cost was too exorbitant and that Canada already had more territory than it knew what to do with.[14] It was practically an echo of objections to Britain's transfer of the Arctic over two decades earlier.

The prime minister also spoke. "If a son of Canada were to plant the flag of his country at the North Pole, if he were to achieve what so many brave men have struggled in vain to achieve, there is not a Canadian heart that would not beat with pride at the thought of it."[15]

However, Laurier concluded in a typically bureaucratic, noncommittal style that the government would give the project "due consideration."[16] One consideration was the fact that the total budget for immigration was $400,000. A contribution of $100,000 for a polar expedition was an exorbitant amount.

FOREIGNERS IN THE ARCTIC

In 1898, while Bernier was soliciting the prime minister about his plans for a North Pole expedition, two foreign expeditions were hauling heavily loaded sledges over ice hummocks in the Far North.

The Pole-obsessed American explorer Lieutenant Robert Edwin Peary was exploring the northern tip of Greenland before crossing Nares Strait and investigating Greely's abandoned Fort Conger on the northern tip of Ellesmere Island. At the same time, a sixteen-man Norwegian team led by Otto Sverdrup was exploring the entire Ellesmere Island region. Both parties were operating in the High Eastern Arctic without Canada's permission being either requested or granted.

The race for the Pole by foreign expeditions was not a serious matter to the Dominion government. What was worrying was that these exploration parties were in the Arctic with the potential of claiming land. Wakeham's proclamation at Kekerten the year before had no influence on these interlopers exploring farther to the north. Sverdrup and Peary were likely not even aware of the flag-raising event at Kekerten, though. In reality, Wakeham's proclamation had been an entirely ineffective ceremony; a mere token gesture to give notice to the whalers and Inuit of Baffin that Canada was in charge.

The forty-two-year-old Peary was on a four-year expedition (1898–1902) in glorious pursuit of the Pole. His exploring partner Matthew Henson describes him as six feet tall, with "heavy, bushy eyebrows shading his 'sharpshooter's eyes' of steel gray.... He has a voice clear and loud, and words never fail him."[17] Peary was an imposing character: determined, ambitious, and single-minded.

Peary sent a letter to the Arctic Club in New York from Etah, Greenland, dated August 7, 1898, just prior to setting off on his polar trek. He wrote, "I feel confident that the desired object will be gained, and the world's last great geographical prize won for the Stars and Stripes."[18] Claiming land was not part of his expedition's mandate.

Sverdrup, however, wanted to claim land for Norway.

Otto Neumann Sverdrup, like Robert Peary, was experienced in Arctic climes. The red-bearded Sverdrup was noted for his tremendous mental and physical strength, and was regarded as silent and calm. He was held in high esteem by the men who worked and lived with him on his expeditions. Wanderlust flowed in his veins. He went to sea at age seventeen, shipping aboard American, as well as Norwegian, vessels. By the time he met Fridtjof Nansen, he was a sea captain. Sverdrup joined Nansen's 350-mile ski expedition across the Greenland icecap. He was later made captain of the *Fram*, and left in command of the expedition when Nansen and Johansen set out to ski to the Pole.

In 1898, Otto Sverdrup took up the gauntlet from Nansen and decided to explore the "white spaces on the map." He planned to map the northern coast of Greenland. Sverdrup received permission from the Norwegian government, which owned the *Fram*, to use it for his expedition. Sverdrup was forty-three when he and fifteen others cast off from the dock at Christiania, Norway, on June 24, on their four-year expedition.

Peary's expedition was then based in Greenland, and he was unnecessarily protective and territorial of what he considered the "American route to the Pole." Believing that Sverdrup was honing in on his plans, he wrote to Sverdrup to discourage him from exploring Greenland.

Weather conditions worked in Peary's favour, however, as Sverdrup was forced by the mass of pack ice coming down into Kane Basin to winter at a protective harbour on eastern Ellesmere Island. Sverdrup then decided to confine his explorations to the Ellesmere region. Fortunately, as a result of this decision, Sverdrup's party made the greatest geographical addition to Arctic maps in decades.

Later, when Peary was sledging around Ellesmere, he met Sverdrup and a companion at their camp at Fort Juliana. Peary's conversation with them was unusually brief and he refused the cup of coffee they offered. This is oddly rude behaviour for one living in a remote latitude. Peary did not approve of Sverdrup exploring Greenland, but had no problem exploring Ellesmere Island where Sverdrup was.

On this expedition, Peary suffered such extreme frostbite that eight of his toes had to be amputated. However, he succeeded in laying the groundwork for his future attempts on the Pole, organizing a number of small sledding teams to set up food caches in advance of his main team.

Sverdrup's expedition, mostly made up of scientists, studied the various plant and animal species of the islands, kept meteorological records, and returned with an enormous collection of specimens and scientific data. The results of their studies were eventually published in five volumes. Sverdrup also published his own two-volume narrative of the expedition, *New Land: Four Years in the Arctic Regions*, in 1904.

Using the *Fram*'s anchorages as their base, Sverdrup and his men made land expeditions to explore the coast, mapping the fiords and peninsulas of the massive Ellesmere Island and the northern coast of Devon Island. They also added three islands to the map named after the expedition's patrons — Axel Heiberg, Ellef Ringnes, and Amund Ringnes — as well as King Christian Island, named after Christian IX of Denmark. On over fifteen major sled journeys, Sverdrup's team mapped 1,750 miles of coastline and, in all, explored 100,400 square miles.

They also found perfectly preserved remains of a forty-five-million-year-old mummified boreal forest on northeast Axel Heiberg Island, to the west of Ellesmere. Tree trunks, stumps, matted leaves, and roots were amazing evidence of the lush forest that once grew to a height of one hundred and fifty feet. This discovery led Sverdrup's men to surmise that the mean annual temperature at this high latitude was once about 65°F.

Sverdrup wanted Norway to claim the land his expedition had discovered. But Oscar II, King of Norway, wasn't interested in valueless, barren land in the High Eastern Arctic, so no official claim was made. If it had, Canada would have forfeited any right to the area. Not having explored, claimed, or inhabited the land, its claim would not have met any of the criteria for sovereignty.

It wasn't until Otto Sverdrup and his men emerged from the Arctic in September 1902 and were greeted in Oslo as heroes for their work that the Dominion government became aware of the full extent of the expedition's activities. Even if the Dominion government had been aware, though, the fledgling country did not have the resources, financial or human, to address them. The Laurier government had committed aid to the British in the Second Boer War, and troops were sent to help in the fight from October 1899 to 1902.

THE BOUNDARY DISPUTE AND OTHER PRESSING MATTERS

Bernier continued to speak to filled concert halls and hotel ballrooms about his plan for a North Pole expedition. His proposed voyage to the top of the world brought the Arctic to life for Canadians. Although individual MPs rallied around the idea of financing his expedition, collectively the government was preoccupied with other issues in the North. Foremost, Canada's relations with its southern neighbour were getting increasingly tense as the situation was unravelling with the Alaska-Yukon border.

On January 24, 1903, the United States and Canada agreed to boundary dispute arbitration with a tribunal of six members. Each side was to appoint three "impartial jurists of repute."

For the Canadian side, two prominent lawyers were appointed: Sir Louis Jette, a sixty-seven-year-old retired judge and lieutenant governor of the province of Quebec, and forty-nine-year-old Allen B. Aylesworth, King's Counsel from Toronto and a leader of the Ontario bar. Baron Alverstone, Lord Chief Justice of England and the highest legal expert in Britain, was the third member of the British-Canadian tribunal. To uphold the American interests, President Theodore Roosevelt appointed Elihu Root, secretary of war; Henry Cabot Lodge, Republican senator from Massachusetts, known as the imperialist faction of the Senate; and George Turner, former senator and Supreme Court associate justice for Washington.

The choice of men appointed to take the American side was anything but "impartial." All three had expressed firm and unalterable opinions on the Alaskan boundary "upon the floors of Congress."[19] The Canadian government objected vehemently that the public views of these men made them unable to consider the question impartially. (The two Canadian jurists were hardly non-partisan either, as both men were Liberals.) However, before the government's protest had been taken into consideration, the British ratified the agreement.[20] It would take nine months for the tribunal to come to a resolution.

In April 1903, Sverdrup, back from his expedition, was honoured at the Royal Geographical Society in London and received the R.G.S. Gold Medal for his work in the Arctic. Admirals Sir Clements Markham, Sir Richard Vesey Hamilton, and Sir Leopold M'Clintock, veteran Arctic officers in the Franklin search, were present at the event.

M'Clintock rose to make a speech: "We looked upon that part of the Arctic regions as so peculiarly our own that we spoke of it as if the Queen's writ was free to run through it to the North Pole. But we can no longer make that boast; Captain Sverdrup has been there, and he has discovered other lands farther north, so that we cannot look for any immediate increase to the British Empire in that direction."[21]

Sir Leopold's remarks caused a collective Canadian blush. It was an embarrassment for the Dominion government that a Norwegian had mapped a large section of High Arctic land that Canada was supposed to have been in control of since 1880. Yet no Canadian had even set foot on any of the territory that Sverdrup had surveyed.

HERSCHEL ISLAND

The government was also becoming increasingly sensitive to other countries making money off Canada's natural resources. Lieutenant Gordon had initially rung the alarm bells about American whalers in Hudson Bay. Wakeham had calmed any concerns of foreign whaling in the Eastern Arctic because he noted that the region's resources had already been exhausted.

However, large numbers of American whalers were still hunting in Canadian waters. In the Western Arctic, on a small island just off the Yukon coast, a profitable whaling industry was being carried out. Once again, the American whalers paid no tariffs and had no whaling licences. It was a free enterprise.

In 1889, bowhead whales were discovered to be abundant in the Western Arctic, attracting American whalers. However, the area was only accessible for a brief period in the summer months, from July until September. The thirty-five-square-mile, treeless Herschel Island, just three miles off the Yukon coast and northeast of the Alaska boundary, offered the whalers an ideal winter haven. By the early 1890s, whalers began over-wintering in the region in order to get an early start on whaling when the ice broke up. Staying over one winter also gave them two summers of whaling, making it a more profitable voyage.[22]

Pauline Cove, on the southeast side of Herschel, offered a natural harbour, deep enough for the large whaling steamships to anchor in, pro-tected from the northerly winds and drifting ice pack. Here, the American whalers built warehouses and dwellings, and by 1892–93 there were 160 whalers living year-round at Pauline Cove. The whalers were keen to trade with the locals, and the population increased when Inuvialuit also set up camps there. Though most of the crews lived aboard their ships, the transient population of the island swelled to 1,500 at the peak of whaling activities.[23] By 1896, 13,450 whales had been caught, with a value of $1,345,000. Trading furs with the Inuvialuit added another $140,000 to the revenue.[24]

Reports of the whalers' influence on the Inuvialuit spread southward, and Anglican missionaries came to the area. The missionaries confirmed earlier reports that the captains and mates of the whaling vessels were purchasing young girls for ill usage, some as young as nine years old, and complained to their superior, Bishop Bompas, of this mistreatment by the whalers.

Bompas was disturbed by this news and wrote to the federal gov-ernment in 1896, requesting their assistance.[25] The government was familiar with the bishop, having received his requests for assistance to deal with the immoral Yukon miners. Although these complaints of American whalers corrupting the Inuvialuit and destroying their social structure rankled the government, it was unable to address the situation on Herschel Island. It could ill afford to send police there until the gold rush ended in the Yukon.

In 1903, American whalers were still hunting in Canadian waters. These men apparently had no interest in claims to Canadian territory. They were there purely for economic gain. Yet because they had set up a community on Herschel Island, erecting buildings, grounds for occupation existed. At that time there were no Canadians, other than missionaries, living permanently on Herschel Island. The government realized it was helpless should the United States decide to make overt actions to lay claims or should any other foreign country exert its power anywhere in the Arctic.[26]

Complaints by missionaries about the whalers, combined with Sverdrup's expedition to the Arctic and the final arbitration of the Alaska-Yukon dispute, became the impetus for Canada to flex its sovereign muscles to preserve its nationhood. The government decided to send two police expeditions north. So, while Bernier was promoting a trek to the North Pole, the Dominion government was quietly contemplating sending expeditions of its own to the Arctic. These expeditions, however, would not be glorious voyages of discovery. Their main purpose would be to assert Canada's authority in its northern regions.

CHAPTER SEVEN

Northern NWMP Posts

The success of the mounted police in the Yukon fortified the government's decision to send them to the trouble spots farther north.

A convincing Department of the Interior memorandum to North West Mounted Police (NWMP) comptroller Fred White justified a police expedition in the Northwest Territories, stating, "It is feared that if American citizens are permitted to land and pursue industries of whaling, fishing, and trading with the Indians without complying with the revenue laws of Canada and without any assertion of sovereignty on the part of Canada, unfounded and troublesome claims may hereafter be set up."[1]

It had taken close to two decades for the government to come to this decision. Gordon's first report had noted the detrimental impact the American whalers were having in Hudson Bay nineteen years previous.

In May 1903, Minister of the Interior Clifford Sifton advised Opposition leader Robert Borden that the Canadian government proposed to send two expeditions of NWMP to the North. One would set up a post each in the Mackenzie Delta and on Herschel Island, and another expedition would set up a third police post in Hudson Bay. Sifton told Borden that for reasons of state, there would be no discussion of the cost of these expeditions in the House. Borden agreed and the item went through without debate.

The Mackenzie Delta/Herschel Island expedition of 1903 was immediately organized.[2] Superintendent Charles Constantine, the inspector who had straightened things out with the miners in the Yukon, led the police detachment. Constantine, four constables, and Sergeant Francis J. Fitzgerald, a non-commissioned officer, left Fort Saskatchewan on May 30, 1903. They travelled by rail to Athabasca, then by steamers up the Slave and Mackenzie Rivers and on up to Fort McPherson on the Peel River. The rivers wound north through breathtaking scenic country. But it was no arable paradise. Rock, muskeg, and swamp were the predominant geographical features — not a region to entice farmers.

The police arrived at Fort McPherson north of the Arctic Circle after travelling for over a month. The Hudson's Bay Company, which had operated a trading post at Fort McPherson since 1849, welcomed the police. Constantine rented one of the company buildings for their Mackenzie Delta detachment, and the police established law and order. But the post at Fort McPherson was only half the job that summer. A second post needed to be established on Herschel Island. While Herschel was reasonably accessible by whalers circumnavigating Alaska, into the Beaufort Sea, it was more difficult to reach for travellers coming up via the land route from the south.

In August 1903, Sergeant Francis Fitzgerald and Constable Forbes Sutherland left Fort McPherson in a small boat and headed north. The one-hundred-and-eighty-mile journey became more perilous once they reached the inhospitable coast of Mackenzie Bay leading to Herschel Island. The two men arrived safely, though, and decided to set up a post immediately.

However, the NWMP had no proper boat to transfer goods up to the new post. Fitzgerald convinced the missionary on Herschel to lend him the mission's steam launch to bring supplies from Fort McPherson. Unfortunately, on the return journey, the launch was wrecked in Mackenzie Bay and most of the supplies were lost. This left the police on the island in straitened circumstances, not to mention the inconvenience to the mission, which was also now without a boat.

Of the six existing buildings on Herschel Island, two were owned by the Anglican mission and the other four by the American Pacific Steam Whaling Company. Fifteen sod houses were also owned by the company and occupied by whalers. There was no other available housing there. Pitching a tent was out of the question, so the police rented one of the sod huts from the whaling company and spent the first winter warmed by coal purchased from the whalers.

The NWMP were on Herschel to emphasize Canada's control over the region. They were there to collect customs duties from the American whalers and halt the liquor sale to the natives. However, they depended on these same whalers to provide them with supplies and housing. They, in fact, were completely dependent on the men who they were there to police. These were indeed awkward circumstances under which to establish government authority.

The police were in no position to affect whaling operations. The whalers were not adversaries, though, and the captains of the ships were glad to have police to control the unruly crews. Customs duties were collected intermittently, with the police relying on the whalers' honesty in paying. On occasion, the police feigned ignorance of ships that avoided paying duties by not stopping at the island, because they had no boat or means of intercepting them.[3]

Carrying out policing operations on Herschel was, without a doubt, a challenging situation. Nonetheless, the first police post was established on the Arctic Ocean.

AN EASTERN ARCTIC EXPEDITION

As a handful of mounted police set up posts in the Western Arctic that summer of 1903, a larger expedition was organized to set up a post in the Eastern Arctic, on Hudson Bay.

A detachment on Hudson Bay would further shore up the government's official presence. Customs licences would be issued and Canadian regulations distributed. However, it would be more than just a policing expedition. Similar to the previous government expeditions to Hudson waters, this one would also be of a scientific nature. The expedition would come under several departments: Marine and Fisheries, the Interior, and the Geological Survey of Canada. Marine and Fisheries was the main department for the logistical demands, such as procuring and outfitting the ship. Whereas commanders Gordon and Wakeham had been employees of the Department of Marine and Fisheries, this time the expedition commander would be a member of the Geological Survey. This expedition would not be a four-month summer cruise

138

either, but one of over a year's duration, spending the winter frozen in the ice of Hudson Bay.

Sixty-two-year-old Robert Bell, who had participated on the four previous government expeditions to Hudson Bay and Strait, was now the acting director of the Geological Survey. It was decided that Albert Peter Low, twenty years Bell's junior, was the ideal candidate for expedition commander. Low had previously been part of a government expedition, exploring the south shore of Hudson Strait during Wakeham's 1897 voyage.

Albert Peter Low was a geologist with iron-man abilities. He had an incredible passion for fieldwork, and his ability to thrive in the wilderness under harsh conditions earned him the reputation of being an intrepid explorer. Low graduated in 1882 from McGill University with a degree in geology, and moved to Ottawa where the new Geological Survey of Canada headquarters had recently been established. Low's work for the survey took him hundreds of miles away from the capital to remote, uncharted territories. He headed several mammoth expeditions into the wilds of Labrador, Northern Quebec, and Ontario.

Natural Resources Canada, courtesy of the Geological Survey of Canada, GSC 72071

Geologist Albert Peter Low commanded the expedition to Hudson Bay and the Arctic islands in 1903–04. This photo was taken in 1929 when he was head of the Geological Survey of Canada.

During the winter of 1884, while exploring the shores of Lake Mistassini, east of James Bay in northern Quebec, the twenty-three-year-old Low got into a heated dispute with another in the party over who was leading the survey expedition. Determined to resolve the issue, Low packed up, strapped on his snowshoes, and tromped three hundred and ten miles over desolate, frozen terrain to Quebec City, caught a train to Ottawa, and took up his case with his superiors at the Geological Survey. He then headed back to the survey camp, arriving five weeks after leaving the expedition with a letter that stated he had full authority for the expedition. His extraordinary determination and drive served him well in his fieldwork.

Between 1892 and 1896, Low and his team of survey scientists explored thousands of miles of Labrador's formidable and rugged terrain, mapping 12,470 miles and traversing hundreds of lakes and portages by foot, canoe, dogsled, and snowshoe. As well, he discovered vast deposits of iron ore, which led to the development of iron mines in Labrador.[4]

In June of 1903, when Minister of Marine and Fisheries Joseph Raymond Préfontaine appointed Albert Peter Low commander of the 1903 Dominion government expedition to Hudson Bay and beyond, no one doubted he was amply qualified for the position.

The ship chosen for the expedition was the SS *Neptune*, the same *Neptune* used by Lieutenant A.R. Gordon on his first cruise to Hudson Bay in 1884. It was still considered the most powerful sealer in the Newfoundland fleet. Although Gordon had not considered the ship ice-worthy enough for his 1885 voyage, the marine experts pronounced the thirty-year-old *Neptune* "quite sound throughout, and of amazing strength."[5] It was considered fully suitable to overwinter in Hudson Bay and became the expedition ship.

Carpenters and machinists were put to work round the clock to get the *Neptune* ready in six weeks. The bow's eight-foot-thick sides were also reinforced with a heavy sheathing of iron plating. The ship had accommodations for a small crew only, which had also been Gordon's complaint about it. During the renovations, the area between decks was converted into storerooms and sleeping quarters for the petty officers and mounted police. New staterooms and a saloon were created for the scientific staff, plus a separate surgery for the doctor. In making the new sleeping quarters, a small airspace was left between the berths' walls and the sides of the ship to provide insulation against the ensuing cold. As well, all the exposed ironwork inside the ship was covered with wood. The benefit of this was proven during the coldest part of the winter when no frost was evident on any part of the ship that had been renovated, whereas, on the exposed interior areas, a thick coating of frost blanketed the sides.

After three decades as a sealer, the *Neptune*'s interior wooden sides were saturated with seal oil, which, despite the thorough cleaning, could not be expunged. The expedition surgeon, Dr. Lorris Borden, commented that the coal dust bonded to the seal oil saturated walls and formed veritable cement. Fortunately, this later proved an impenetrable sealant when the ship struck rock and the stem plate was torn away. The oil-and-coal-dust coating prevented any water from leaking in.[6]

Commander Low's police counterpart on the expedition was the NWMP inspector John Douglas Moodie. The fifty-five-year-old Moodie was the second senior inspector in the NWMP. He was the epitome of an indomitable policeman: an intense, forceful character with a physique to match. His tall, strapping frame boasted the strength and endurance necessary to perform his duties. He had proven his mettle in 1897, when he'd led a fifteen-month patrol of the overland route from Edmonton to Dawson to quell any lawlessness arising from the influx of questionable prospecting characters in the Yukon.[7]

Moodie was in charge of the expedition's police contingent of a staff sergeant and four constables, who would set up the first mounted police post on Hudson Bay. Moodie's appointment to the Hudson Bay expedition promoted him to the rank of superintendent. With this promotion, his pay increased to $1,400 per year. Plus, his wife was given a living allowance of seventy-five cents a day in his absence. Despite being promoted to superintendent, the ship's company referred to him as Major Moodie.

The expedition's scientific staff was a small team of six that included Commander Low as geologist. Professor Andrew Halkett was the naturalist from the Department of Marine and Fisheries. C.F. King of the Geological Survey was the meteorologist and topographer, who would be assisted by the expedition photographer, George F. Caldwell. Dr. Lorris Elijah Borden, the ship's surgeon, was also the botanist. His assistant was Dr. G.B. Faribault. These men, as well as Purser M. Ross and NWMP staff sergeant Dee, would be mess mates.

Dr. Borden was the youngest of the officers, being twenty-six and a recent graduate of medicine from Dalhousie University. His passage aboard the ship was secured with the good word of his uncle, Sir Frederick William Borden, minister of Militia and Defence. Borden was hired in June at a salary of one hundred dollars a month, comparable to what he could earn at home.

Part of Borden's task was to assess the health of the Inuit living around Hudson Bay. He was to report on all diseases they suffered from, especially cancer, syphilis, and tuberculosis. Borden also conducted medical examinations of the entire crew to determine the state of their health and their physical fitness level. The only man he did not examine was his assistant, Dr. Faribault, who arrived just prior to the ship's departure. Borden kept a diary of the expedition, which gives insight into the ordinary, daily events not included in Low's official report.

The *Neptune* was in capable hands, as sailing master Captain Sam W. Bartlett had extensive experience in Arctic waters.[8] Bartlett had a crew of twenty-nine experienced men. With Low, the scientific staff, Moodie, and his five mounted police officers, the expedition counted forty-two men.

The officers boarded the *Neptune* at 2:30 p.m. on August 22. Anchored at the government wharf ready for sea, the ship was a sight. It was heavily loaded and fully provisioned with two years' worth of supplies for both the expedition and the police detachment. Every inch of deck space was taken up. Oil barrels and tins covered the quarterdeck. Lumber and building materials for the police detachment were piled on the afterdeck and both sides of the bridge. The most eye-popping of the stores hung in the ship's rigging. Not having a large refrigeration unit, fresh carcasses of meat hung from the masts and yardarms and by the sails' ropes.

A crowd gathered on the dock to see the expedition off. Speeches were delivered with handshakes all round. At 7:00 p.m. the ship cast off from the dock to a grand send-off. It didn't proceed very far, though, anchoring in the harbour to set the compasses. All hands were then busy, securing the heavy deck load and getting ready to put to sea the next morning. At noon on Sunday, August 23, 1903, they weighed anchor, and the old sealer quietly slipped out of Halifax harbour on a course for Hudson Bay.

LOW'S EXPEDITION, 1903

The Americans were quite interested in the goings-on of this expedition to Hudson Bay. An August 9, 1903, *New York Times* article reported, "So far that portion of the Dominion has been left to look after itself, and the result has been that the Americans have been making a very good thing out of the fisheries for many years past. The result of the expedition will be to drive the Americans out."

Driving the Americans out was not the intent of the expedition at all, though monitoring the whalers and notifying them of the Canadian government's authority was.

The *Neptune* travelled up the grandly picturesque Labrador coast to the Hudson's Bay Company post in Nachvak, where Low planned to pick up the Inuit interpreter Harry Ford, who had been interpreter on Wakeham's expedition five years previous. At Nachvak he learned Ford had moved to Port Burwell.

A trading post had been established at Port Burwell by a Newfoundland trading company in 1898. Ford turned out to be one of the post's employees, and Low negotiated with the agent to hire him for the expedition. His translation skills would be sorely missed by the post, as much of its business was in trade with the local Inuit families.

The following day, the expedition continued northward through fog to Cumberland Sound. The fog lifted on September 4, and they found themselves twenty miles east of Blacklead Island. The ship anchored in a bay fringed by a high, rugged coast. The expedition members went ashore and took photographs of the scenery while Major Moodie explained to the missionaries and whaling station agent the Dominion government's intentions. Blacklead's population of one hundred and fifty people was not much larger than when Wakeham had visited. However, when the *Neptune* arrived, the majority of the community was out on the land, hunting caribou. Low noted that the place was overrun with dogs. The rocky land lacked drainage, so the refuse from the whaling station and Inuit encampment, combined with excrement from the dogs, never washed away and succeeded in making the area foul and filthy.

The Inuit, still employed by the whaling station, were given biscuits, coffee, and molasses, but supplied their own meat, which was actually the most nutritious part of their diet. Low says, "The men are paid irregularly for their work, usually in tobacco, ammunition and clothing, and they receive extra pay when a whale is captured. Of course the pay alone does not at all represent the value of the whale, but the expense of the station, and the few whales killed prohibit a large expenditure."[9]

The Reverend Edmund James Peck, a Church of England priest, was in charge of the mission. He had arrived at Blacklead in 1894 anxious to bring Christianity and literacy to the Inuit of Baffin Island. His mission took him around the Cumberland Sound region, where he administered to about five hundred people. Peck was a talented linguist, becoming fluent in Cree and then Inuktitut, earning the name Uqammaq — the one who talks well. Peck translated the Bible into Inuktitut, wrote a book on Inuit grammar, as well as an Inuktitut-English dictionary, and taught the people the syllabic writing system created for the Cree living in the James Bay area. Although Peck was a Christian with strong Victorian principles, he became a devoted researcher of shamanism practices and documented 347 *tuurngait*, shamanic helping spirits. Dr. Lorris Borden described him as "a very fine looking old gentlemen," though the white-bearded Peck was only fifty-four at the time of their visit.

On Sunday, September 6, the *Neptune*, with a pilot from Blacklead, left early in the morning for Kekerten, forty-five miles up the sound, where Wakeham had made his proclamation five years previous. A three-masted Norwegian schooner was anchored there loading whale oil, bone, and skins. The captain of the schooner and Mr. Noble, who owned the station, came aboard the *Neptune*. Only two whales had been taken that year, but the numerous fox, wolf, and walrus skins, plus three thousand seal pelts, would bring a handsome profit.

Moodie explained to Noble that collection of taxes and duties would commence on January 1, 1904. He also made it clear that a government vessel would visit annually. The job of spreading the administrative word of the Dominion government accomplished, Low's expedition headed back to Blacklead that night. Here it picked up Captain Jackson, the new master of the Cape Haven whaling station, along with his large whaleboat and its crew of five Inuit men and one woman, and dropped them off on the way to Hudson Strait.

On Tuesday, September 8, with the official business in Cumberland Sound completed, the *Neptune* headed south, rounded the rocky shores of Resolution Island, and steamed westward into Hudson Strait. The steamship proceeded along the strait's south shore. The next evening it arrived at Cape Wolstenholme and anchored at Erik Cove, where the crew filled their casks with fresh water at a stream. The ship's steam engines, and its expedition of over forty men, consumed a lot of water. Throughout the expedition, searching for fresh water was a regular chore.

The *Neptune* pushed through snow squalls past Digges Island into Hudson Bay, and encountered its first large field of ice early in the morning of Monday, September 14. It steamed slowly through it, but the ship smacked into larger cakes, jolting its cargo and the sleeping travellers on board. It cautiously approached Southampton Island, on Hudson Bay's northwest side, using the lead to take depth measurements every hour to sound out the dangerous reefs charted for several miles from it. The ship lay five miles from the land for the night, surrounded by scattered pans of ice.

Low's instructions were to find and winter close to the American whaling ship known to be in Hudson Bay. Whalers had formerly wintered at Marble Island, but the lack of fresh water ended that. Cape Fullerton, farther north, across from Southampton Island and at the mouth of Roes Welcome Sound, had become the more common overwintering spot. With the weather worsening and thick fog descending, the ship anchored in a sheltered bay on the west side of Hudson Bay between Chesterfield Inlet and Fullerton Harbour. Low observed how sluggish the compass needle now was, owing to the proximity of the north magnetic pole.

One afternoon, the men heard shots fired and could see people on the shore six miles away, waving hats and coats to signal the ship. The steam launch set out to meet them and soon returned with a group of Inuit from Chesterfield Inlet. They had been at Cape Fullerton and reported a whaler there. The men were now on their way inland to kill caribou for winter clothing.

Two of the men introduced themselves as Scotty and Gilbert. They spoke some English, having been employed by Scottish whalers. Low doesn't give these men's real names, only the English names that the whalers had bestowed on them. Both men were hired by the American schooner that Low's party was searching for.

Upon hearing that there were caribou skins available, Low decided to take the launch up Chesterfield Inlet to where the Inuit had an encampment to try to procure some for winter clothing for his men. Old Scotty consented to pilot the steam launch up the river, while Gilbert would pilot the *Neptune* into Fullerton Harbour. On the morning of September 23, Low, with a crew of six, including Scotty and interpreter Ford, set out in the launch. The next morning, after steaming seventy miles, they came upon the first Inuit settlement on a bay at the north side of the inlet. They found only women and children there. The men were all away on the caribou hunt and the women would not part with any of the skins without the men's consent.

Officers of the Neptune. *Low is front and centre. Dr. Lorris Borden is front row, far right.*

Natural Resources Canada, courtesy of the Geological Survey of Canada, GSC 2918

Low's party carried on thirty miles up to the mouth of the river, where they found an encampment of four tents. With a lively barter that extended into the evening, Low gained fifty skins and a large quantity of meat in exchange for gunpowder, tobacco, knives, and metal files.

They started their return journey the next morning. At dark, the pilot grew unsure of their location and advised them to anchor until daylight. Unfortunately, during the night, the tide fell and the launch was grounded on rocks. The men tried to float the boat, but it listed to one side and water rushed in. The precious cargo was quickly ferried over to a nearby island in the twelve-foot dinghy, while some of the men attempted to bail out the launch.

The tide rose again and the "energies of all were devoted to saving everything possible."[10] Daylight arrived some hours later, casting a pale light on the cold, forlorn group. A skim of ice had already formed on the local ponds. After a second failed attempt to raise the launch, it became obvious that the dinghy would have to go to the ship for help.

Everything was moved to the mainland from the island before the small boat set off with translator Ford, pilot Scotty, and seaman Wells to find the *Neptune*. The stranded foursome spent the next few days drying the skins and other items saved from the wreck. They attempted, without success, to hunt and fish. The temperature dropped and snow fell on their hastily rigged shelter, while the unprepared men waited for help.

A SAFE HARBOUR AND A PERILOUS RESCUE

Meanwhile, under Gilbert's pilotage, the *Neptune* headed north up the coast to Cape Fullerton forty miles away, arriving on September 23 at 1:00 p.m. The American schooner *Era* was anchored there. It was the first vessel the expedition men had seen since leaving Kekerten. They'd travelled over a thousand miles without spotting a single ship.

Borden commented on how strange it was to see the Stars and Stripes flying from the schooner's mast. They had anticipated encountering the American ship, though, unlike George Comer, captain of the *Era*, who was flabbergasted at the arrival of the Canadian steamer.[11] Comer immediately went out to meet the new vessel and help pilot it into the harbour.

Comer was astounded that the *Neptune* had a complement of forty-two men, six of them being policemen. There were only nineteen aboard the *Era* that winter. Seven were officers and twelve were seamen, though only two of them had ever been to sea before. The practice of taking only a bare-bones whaling crew north had become common, since the majority of work could be carried out by the Inuit men the captain hired in the North. By the turn of the twentieth century, experienced whalemen were scarce, and often the owners were reduced to using less than honourable means of enticing men to the whaling ships.

Fullerton Harbour, just west of Cape Fullerton, was chosen as an ideal anchorage by whalers as it was protected by a group of small islands. It also offered easy access to the mainland once the harbour froze over. But primarily it was chosen because it was located at the mouth of Roes Welcome, where the majority of whales migrated to each summer.[12]

The following morning Major Moodie assessed the area and decided on a nearby island for the site of the police detachment. Comer noted in his diary that the spot Moodie had chosen was very near the place where his men got water. The availability of water was likely a factor in Moodie choosing it as a suitable location. The crew and policemen promptly started moving lumber from the ship's deck to the shore and began building the barracks.

All the passengers went ashore to check out the new surroundings that would be home for the next ten months or so. They found the low-lying land of granite rock covered with moss, stunted grasses, and berries. They had brought rifles and lost no time shooting five ptarmigan.

That night, Dr. Borden's sleep was interrupted to attend to the cabin boy, Frank O'Connell. Borden noted, "He is crazy and is a lot of bother," but gives no details about what sort of behaviour the "crazy" young man exhibited.[13] Later in the day, Borden says the cabin boy was getting worse. He was up a second night with him. The boy was irrational, and threatened to drown himself. Borden says he would be confined if there was no improvement. That is the last mention of O'Connell until the spring.

By September 26, the frame of the mounted police house was up.

Comer's men were also erecting a house on the afterdeck. This was common practice for ships overwintering in the Arctic. A ship's open deck was virtually unusable in the winter, so a large roofed-in area was constructed over it to provide extra sheltered space for carpentry work or boat repair in the cold winter days. The walls were built of wooden planks and the main boom was used as a ridge pole to support a canvas-tented roof. The covered deck also offered an ideal area for dances and entertainment through the long winter nights.

On September 28, Borden, Caldwell, and King paid a visit to Captain Comer on the *Era*. He talked much about the Inuit and tried to convey an understanding of them. Sadly, Borden never came to share Comer's genuine concern for the people of Hudson Bay. Throughout his diary, his interest is more of a scientific nature and not a humanitarian one.

Comer, on the other hand, had a strong appreciation of the Inuit. His years in the Hudson Bay region brought him in contact with many of the different groups that lived around the west and northwest side of the bay. He got to know the people well, hiring them to work for the ship. And to many Inuit, Comer was a true friend. No doubt his sincere interest gained their trust so that they readily shared their stories and customs with him. Comer took great care to faithfully record their stories, customs, legends, and myths, taking photographs and recording their songs and speech, on a graphophone. Several museums, including the Museum of Natural History in New York, were interested in this ethnographic information he gathered. He gathered such extensive information about the people he met that he was looked upon as an amateur anthropologist. To many less liberal-minded souls, he was simply "native crazy."

The forty-five-year-old Comer first travelled to the Arctic in 1875 as a green seventeen-year-old aboard a whaling ship. He then worked aboard sealers in the Antarctic from 1879 until 1889. He returned to the North in 1889 as first mate on the *Era*, supplying the American whaling stations at Spicer Island west of Big Island in Hudson Strait, Cape Haven, and Blacklead Island in Cumberland Sound. Between 1893 and 1902, Comer made four voyages to Hudson Bay, overwintering there each time. Twice he stayed for two winters. By the time the Canadians steamed into Fullerton and anchored beside him, Comer was an experienced old hand at living aboard ship in the Subarctic.

By September 30, the NWMP house was roofed and the windows were in. All that remained to do was shingle and side it. The fifteen-by-twenty-four-foot building was divided into three rooms: a large one and two smaller ones. A storehouse was later built, along with a coal shed and a lean-to kitchen that was twelve by sixteen feet with a large porch. Moodie intended to add a separate barracks and quartermaster's store the following year.[14]

On October 1, the boat with Ford, Wells, and Scotty arrived from Chesterfield Inlet with news of the wreck of the launch. The three men had travelled four days, a gruelling one hundred miles in an open twelve-foot boat through snow squalls and miserable cold, to reach the ship.

Captain Bartlett called upon Comer's navigational expertise in the region. Comer willingly volunteered his services, soon coming aboard with three Inuk, his boatsteerer, and one of his whaleboats. The *Neptune* started off at once to rescue the stranded men. The sea was rough with a strong wind blowing. Under steam they travelled faster than the men rowing the dinghy had, and reached the mouth of Chesterfield Inlet that night.

The moon was obscured as clouds scuttled across it. A snow squall blew up in the night but subsided somewhat early the next morning as they got underway. The ship plunged ahead through a big sea into the inlet. Both captains were on deck with the Inuit guides pointing the way.

Violent seas crashed over the decks, its icy spray freezing halfway up the mast and bridge. Navigation was difficult and twice the ship struck reefs about ten miles offshore of the inlet's north side. The third time it happened, the solid grating sound was accompanied by the ship keeling over on its right side. The engines were ordered full speed ahead and the ship slipped off the shoal. This was as close to a disaster as any of them wanted to come. The chance of the ship surviving being stranded on its side in such a violent sea was slim, and scared all on board. The ship could have rolled and capsized with no probability of rescue.

Soundings were then made every few minutes. When they were in deep enough water, they headed to the south side of the inlet. They anchored ten miles from Dangerous Point, where Low's group was stranded. A boat was lowered to reach them, but it returned without finding them. The next morning Comer, with his whaleboat and men, set out for Dangerous Point. They arrived to find the four men had managed admirably. This was the first time Comer met the commander of the Canadian expedition, and likely not the introduction that Low had intended for the American they were in Hudson Bay to monitor.

Shortly after Comer's boat left the *Neptune*, all boats were lowered with all seamen and mounted police to look for Low's party. The first mate was left in charge of the ship with Major Moodie. Dr. Borden, Caldwell, King, Halkett, and Murphy, an injured seaman, were the only others left on board. It was a quiet ship once the men had all gone, with nothing for those left to do but wait. None of the rescue parties returned that night. The following morning, in an excessively rough sea that crashed over the deck, the men on the *Neptune* spotted Comer's whaleboat rowing towards them.

Borden said it made him sick just to watch the whaleboat rising on a white-capped crest, then showing its keel before disappearing from sight in the wave's trough. A wooden keg with a rope tied to it was played out from the ship as a sort of rescue buoy for the boatmen to haul themselves in with. The men had a difficult time coming aboard in the rough sea. They were soaked with icy sea water and exhausted. Low was one of them.

Low told how they had attempted to reach the ship the day before but their progress was severely halted by a sudden snowstorm and they had to stop for the night on an island. They made a shelter by leaning the sail against a rock, but it was so tight the men were forced to stand all night. In the morning, it took them two hours to dig the sail out from under the snow. They reached the ship a harrowing twenty-four hours after leaving the makeshift camp at Dangerous Point.

The gale blew for three days. On October 6, the rest of the men managed to return to the ship with most of the wares from the camp in their boats. They had endured a rough time, camping out in the snow under the boats. On the eighth, the ship steamed up the inlet and anchored close to the sunken launch. They were able to float it on the midnight tide by "putting empty tierces [wooden casks] in her and fastening them down."[15] By 7:30 the next morning, they'd rigged the launch up on spars and carried it between the boats out to the ship. It was a difficult operation, but with the help of Comer and his men it was hoisted on board.

The *Neptune* finally steamed ahead for Fullerton Harbour. The snow squalls and strong winds slowed the ship's progress, but it finally dropped anchor at Fullerton on October 11.

CHAPTER EIGHT

FULLERTON HARBOUR, 1903

The days noticeably shortened by three minutes, while the temperature dropped several degrees daily. Men from both ships immediately began to prepare for winter.

Blocks of ice were cut from frozen ponds to melt later. The ice blocks were hauled to a point near the shoreline. After the bay froze over, they would be moved and stacked close to the vessels for easier access. The *Neptune* men cut and stacked two hundred tons of ice.

Moodie and the policemen were busy finishing the police post, soon referred to as Government House. The schooner's carpenter, who was a house builder by trade, as well as Comer and some of his crew, assisted them. Like Herschel Island, this was another case of the NWMP needing the help of the men they were there to police.

Comer was invited to dine aboard the *Neptune* every Sunday during the winter. He and some of his crew began attending the "divine service" of the Church of England that Major Moodie presided over.

By Monday, October 19, the harbour was fully frozen over. The ice measured several inches; not thick enough to support a man's weight, but within a week it was two feet thick. At the shore, however, the tide still fell eighteen feet and the ice would break and overflow, so it took longer before it was frozen completely to the shore and safe enough to traverse. Snow drifted deeply on the land, and the Inuit began building their snow houses.

With ice saws, the crew of the *Era* cut a ship-wide channel in the new ice. The ship was manoeuvred into it so that its bow faced north. This way, the ship would receive sunlight on both sides, keeping it evenly warm, and the sun would melt the ice equally on both sides in the late spring. Once the ice froze firmly around the hull, it would hold the ship in place, and the anchor would be hauled up and kept on board until needed when the ice melted the following summer.

The *Neptune*, which lay about 225 feet from the *Era*, copied the schooner and was also swung around to face north a couple of days later. The *Neptune* crew also roofed over the deck. Two boats were taken ashore to a nearby island in the event that some hazard, such as fire, would force the men to abandon ship. Extra supplies and clothing were also stored on shore in case of emergency.

Flags were draped in cabin gun racks and efforts were made to present a more respectable appearance. Routines were established to keep the men occupied and amused during the long winter months. They kept trap lines, and some tried their hand and patience at ice fishing. These activities got the men out in the fresh air and forced them to take exercise. It gave them something to do, as well as a little extra fresh meat.

A newspaper called the *Northern Satellite* was launched aboard the *Neptune* on October 23. It was a typewritten, three-page bulletin about life in Fullerton Harbour, edited by George Caldwell, the ship's photographer.

The men of the 1903 expedition standing or sitting on the snow banked against the Neptune. *Commander Low is front, centre, and turned to the right. Captain Bartlett is second from left.*

J.D. Moodie, Library and Archives Canada, PA-053567

Captain Comer was encouraged to submit articles as well, and happily did so. Publishing newspapers had become a tradition for ships wintering in the Arctic since the publication of the *New Georgia Gazette* or *Winter Chronicle*, aboard Captain William Edward Parry's ships, which overwintered at Melville Island from 1819 to 1821.

Wednesday evenings were reserved for lectures in the officers' saloon. Professor Halkett lectured on the evolution of fishes. Major Moodie spoke about his Yukon trek from Edmonton to Dawson. Dr. Borden lectured on the prevention of disease. Commander Low gave a lecture on Hudson Bay explorers and resources, and another on his expeditions in Labrador. Captain Comer even gave a lecture on his sea elephant voyages in Antarctic waters. The diversity of subjects and extent of the lecturers' experiences made for stimulating and educational evenings.

Dances, regularly held on Thursday nights, were one of the on-board entertainments. Harry Ford was the fiddler. Comer lamented in his diary that no one aboard the schooner played an instrument. Nonetheless, dances were hosted aboard the schooner when the temperature plummeted below -40°F. The *Era*'s deck house had been covered in better than that of the *Neptune*'s and offered a more comfortable venue. The local Inuit also attended and enjoyed the entertainment aboard both vessels.

On Sunday, November 1, the *Neptune*'s assistant Dr. Faribault began acting strangely. After the church service, Faribault got up and read an extract that Dr. Borden said, "was the most utter rot." He showed up a little later with a cake and offered pieces to the men. Purser Ross saw his name on the cake and knew Faribault had taken it from his room. Then the assistant doctor took everything off his bed and piled it, and all the furniture, in the saloon on the table. His behaviour was disturbing, so the doctor gave him bromides and morphine to quieten him. The night watchman was also ordered to keep an eye on him.

By Tuesday, Faribault had turned aggressive and violent, having enraged outbursts one moment, then acting calm and chatty the next. Then he set fire to some paper in his room. This was a serious matter, taken as proof that Faribault could do bodily harm to himself, others, and the ship. Constables Caldwell and Conway were posted to sit up all night and keep an eye on him. Borden gave Faribault a stronger dosage of morphine, which had little effect. Borden certified the man insane and it was agreed, for everyone's safety, that he needed to be specially confined and constantly monitored. Construction began on a small room on deck for Faribault.

On November 4, Faribault was considerably agitated and spent the whole night up, sweeping the decks and working. He imagined getting telephone calls from people. He ate nothing and slept little. Physically, he looked healthy and perfectly normal, but he had lost all reason. The following day, the room on deck was completed and Faribault was confined to it, with a policeman posted outside. He was now under the charge of the police.

Faribault's new room of six by eight feet was kept locked and had a grate in its door. It was a cell. The following day, Faribault was so "noisy and dirty" that he had to be put in a strait jacket.[1] His constant ranting was unnerving to all on board, and in the quiet he could even be heard by people on the other ship and on land.

Moodie recommended in his report that the men who guarded Dr. Faribault and endured "the yells of, at most times, a raving maniac ringing in their ears," should be given an additional twenty-five cents per day for maintaining their good temper and kindness in the handling of the patient. He suggested that this pay increase be registered under the heading of "Attendants in Asylum."[2]

By the first week of November, meals were reduced to two a day: breakfast at 10:00 a.m. and supper at 4:00 p.m.

ASSERTING CANADA'S AUTHORITY

Monday, November 9, was King Edward VII's birthday, and the Canadians celebrated in style. Flags flew salubriously from the *Neptune* and Government House on the island, as well as on the schooner. A salute was fired from the small cannon on board and fireworks lit up the night sky.

The following day, Major Moodie sent a proclamation to Comer, notifying him that as of January 1, 1904, all foreign vessels were required to pay duty on all chargeable goods brought into the country. In addition, killing muskox and trading or taking muskox skins from the natives was now forbidden.

Comer was incensed. He wrote in his journal, "I am feeling considerably offended by Major Moodie's forbidding me to let my natives go out after musk-ox, while there has been nothing done to prevent other parties from hunting them or even trade for one. It looks very strongly like a slap at the American vessel, as we are the only one here."[3]

Comer was right about being singled out, but it was unintentionally so. When the *Neptune* stopped at Blacklead and Kekerten Islands and Cape Haven, Moodie had notified the whalers and agents of the rules coming into force in the New Year, requiring them to pay duties and taxes. It was only after arriving at Hudson Bay, though, that he became aware of the plight of the muskox and inserted the ban on them into the notice he delivered to Comer. Moodie had quickly assessed that the muskox was steadily being decimated by trade with the whalers.

In his report to the Dominion government, Moodie says,

> I found the slaughter of these animals for the sake of their skins was much greater than supposed. The United States schooner *Era* took home over 350 skins on her last voyage…. These animals are becoming scarcer every year, and even the whalers agree that at the present rate of killing, they will soon become extinct on the west coast of Hudson bay. The only means of preventing such extermination is to treat them as the buffalo is treated, by prohibiting the export of the skins, &c., and prohibit the having in possession by any person other than native.[4]

However, the *Era* was the only American vessel that Moodie was able to notify that fall. He intended all vessels to be aware of it, but without appropriate sleds and dogs, the mounted police could not contact the American whalers to the north. However, Moodie's waiting until the ships were frozen in before delivering his proclamation meant that Comer was physically unable to leave the vicinity before the laws came into effect, forcing him to pay his taxes. Moodie had also reasoned that if he had given "considerable notice," the whaler might have urged the collection of as many muskox as possible before the ban came into effect, undermining what the ban was intended to do: protect the muskox.[5] On the other hand, for years the Americans had made a fortune in whales and skins without paying one cent to the Canadian government. It had been a long time coming. Unfortunately, Comer was the one to feel the brunt of the law.

Moodie was just starting to exert his authority in Fullerton, though. On Saturday, November 14, he held a "powwow" at Government House with as many of the local Inuit men and boys as possible. Borden, photographer Caldwell, and all the policemen were witnesses. About twenty-five Inuit men were present. Seven or eight gallons of tea were boiled and twenty-one pounds of hard tack and other biscuit served up. Each Inuk was also given a clay pipe and a fig of tobacco.

Borden wrote in his journal that Moodie told the men gathered there that a big chief ruled over them all, and that Moodie had been sent by this big chief "to see that they did what was right and settle all quarrels and punish all offenders."[6] He told them that they were no longer to sell or trade muskox, but only kill them for their own food. Moodie also questioned them about rumours he had heard about cannibalism, infanticide of baby girls, and killing members of their tribe when they were too old to travel. Not surprisingly, Moodie received evasive answers. Borden said it was "very interesting to see the natives standing open mouthed with varying expressions as the interpreter told the above."[7] Then Moodie handed out woollen underclothes to each man, and gave the younger boys a small box containing a toque, a pair of mitts, and a sash.

No wonder they had stood open-mouthed. The Inuit had been trading with the whalers for several decades with no restrictions on their actions. And here was a uniformed outsider suddenly imposing strange rules and handing out underwear. Despite the bizarreness of the ceremony, the Inuit reacted with utmost politeness, thanking Moodie and even giving him a cheer.

The long underwear the major had issued turned out not to be such a fine gift. The Inuit found the woollen underwear quickly became saturated with their sweat and grew cold with the damp. Their own loose fur clothing allowed perspiration to evaporate readily. Many of the men caught colds as a result and a few even developed pneumonia. Fortunately, no one died.

The men from the *Era* enjoyed the dance aboard the *Neptune* that night, but Comer was noticeably absent. He nursed his wounded pride for several weeks, turning down offers to dine aboard the *Neptune*. He felt that he and his crew had been very generous in their help to the government ship. He had aided in the rescue of Low and his men at Chesterfield Inlet with much risk to his own men. His crew had also helped Moodie build his post. In fact, Comer was so upset by Moodie's sudden assertion of police authority that Borden had to administer a mild sedative for his nerves.

The men banked snow along the sides of the ships, which would act as a windbreak and insulation as the temperature plummeted through the winter. Thick ice was cut out to fit over the windows to let the light in. The effect of this white insulation was felt immediately as the temperature on board rose ten degrees.

The snow around the *Neptune* was about six feet thick and level with the deck. After dinner on November 18, the men heard a great cracking sound. The weight of the packed snow had broken the ice and the huge bank was swallowed up by the frigid salt water. They would have to wait for the ice to re-form before banking more snow around the ship.

On November 21, Comer took a letter with his grievances over to the steamer for inclusion in the *Northern Satellite*. He was disappointed when he saw that his published piece had been edited, removing the important part about the law being unjust. On Thursday, November 26, American Thanksgiving, Commander Low sent an invitation to Comer to come to a dance on board the steamer that night. Comer, feeling further slighted, declined.

Comer had his own system of law, one that had long been held by mariners. As captain, he was master after God and his rule was law. This was necessary to keep order aboard ship, and the captain had the right to enforce punishment as he saw fit.

A rumour circulated that Comer had put a man in irons because the sailor had suffered frostbite on his foot and refused to let Comer treat him by cutting the dead flesh off his toe. Comer put him in chains and cut it off his foot anyway. Borden later confirmed this story.

Borden had been prepared to treat the local Inuit for a variety of illnesses and ailments. He hadn't anticipated, though, that his services would be required aboard the *Era*. On his first visit to the schooner to attend a sick man, he was appalled by the living conditions. The interior of the schooner was constantly damp, owing to the fact that the fifty-six-year-old ship had been leaking since it left port and the pump ran constantly.

Fourteen men slept in the forecastle, which was no bigger than ten feet square, with no room to stand. Oil lamps burning in the room combined with the odour of the unwashed men made it stifling. And the bedbugs were so thick on the invalid that Borden could barely find a part of his body free of them to examine the man properly.

Saturday, December 12, was a stormy day. Winds whistled round the ship at thirty miles per hour. All the men had been busy writing letters home. A bag of mail was being sent by dogsled to Churchill. Unfortunately, the blizzard prevented that. The men's disappointment in the mail delay quickly evaporated when they realized that the cabin boy Frank O'Connell was missing. He had mentioned going ashore. The weather had been too bad to go out, but it became obvious that the young man had left the ship anyway.

A search prevailed. All hands, including police, local Inuit, and men from the schooner, went out to search for the lad, but the blowing snow made visibility poor and he wasn't found. The mailbag was opened and a notice of his disappearance added to it.

The next day almost the entire population of Fullerton Harbour was out looking for O'Connell. One Inuk reported finding tracks three miles from the ship in a southeast direction. Captain Comer came on board that night, the first time in weeks. Comer, Moodie, and some of the Inuit men took a sled and went to examine the tracks. They found that the boy had wandered and turned around several times but generally walked before the wind. O'Connell's tracks were traced seven miles from the ship to the thin ice near the floe edge, where they disappeared. The men concluded that he had mercifully met a swift death in the icy waters.

In his published report of the expedition, Low wrote that "James O'Connel, a cabin-boy of weak mind" wandered away in a snowstorm.[8] This is a sad mention of the incident. Not only is the cabin boy's last name spelled incorrectly, but Low gives him the wrong first name as well. Low might simply have said that the lad had got lost in a snowstorm, instead of pronouncing O'Connell "of weak mind." Yet there is no mention in official records of his mental condition. However, this was the same O'Connell who had told Borden in early September that he wanted to drown himself. The inference, at any rate, was that O'Connell's wandering in the storm was intentional.

A few days before Christmas, Comer met Commander Low out walking. Comer was honest with Low, telling him how offended he was that the *Era* had been picked out to first assert the new laws. Low replied diplomatically, explaining that there was no personal feeling against him. Low further patched it up by sending over two large hams, one for the men and one for the cabin for a Christmas dinner.[9]

It is incredible that two southern ships were locked together in ice in the Far North, and yet men held animosities against each other.

On Christmas Eve, the *Neptune's* deck house was draped in flags, including the Star-Spangled Banner borrowed from the *Era*. Dancing ended at 2:00 a.m., but further celebrations continued until four o'clock in the morning, when they drank a toast to the schooner and the health of all. A fine dinner was enjoyed on Christmas Day, and toasts made to the King of England and to the president of the United States. The evening ended with another dance enjoyed by all the residents of Fullerton Harbour.

At that time, Aivilingmiut resided in the northwestern Hudson Bay region of Repulse Bay, Wager Bay, and the Boothia Peninsula. Iglulingmiut resided in the northern Foxe Basin. The Qaernermiut lived in the Chesterfield Inlet area between the treeline and Baker Lake, and relied on the barrenland caribou for livelihood, unlike the more northern people who lived mainly off the ocean mammals such as walrus (*aivik*).

Comer and Low agreed on which tribe would help which ship. This meant the people would provide the vessels with fresh meat and clothing. Each vessel would then take on the responsibility for the families of the "ship's natives." It was agreed that the Aivilingmiut would work mainly for the *Era* and the Qaernermiut would work for the *Neptune*. A dozen more worked for the schooner than for the steamer, as more men were required for whaling activities. The men hunted for the ships, contributing to the fresh meat supply, while the women made the men clothing.[10]

Men of both vessels needed caribou-skin clothing to work and survive in the Arctic. The combination of men from the two ships, which added up to sixty people, required about three hundred caribou to make enough clothing for them all. It takes about three caribou to make a suit, and some of the men would have two suits each. The women also made sealskin boots. As well, a few hundred pairs of mittens and boots could be worn out in a single winter.[11] An incredible number of animals were needed to clothe and feed the ships' companies.

Comer charged his men one dollar a piece for each fur-skin suit. This was a pittance considering the amount of time the women spent making the outfits, not to mention the time and energy to hunt them and the value of the fur. The people were not paid in cash, which had no worth there, but in items that cost virtually nothing to the *Era*'s owner to send up as payment or for trade with the Inuit. The value of what the Inuit received for the suits was much less than a dollar per suit.

FULLERTON HARBOUR, 1904

On January 4, the customs house opened and Comer diligently went over with a report and manifest of the *Era*'s cargo. He paid $94.60 in duties, signing on behalf of Mr. Luce, the ship's owner.

The New Year did not start brightly for Captain Comer. The men came aft to complain of the soft bread they were being fed. Comer noted it was quite heavy but fit to eat. Borden noted the *Era*'s pitifully inadequate food supply in his journal: salt horse, hard tack, blackstrap molasses. There were no potatoes, canned fruit, or vegetables on board, though these items were on the ship's provision list. Once Borden visited the *Era*'s food cache on shore, and the stench of the molasses was so vile that he had to run some distance to rid himself of the smell. He suspected that the food had been bought by the schooner's owners at a discounted price. He was right. In November 1905, Comer opened a new cask of bread for the men and found it "quite buggy." He noted in his diary that it was purchased from the government after the Spanish-American War (which had ended in 1898). Comer kept his own stock of items that had been given to him as gifts before he left.

This poor food quality was largely responsible for two of the *Era*'s men becoming seriously ill in early January. Borden suspected the man with "Mouth & gums sore. Breath foul. Pains in chest & limbs," was suffering from scurvy.[12] It was surmised that the incidence of scurvy on the *Era* was a result of the lack of antiscorbutics, like lime juice. Also, the fact that the local wildlife was being hunted to feed more men than usual meant that the fresh meat supply was further taxed. It is puzzling, though, knowing men on the schooner were suffering from scurvy, that more effort wasn't made to ensure that they were given more fresh meat or lime juice from the steamer, although presents of food were made to the *Era* on special occasions.

The ice around the ships was now thirty-nine inches thick, and the Inuit moved from the shore into igloos nearer the vessels. In the moonlight, the igloos looked like marble beehives.

At the end of January, one of the little boys at the settlement died. Borden wanted to do an autopsy on him but the women wouldn't let him. The chief assented to a post-mortem but the mother of the child did not. She wrapped him in deer skin, hair side in, and buried him onshore with rocks over his little body to prevent the dogs from getting at it. Borden was irritated with the women denying him a post-mortem. He blamed their reticence on superstitions. However, many mothers back in his native Nova Scotia would also have refused him an autopsy on their child.

At one point, Borden snuck out at night and collected a skeleton to bring back in the name of science, without any permission from the family of the deceased. Comer at least respected the people's customs. He brought back bones and skulls for various museums, but made certain that he left a present at the graveside for the person whose grave he had robbed.

The temperature reached sub-forties in February, and ice in the bay was fifty-five inches thick. By March, the sun had returned, and anyone out enjoying the sunshine had to wear coloured glasses as protection from snow blindness, a temporary but painful condition caused by the glare off the snow. Days were lengthening and the weather had warmed to -11°F.

On St. Patrick's Day, both vessels set their colours, flew their flags, and had a football, or soccer, match on the ice between the ships. The playing-field ice was sixty-two inches thick. Borden, who was the referee, noted that it wasn't a "very swift game," but it broke the monotony. The steamer team won: one to nothing.

On March 22, Borden was called to see Dr. Faribault, who had gotten up, eaten his breakfast, had a smoke and a bath, and gone out for his morning exercise. However, his police officer attendants noticed that he was unusually drowsy, and after sitting in his chair he fell into an unconscious state. He was put to bed and suffered a number of convulsions during the day. Borden administered morphine and atropine, which seemed to lessen his spasms. Faribault's eyes remained open but with no sign of consciousness. His right side seemed paralyzed. He was comatose the next day, but became semi-conscious on the twenty-fourth.

On March 25, one of the men aboard the *Era* mouthed off to Comer. Comer put him in irons for his insubordination. Two of his men went over to the *Neptune* and complained of the captain's ill-treatment of their ship-mate to Major Moodie. Moodie sent Comer a note, requesting he come aboard the *Neptune* as soon as possible. Furious, Comer ignored the note. He called his crew together to find out who had squealed. Five admitted to it and he confined them all in the hold. Then he marched over to the steamer to confront Moodie.

It was a heated discussion. Comer was blunt, telling Moodie that he alone was captain of his ship and Moodie had no authority to interfere. Moodie told Comer that no captain had jurisdiction on any vessel in Canadian waters to put a man in irons, asserting that, as he was in a Canadian port, the mounted police had every right to intervene. Comer backed down and agreed to give his men an opportunity to withdraw their complaint.

After Comer told the guilty men to withdraw their complaint "or they would get worse treatment," the two complainants willingly went over to the *Neptune* and withdrew it.[13] Upon their return, Comer stuck the men back in the forecastle. His nose was severely shoved out of joint, having ruled a ship for decades with no one to answer to.

The next day, Comer had the men out doing heavy manual labour. He forbade them to leave the vessel without a permit until they had issued an apology to him. One of his boatsteerers, Brass Lopes, did not take this well and mouthed off to Comer. He was immediately returned to confines in steerage. Comer subsequently prohibited the *Neptune*'s men from coming aboard the schooner until his own men showed him more respect. The *Era* men were compliant and held their attitudes in check. Comer then reinstated their privileges. However, his feeling of animosity against Moodie had been fired up again, and Borden had to prescribe a tonic to relax him.

Comer had a valid concern about his men being disgruntled. He knew full well that feelings of discontent could foster mutiny. Comer conceded that the men on board the Canadian government steamer nearby were provided with every comfort, which made his own men's lives seem meagre in contrast. He reminded his men, though, that they did have all the necessities of life.

However, they lacked nutritious food. By the end of March, two men were bedridden. Scurvy was no doubt the cause. One suffered noticeably, with swollen legs covered with black and blue spots. Both men's gums were red and spongy, with black tongues and foul breath. One man was definitely on the decline, vomiting black liquid. Comer took the graphophone down to the forecastle for the ill sailor's amusement.

On the morning of April 6, W.P. Maynes died. It was the first death aboard the *Era* since Comer had become captain in 1889. On the death certificate required by Moodie, Borden listed cause of death as "natural causes," although there was no doubt he had died of scurvy complicated by bronchitis and pneumonia. Comer said age and general health was against the man, noting he had been "shipped while under the influence of liquor."[14] Maynes was fifty-five.

At two o'clock that afternoon, a Roman Catholic burial service was read for the deceased aboard ship by one of his mates and attended by the men of the steamer. Maynes was buried beneath a mound of stones on a nearby island.

Three days later, Comer auctioned off the dead man's clothing. He collected $10.50. This was common practice aboard ship. The men appreciated the added shirt or pair of pants that they could buy from their deceased mate's articles. The money would eventually be given to the man's family.

SURVEYING AND WHALING

The days lengthened to twelve hours and the thermometer rose to 26°F. Several of the *Neptune*'s men embarked on survey expeditions in the area. King surveyed the harbour and Caldwell headed north with two other Inuit men and a woman to Wager and Repulse Bays. A number of the charts of the region contained inaccuracies that the men were sent out to correct.

On April 27, a second death among the southerners occurred when Dr. Faribault passed away. Colours were lowered to half-mast on both vessels.

Borden did an autopsy and found Faribault's brain "interesting," noting its texture was soft and the nerves looked exceedingly pale. Borden concluded that the assistant doctor had suffered from syphilis acquired years before as a post-graduate student in Paris. Faribault was laid to rest that same evening close to Maynes' grave. His coffin was also covered with stones.

May brought warmer weather, and on the fourth, the deck house was taken down. Commander Low left with two Inuit men on a trip to Chesterfield Inlet to carry out a survey of the coast. In 1894, James Tyrrell, who had accompanied Gordon in 1885–86, had surveyed the coast with his brother, Joseph, from the North Saskatchewan River down to Churchill, completing an epic 3,200-mile canoe and snowshoe trek. Low's survey would connect Tyrrell's northern point with that of Caldwell's survey, being carried out to the north. Low's group was gone about ten days, during which they were practically buried in their tent by a tremendous snowstorm.

Early in the morning of May 11, the *Neptune* woke its sleeping inhabitants with a formidable groaning. The ice had melted around the hull and no longer gripped the ship's sides. The ship came up about fifteen inches. This freedom from the ice buoyed not only the ship, but the men's spirits. For Comer, this meant that whaling would soon begin. The Inuit moved off the unstable, melting ice to the cape to set up their tupiks and be closer to the sea's hunting grounds.

Comer's men set out on whaling excursions. His contemporaries hunted the migrating whales from the floe edge, but Comer's method of whaling was to go in search of the whales in small whaleboats. He devised special covers for the boats so that at the end of each day the men could haul the boats up on the ice and erect a canvas cover as a makeshift roof to sleep under.

Comer's hunting techniques would take the boats miles from the ship, navigating through ice-strewn waters, even chasing a whale one hundred miles from the *Era*. As they could not drag the carcass back to the ship with these small boats, the men would just hack the baleen, the valuable part of the whale, from its mouth and leave the rest of the leviathan to sink in the bay or rot on the ice.[15]

All surveying parties returned to the ship by the end of May. The winter darkness had departed and twilight reigned, offering enough light to read a book on deck at midnight.

On May 23, Commander Low gave Comer a tierce of lime juice. A tierce was a cask of about thirty-five gallons. It seems strange, in light of the two occurrences of, and one death from, scurvy that Low would give Comer the lime juice at this date. Perhaps, being only months from the end of his cruise, Low calculated they would not need it, and hoped it would help ward off further cases of scurvy aboard the *Era*.

In mid-June, Comer and his men planned a longer whaling cruise to Southampton Island, forty-five miles east of Fullerton Harbour. Comer invited Low along. Low accepted and borrowed two whaleboats from Comer. The *Neptune* contingent of ten men, five per boat, included two sailors and six Inuit men, plus Low and Borden. Low intended to make geological, zoological, botanical, and archaeological studies of Southampton Island. They would return the first week of July, while Comer and his three boats would continue hunting whales along the Southampton coast.

Low paid Comer a rent of sorts for the use of the two boats, giving him $25 worth of food. He sent over cases of canned fruit, meat, and pickles to the *Era*. This went a long way to improving the diet on the American ship.

A.P. Low, Geological Survey of Canada, GSC 2891

Returning from Southampton Island, June 1904, where Low and five others had joined Captain Comer's whaling excursion to conduct their own scientific research.

Six boats made up the fleet that left Fullerton. It wasn't easy going. The men sailed, and rowed when there was no breeze. The weather blew up nasty gales. They contended with rain, snow, and fog. They battled ice, using oars, paddles, and boathooks to push or pull their way through the floes and slushy water. There were perilous moments when ice floes suddenly changed direction with the tides and came careening together. When it looked like they might be caught between these moving ice pans, the men paddled a hasty retreat and hauled the boats up onto the nearest ice pan to avoid being crushed.

Birds began returning to Hudson Bay and the men saw all kinds of winged wildlife. They shot a bear and managed to go ashore a number of times. No whales were spotted, though. The *Neptune*'s and *Era*'s whale-boats parted company on June 22. Comer and his men continued on their whale hunt, while Low and his men carried out studies on Southampton Island. Ice still lay between them at the floe edge and the island's shore, forcing them to tromp through the knee-deep slush and water floating on top of the ice.

On Thursday, June 23, the Canadian contingent went ashore south of Cape Kendall. They erected a mound of stones and Low placed a box with a document in it. Then he held a formal ceremony taking posses-sion of the island for Canada. The men hoisted the flag above the cairn, recited the proclamation, gave three cheers, and sang "God Save the King," then Low stowed the box in the cairn.

The proclamation in the box declared, "In the name of our Gracious Sovereign King Edward VII and on behalf of the Government of Canada, I renew and take Possession of this Island of Southampton for the use and Property of the Dominion of Canada. God Save the King. [Signed] AP Low."

As Hudson Bay was viewed as an inland sea, its islands automatically belonged to Canada, so the necessity of this ceremony is puzzling. However, with the American activity in that vicinity, the government likely thought that a show of the flag would be a reminder to foreigners of who was in charge.

Low's party arrived back at Fullerton Harbour on July 2, and walked the three and a half miles over the ice from the water's edge to the ship. Although enormous holes had appeared in the ice since they left, it was still forty-five inches thick in areas.

On July 6, after the crew had spent a couple of days cutting the ice around the hull, the ship finally "rolled" once more on the water. It had been frozen in for nine months. It would still be two weeks before the ice melted sufficiently for them to leave their winter quarters. The *Neptune* was alive with activity in preparedness for its eastward voyage, and was painted and overhauled.

Angekok, the chief of the Aivilingmiut, came aboard with news that the mail, which had been sent out in December destined for Ottawa, had never arrived at the Hudson's Bay Company post at Churchill. It was apparently not delivered because the people who were to take the mail there were nervous about encountering the native people who lived in the area. The Inuit and First Nations did not get along and had been warring foes in the past, so their anxiety about encountering them was well-founded.

At any rate, the news threw a wrench into the works, as Moodie had made a number of requests about living and policing in the area. The mail not reaching its destination meant these requests would not be met. The only thing to do was to await the arrival of the relief ship and see what plans had been made without his input.

The Neptune *dressed for Dominion Day 1904, still frozen in the ice in Fullerton Harbour, Hudson Bay. The* Neptune *was the first Canadian expedition ship to overwinter in the Far North.*

On July 10, the Inuit held a party in honour of the *Neptune*'s departure. The people were full of good wishes for their safe return home. The police moved into their barracks on shore in preparation for another year as the official authority at Fullerton Harbour. Major Moodie would accompany the ship on its voyage through the archipelago to carry out his duties, imposing the law of the land, but intended to return with the supply ship in the fall. The five young officers would remain at the new post at Fullerton to carry out their duties for the summer.

Water lay on top of the quickly melting ice. The men tried to speed up the opening of a channel by sawing the ice ahead of the ship. By July 14, the crew was "swinging the ship and adjusting the compasses." At 2:00 a.m. on July 18, the ship weighed anchor and steamed slowly through the sawn and melted channel to Hudson Bay. The men of the *Era* were also awake and on deck to see their comrades safely off. They gave three cheers and the men of the *Neptune* returned the cheer. Both ships saluted with their flags.

Borden was not sorry to bid Fullerton farewell, saying it was one of the "most dismal, dreary & out-of-the-way places in the world."[16] The men of the *Neptune* were glad to be leaving Fullerton Harbour. However, they weren't homeward bound yet, nor was it the last they would see of the place. Their work in the North was just beginning. It would be another three months before they would sail into Halifax harbour.

CHAPTER NINE

A Ship for Bernier

While Low was preparing for his voyage to Hudson Bay in 1903, Bernier was busily lecturing and petitioning for his North Pole expedition. The public was still rooting for him.

On Friday, July 10, 1903, a cartoon on the front page of the *Toronto Daily Star* showed an English bobby-style policeman directing a queue of perspiring men, in shirt sleeves and suspenders, waiting outside a brick building. The sign on the building says, "Wanted, Recruits for Captain Bernier's Expedition to the North Pole." Judging by the cartoon, there was no lack of volunteers for his North Pole expedition — at least not during the mid-summer heat.

Bernier had realized that the government would not fund him the entire amount for his expedition. So he changed his tactic. He proposed that the Department of Marine and Fisheries provide him with a boat, and he would procure, by public subscription, the crew and necessary provisions for his polar expedition. The cost to the government would then be between $60,000 and $70,000, a substantial reduction from his initial request for $120,000.

Bernier also suggested that after his expedition, the ship would be returned to the department for use in the fishery protection. This time, Bernier's tenacity seemed to be rewarded. Lord Strathcona donated $5,000 to his expedition treasury.

Lord Strathcona's endorsement was a significant one. The Scottish-born Canadian, Donald Smith, had moved to Canada as a young man to work for the Hudson's Bay Company at the post at Nachvak Fiord. He had amassed a fortune building railroads, and had nailed the last spike in the Canadian Pacific Railway in November 1885. Throwing his support behind Bernier lent the project much credence.

On September 30, 1903, Bernier's ally, the Honourable John Charlton, made a second long, impassioned plea in the House of Commons for support for Bernier's North Pole expedition. Charlton's praise of Bernier was ebullient. He even compared Bernier's persistence to that of Christopher Columbus, going from court to court to seek a patron for his voyage of discovery.

Charlton argued that the ship would be owned by the government and therefore available for future use by it: "She would be the kind of vessel that would be exactly wanted in patrolling Hudson bay, in making voyages among the islands north of Hudson bay, and taking possession of newly discovered lands in that region."[1]

A HOT WEATHER SUGGESTION FOR CAPTAIN BERNIER.

Cartoon on the front page of the Toronto Daily Star, *Friday, July 10, 1903, spoofing the number of men interested in joining Bernier's polar expedition during that summer's heatwave.*

Charlton's speech was seconded by the Honourable Raymond Préfontaine, minister of Marine and Fisheries, who said, "If by risking the sum of $80,000 which would be the cost of the steamer to be built for the expedition, and which could be used for something else when it returns, the exploration of that territory could be helped on, I think, personally and as a member of this House, that the people of this country would approve of it."[2]

The Honourable Arthur W. Hackett, Independent Labour representative for Winnipeg, responded vehemently, "I very much fear that the country will question the sanity of this House when it finds that after sitting here for seven months we have nothing better to talk about than discovering the North Pole."[3]

In the end, Préfontaine was evasive on the government's official stance: "There have been so many important matters demanding the attention of the government that this question has not been specifically taken up by the cabinet."[4]

The discussion concluded and members agreed to a motion to consider putting funding toward the purchase of a boat for Captain Bernier's North Pole expedition. It was not the definitive answer Bernier wanted, but it was another step closer to the realization of his dream.

Alaska Boundary Resolution

As Préfontaine had mentioned, other "important matters" jockeyed for the government's attention and its coffers. These were matters that Bernier would undoubtedly have been aware of. Not only were they debated in the House of Commons, but the newspapers were full of them. One that occupied a great deal of newsprint was the resolution of the Alaska-Yukon boundary.

For nine months, the arbitration tribunal studied the legal aspects of the dispute. Both sides were in agreement on the boundary dividing Alaska and the Yukon at the 141st meridian. The mountain range running down the coast of British Columbia remained the contentious part of the boundary in question.

The arbitration meetings were held in October 1903 in the Foreign Office in London, England. Canada was confident that the British judge,

Baron Alverstone, would weigh in on the side of Canada. The government was certain of British support after the help it gave Britain in the Boer War.

However, Roosevelt applied his motto "speak softly and carry a big stick" with regard to settling the dispute. He sent word that if the panel did not "find correctly," he would send in marines to secure U.S. rights. In the end, Britain was more concerned with its relations with the United States than with Canada.[5]

On October 20, 1903, after three weeks of discussion, the dispute was resolved in favour of the United States, with Baron Alverstone casting the deciding vote. Canadian commissioners on the tribunal were stunned. Allen Aylesworth and Sir Louis Jette refused to sign the majority decision and published their own dissenting opinion. It took up three columns of the *London Times*.

It was picked up in the Canadian press, and the headline on the front page of the *Globe* on Wednesday, October 21, 1903, read, "Canadian Interests Have Been Sacrificed by Lord Alverstone." Aylesworth and Jette's protest statement read,

> We do not consider the finding of the tribunal as to the islands at the entrance of the Portland Channel or as to the mountain line a judicial one and, therefore, we have declined to be parties to the award…, but we have been compelled to witness the sacrifice of the interests of Canada, powerless to prevent it, though satisfied that the course the majority determined to pursue, in respect to the matters above specially referred to, ignored the just rights of Canada.[6]

Despite their fervent objections, the tribunal's resolution was passed. As a result, the northern part of the Coast Mountains and the scores of islands scattered down the coast became the Alaska Panhandle. Canada wound up with virtually no coastline or coastal port that would give direct access to northern British Columbia and, from there, to the Yukon. This was a gross humiliation for Canada.[7]

The House of Commons convened at 11:00 a.m. on Friday, October 23, 1903. The Alaskan Boundary Commission was one of the first topics brought up. The subject occupied the discussion for most of the day — and evening. Recess was called at six o'clock for supper. But when the House returned two hours later, the conversation carried on where it left off.

The Right Honourable Robert Borden, leader of the Conservative party, spoke at length, suggesting the matter might have been resolved differently if three Canadian jurists had been on the tribunal rather than two Canadians and one Brit. It appeared that Canada's interests had not been foremost in Britain's negotiations with the United States from the start.

Prime Minister Laurier said, "The difficulty, as I conceive it to be, is that so long as Canada remains a dependency of the British Crown the present powers that we have are not sufficient for the maintenance of our rights."[8]

Laurier was voicing a general feeling that was growing in the hearts of Canadians. There was a sense that policies being drafted in London on Canada's behalf virtually ignored the country's best interests and acted in favour of global considerations instead.[9]

Meeting of the Alaska Boundary Tribunal at the Foreign Office in London, England, October 1903.

For days, the Alaskan Boundary Dispute resolution continued to be the lead front page story across the country. Newspapers hyped the fear that the Americans would not stop at claiming land west of the Yukon, but move into Canada's Arctic.[10]

Minister of the Interior Clifford Sifton, an ardent nationalistic force in Laurier's government, took an anti-American stand. He had been in London for the arbitration meetings, and, having just witnessed their manoeuvrings firsthand, was determined to keep the Americans from gaining more Canadian ground. Shortly after the outcome of the Alaskan Boundary Dispute, he commissioned chief astronomer Dr. William F. King to compile a report on Canada's title to the Arctic islands. Rather than dispelling the government's concern, King's report, released to senior ministers on January 23, 1904, revealed fractures in Canada's supposedly solid claim in the Arctic.[11]

In his report, King analyzed the documents and maps held in the Dominion Archives regarding the transfer of land to Canada by Britain in 1880. He showed that Hudson Bay and Hudson Strait were indisputably Canadian waters, but concluded "that Canada's title to, some at least of the northern islands, is imperfect."[12]

King's report, the resolution of the Alaskan boundary, Herschel Island, and Sverdrup's four-year presence in the Ellesmere area, as well as the continual presence of whalers and American explorers in the North, forced the government to realize that something more had to be done before a foreign country decided to lay claim to the Arctic.

On Thursday, November 19, 1903, Toronto's *Globe* ran a piece under the headline, "What Other Flag?" which said, "One result of the Alaskan award will be the financing of Capt. Bernier's proposed arctic expedition by the Canadian government on condition that the British flag be hoisted on the most northerly islands of the Arctic Archipelago."

MP Charlton had failed to convince the government to finance an expedition to the Pole, but his suggestion of using the vessel for other Arctic work was taken up. By March, the government had given Bernier permission to purchase an ice-strengthened vessel.

Bernier contacted B. Nordahl, a ship's broker in Christiania, Norway, about an existing ice-worthy ship. Nordahl informed Bernier that the *Gauss*, used for a German scientific expedition to the Antarctic, was for sale. The *Gauss* was built in Kiel, Germany, as a research ship to gather magnetic and meteorological information. It was part of an international team, with British and Swedish contingents, to study the Antarctic. However, the 1901 German National Antarctic Expedition was not viewed as a great success, since the ship had advanced only as far as 66°40'S, while the English had reached 82°17'S.[13] Thus, upon its return, the *Gauss* was put up for sale.

The Canadian government paid the German government £15,000, or $75,000, for the ship. It was a deal. The *Gauss* had cost $137,000 to build three years previous. This was the first ship that the Dominion government had purchased for a northern expedition. For the previous five expeditions to Hudson Bay, the vessels had been leased.

On Saturday, March 5, 1904, the *Globe* reported,

> Captain Bernier, who is desirous of discovering the north pole for Canada, is to realize part of the great ambition of his life.... The *Gaus* [sic] will not go immediately to the arctic region. As early as possible, say about the end of May or June, she will take relief stores and coal for the Government steamer *Neptune*, at present wintering in Hudson's Bay. The two vessels will meet at Lady Jobs Harbor, on the northwest coast of Labrador, in July next. After transferring her cargo to the *Neptune*, the *Gauss* will be engaged in survey work on the coast of Labrador until about October. She will then start on her long journey to the mouth of the Mackenzie River. Proceeding due south, the *Gauss* will weather Cape Horn, and then steam north until she reaches Bering Sea. The drift of the eastward current and her own steam will carry her swiftly through the straits into Beaufort Sea. On arriving off the mouth of the Mackenzie, Captain Bernier will report to the commander of the Mounted Police post. Flying the British flag, she will cruise in northern waters and assert British sovereignty. Illegal trading on the part of American sealers will be suppressed, and customs duties collected for goods brought into Canadian Territory.

The newspaper had spelled out the government's plan: Bernier would head into the Arctic to establish sovereignty.

However, Bernier was undoubtedly thinking of a polar voyage as he organized the ship's supplies. The Department of Marine and Fisheries called upon his expertise to make a requisition for all supplies that would be required for the expedition. Bernier studied the supply list of the three other recent polar expeditions — American, German, and British. Bernier based most of his list of provisions on Robert Falcon Scott's Antarctic expedition aboard *Discovery*. Bernier calculated every item, such as how much meat, biscuits, flour, sugar, et cetera, would be needed for fifty men for twelve hundred days, or three years.

In April, an article in Ottawa's *Citizen* mentioned, "Capt. Bernier's hopes are that when he has victualled his ship at Herschell island he will be able to steer his course due north, keeping to the 30th meridian of west longitude and so reach the pole."[14]

But these were clearly Bernier's "hopes." Nothing in his orders from the government indicated that the ship would be permitted to make a polar cruise after visiting Hudson Bay. In fact, the expedition was known in government correspondence and newspapers at the time as the "Hudson Bay and Mackenzie River Expedition."[15]

As per instructions, Bernier and his crew went to New York on Sunday, April 10, and boarded a Hamburg American liner for Bremerhaven, Germany, to pick up the new Dominion Government Steamship. On May 7, the *Gauss* cast off from the Bremerhaven docks. A course was charted across the Atlantic for Canada.

The *Gauss* was a three-masted barquentine, which meant its fore-mast was rigged with square sails, and the main- and mizzen-masts were rigged with triangular fore and aft sails, with its smoke stack positioned between the main- and mizzen-masts. The *Gauss* was an impressive sight as it sailed up the St. Lawrence to the dry dock at Lévis, Quebec, arriving the second week of June.

Bernier arrived from Bremerhaven a disgruntled sailor, though. Unfortunately, he complained to the press. Bernier's crew was hand-picked by the department and did not measure up to the captain's expec-tations. On Friday, June 17, the *Montreal Gazette* ran an article noting Bernier's comments:

He was very much dissatisfied with the personnel of his crew all of which, with the exception of four men had been foisted upon him at Montreal by the Dominion Government. They were landlubbers. They thought because the *Gauss* was a government vessel they were going on a picnic ... In his thirty-five years experience as a ship's master he never heard of such a crew. Finally he declared with emphasis that in the future he would have the shipping of his own men or know the reason why.

Bernier was likely justified in his complaints. However, he had created intense public interest in his northern expedition. The cartoon in the *Toronto Daily Star* was not too far wrong in suggesting that everyone wanted to go along. The government was inundated with requests from men volunteering to go with Captain Bernier.

When Senator Landry asked if the government planned to give the commander of the *Gauss* complete liberty in choosing his crew, Préfontaine responded, "The commander of the *Arctic*, formerly the *Gauss*, will be provided with the proper crew found qualified by the department for the expedition."[16]

The government was keeping control over the matter. However, their means of qualifying the crew had little to do with the men's marine or Arctic experience. For starters, the government vetted the men by having applicants apply through their members of Parliament. Their applications were simply letters listing their qualifications and the reasons why they wanted to go along on the expedition. The men were also required to include a doctor's certificate to prove they were fit for the job.

The government received stacks of applications from candidates with diverse careers and experiences. One was from a Roman Catholic priest who promoted his skills in "map drawing and sketching from nature," and his ability to "be of service to Catholics on board." He didn't get the job.

Even crew members who had previously sailed with Bernier had to "be recommended by a minister or prominent member of Parliament."[17] Some of these requests were denied and able seamen passed over for those having more solid connections with someone on the Hill. The result was that the crew was less than satisfactory.

Unfortunately, public criticism of his employer was not prudent. Bernier's complaints did not stand him in good stead with the department, nor did it help him get more experienced crew for the voyage that summer.

Preparing for a Northern Expedition

The *Gauss* put into dry dock at Lévis, opposite Quebec City on the St. Lawrence River, to make necessary repairs for the expedition. Its hull was built of oak and pitch pine with a covering of greenheart, a dense hardwood. Bernier had copper sheathing added to the bow and stern for extra protection against ice before it was repainted a battleship grey with white above the waterline.[18] The ship was launched and re-christened the *Arctic*.

The issue of hiring continued. The government held its crew selection cards close to its chest. Deputy minister of Marine and Fisheries Colonel François Gourdeau's letter to J.U. Gregory, a Marine and Fisheries agent, put it very succinctly: "In regard to the crew of the *Arctic*; at present you will hire by the day the men that are necessary on board this vessel, on the full understanding that they are not in any way permanently engaged."[19]

But as the days advanced, it became increasingly necessary to hire men if the *Arctic* intended to sail by mid-August. The rising panic in Gregory's reply on July 13 is discernible: "Concerning the DGS *Arctic*, I would respectfully suggest that the engagement of a crew for this vessel takes place as soon as possible. Good men are scarce; having nearly all signed articles for the season of navigation and it is quite difficult to get good officers, able bodied seamen and firemen."[20]

Gregory detailed the cost of coaling and provisioning the vessel for an expedition of three years in a memorandum to the deputy minister. The total was $88,000.[21] This cost did not include wages, which would add up to about $8,000 per annum. Bernier as sailing master would receive $150 per month. Each position received wages accordingly, from the chief engineer at $100 per month down to the cabin boy at $20 per month. Historian Fabien Vanasse received $125, which in relation to the tasks of sailing master seems generous.

Fifty-four-year-old Vanasse was a journalist and lawyer who had been a member of Parliament for Yamaska, Quebec, from 1879 to 1891. Indubitably, he was one of the applicants chosen for his political connections.

On July 6, 1904, NWMP Comptroller White wrote to Minister of the Interior Sifton:

> The undersigned, while keenly anxious to have a patrol boat to act in conjunction with the mounted police, at the mouth of the Mackenzie River, respectfully suggests whether, under existing conditions, the supervision of Hudson's Bay and the waters north thereof, is not more important and urgent than Mackenzie Bay; and whether it would not be better to assign the *Arctic* to that service; she being built specially for Arctic exploration, and having capacity for carrying supplies for three years.[22]

White's suggestion made sense. By July 29, it had become the government's intentions, as Laurier stated in his address to the House: "The '*Neptune*' is to come back and be relieved and be replaced by another boat, the '*Arctic*,' which will be under the command of Captain Bernier and which is to sail on August 15. This boat will carry an officer and ten men from the mounted police.... Their instructions are to patrol the waters, to find suitable locations for posts, to establish those posts and to assert the jurisdiction of Canada."[23]

It had been officially announced. The *Arctic* would replace the *Neptune* and patrol the Eastern Arctic waters. By now it was apparent that Bernier would not be making any attack on the Pole.

The day Laurier announced the *Arctic*'s mission in the House of Commons, Commander O.G.V. Spain of the Canadian Marine Service, who was overseeing work on the *Arctic*, received a telegram from his superior, Deputy Minister Gourdeau, saying,

> I wish to confirm the instructions you received verbally yesterday from the minister as to the status of captain Bernier on the northern expedition. As you are aware, it has been decided by the minister that the captain of

the *Arctic* will only act as sailing master being entirely under the directions of the officer or officers, who will be selected by the minister to take charge of this expedition and as arranged yesterday you will make this matter clear to captain Bernier.[24]

Spain informed Bernier of this decision on July 30, 1904, adding more salt to the captain's wound. Not only was he not going in search of the Pole, but he would no longer even be commander-in-chief of the expedition. The commander was still to be appointed by the Royal North West Mounted Police (RNWMP). The North West Mounted Police had been given royal designation that June by King Edward VII.

By this time, the ship was almost ready to go. It had been loaded with supplies for three years. Some of this now had to be put ashore so that room could be made on deck for the building materials for the RNWMP post and the ten officers who would take passage aboard the *Arctic*. This reordering of things meant that the *Arctic* was not ready to leave by mid-August. The departure date was postponed and Bernier awaited his sailing orders.

A COMMANDER FOR THE EXPEDITION

Meanwhile, in northern waters, the *Neptune* encountered plenty of drifting ice after leaving Fullerton and heading across Hudson Bay and through the strait.

At times blowing snow and ice closed menacingly around the ship as it drifted eastward with the current. As leads or fissures in the ice opened, the *Neptune* would manoeuvre into them, sometimes charging a mass of solid-looking ice in an effort to punch through it. The ship would ram at full speed to force a path through, jarring the ship and its occupants' nerves, even occasionally knocking them down. It finally made Port Burwell at the eastern end of Hudson Strait on Tuesday, July 25, at 5:00 p.m., a date prearranged before leaving Halifax the summer before.

The re-supply ship *Erik* had arrived only an hour before. The *Erik* carried mail, and the entire company rejoiced at receiving letters from home after eleven months. The ship also brought news that the Dominion government was sending up a patrol ship, the *Arctic*. This would take over the duties of the *Neptune* in Hudson Bay, wintering and keeping an eye on the foreign whalers.

Borden wrote, "A new ship to come up to replace us. The Major is going back all in an uproar but we, as intended, go north as soon as we get supplies aboard."[25]

The major was no doubt in an uproar, knowing that the mail he had sent out in December with particulars about Fullerton Harbour had not reached Ottawa. Moodie realized that information about Hudson Bay, essential to this new patrol ship, had not been received. He needed to convince the government of the necessity of more reinforcements, more posts, and annual patrols in Hudson Bay.

Moodie decided to go directly to Ottawa, file his report with his superiors, and then take passage back to Fullerton aboard the *Arctic*. He needed to get back down south before it left port. So he hastily jumped ship and took passage aboard the *Erik*, which left on August 2 and arrived in St. John's five days later.

Two other passengers besides Moodie also transferred to the *Erik* to return south. The second sailor from the *Era* suffering with scurvy had taken passage aboard the *Neptune* in order to make his way home to New England. The number of men aboard the *Era* had been reduced to sixteen.

The other man transferring to the *Erik* was the *Neptune*'s second steward, D. Tierney. Borden wrote that Tierney "thinks he is not well." The doctor doubted the man's complaints, but Low accepted the man's resignation. Low cut the man more slack than he did the poor cabin boy who drowned the previous December. A man from the *Erik* switched places with Tierney and shipped aboard the *Neptune*. He was suddenly in for an adventure he hadn't imagined when he had signed on with the supply ship.

The *Neptune* left early in the morning of August 3. It headed north into Davis Strait, where Low and his men would begin raising the flag for Canada in the Arctic Archipelago.

Moodie arrived in St. John's on August 7 and gave a brief report of activities in Hudson Bay to the newspapermen on the docks. A *New York Times* article referred to him as "Major Moodie, Governor of Hudson Bay."[26] Moodie later denied that he had presented himself as "Governor of

Hudson Bay," but Comer mentions it in his diary, as does Borden, so he must have suggested this was his title.

Upon arriving in the capital, Moodie immediately reported to Comptroller Fred White. His appearance in Ottawa was ideally timed. The expedition to Hudson Bay was ready to go. The only thing missing was an appropriate commander. Moodie was the ideal candidate. He already had first-hand knowledge of the situation in Hudson Bay and the post there.

The *Arctic* was supposed to leave in mid-August; however, after Moodie arrived, the sailing date was delayed. September approached. Bernier's impatience with the delay was well-founded, as it was getting late in the season to sail into Arctic waters.

On September 9, 1904, Superintendent Moodie received a memo from Fred White, comptroller of the RNWMP, informing him he would be named as the officer-in-charge of the expedition. He would take with him ten officers and Inspector E.A. Pelletier to serve in Hudson Bay for three years. The memo went on to say,

> As you are already aware, the object of this service is to explore and patrol Hudson Bay, and the islands and waters north thereof, and to administer and enforce the laws of Canada therein.
>
> Until otherwise ordered by the Government, the route of the vessel will be limited to Hudson Bay, Hudson Strait, Davis Strait, Baffin's Bay, Smith Sound, Kennedy Channel, Lancaster Sound, and other bays and channels on the west coast of Hudson Bay, Davis Strait or Baffin's Bay.[27]

Moodie was also appointed Fishery Officer and was heading north with more power and authority. The work that the DGS *Arctic* would carry out was considered "as simply an extension of the Fisheries Protection Service of Canada."[28]

On September 12, 1904, three days after Moodie was informed about his position aboard the *Arctic*, Bernier received his long-awaited sailing orders. The orders stated,

Geraldine Moodie, Parks Canada, PC-696.10

Inspector (Major) John Douglas Moodie of the North West Mounted Police commanded the expedition to Hudson Bay in 1904–05 and set up the first police post in Fullerton Harbour, Hudson Bay.

After very serious consideration, the government has deemed it advisable that permanent stations should be established at different places on shore in these northern parts of the Dominion and to carry this out in the best and most effective manner, the sole charge of the expedition has been placed under the command of Superintendent Moodie, of the R.N.W.M.P., an officer very experienced in these northern regions both on water and on land.

Your duties are to be as follows: You will be held responsible for the navigation and the safety of the *Arctic* in every way, but in all other respects she is to be subject to the commands of the Officer in Charge of the Expedition.[29]

It was in writing. Despite Commander Spain having verbally informed him of the change in his position at the end of July, seeing it spelled out on paper meant it was unequivocally official. Bernier was relegated to sailing master.

He had been convincing in his crusade for a Canadian North Pole expedition. He had gained the financial and moral support of numerous Arctic experts, politicians, and the public. However, his experience was that of navigator and ship's captain. He lacked the experience of the whalers, never having ventured into Baffin waters or Hudson Bay. The fact was that even Moodie, as the shipping orders stated, was "an officer very experienced in these northern regions both on water and on land." Bernier was not.

Not only was his dream of going to the Pole denied him, but he was also denied the post of commander, which he had worked so hard to secure. He was furious, but mainly he was humiliated. So he resigned.

A September 13 telegram to Bernier from Deputy Minister Gourdeau reads, "It is rumoured that you are unwilling to accept position of sailing master of 'ARCTIC' for northern expedition under Major Moodie. Wire your acceptance or refusal."[30]

It did not take long for this news to hit the papers. On Thursday, September 15, headlines in the Ottawa *Citizen* read, "Capt. Bernier Resigns. He Will Not Sail the 'Arctic' to Hudson Bay."

The same day, the *Toronto Daily Star* also reported on the resignation: "Not prepared to play second fiddle to Superintendent Moodie of the North-West Mounted Police and to act as sailing master only, Captain Bernier has refused to go with the '*Arctic*' to Hudson's Bay and another navigator will be appointed in his stead."

The government was scrambling to find another navigator to take the *Arctic* north when Bernier changed his mind. He had worked so hard for a northern expedition that he could not turn the opportunity down. He swallowed his pride, and responded to Gourdeau's telegram with his acceptance. On Monday, September 19, Captain Bernier was on the bridge of the *Arctic* when Minister of Marine and Fisheries Raymond Préfontaine made his departing speech. Bernier was reconciled to his role as ship's master for this first Arctic voyage.

The public was as disappointed as Bernier that his dream was not to be realized. The *Toronto Daily Star* wrote, "The captain may be sure that he has our sympathy. The whole world is disappointed at a good man being kept down. And the North Pole openly exalts now that its duly serious pursuer is removed."[31]

Bernier was finally going to the Arctic, although regrettably not on a North Pole expedition. But he would not be "kept down." He just deferred his plans for a polar expedition for another year. The trip to Hudson Bay would be a run-through for the real thing next season.

THE *NEPTUNE*'S CRUISE INTO ARCTIC WATERS

Meanwhile, the *Neptune* sailed northeast across Davis Strait and up the coast of Greenland, passing splendid snow-capped mountains and fiords. The men enjoyed incredible vistas but also grave dangers, passing enormous icebergs, some two hundred feet in height. The ship's northward advance was finally blocked by ice at Smith Sound. They crossed over to Cape Sabine, midway up the east coast of Ellesmere Island. They were at 78°30'N.

Cape Sabine, the site of the Greely disaster, was also the makeshift headquarters for Peary's 1898–1902 attempt at the Pole, eight hundred miles distant. Low, Bartlett, and Borden went ashore and explored the abandoned American base camps. Low, the impeccable scientist, commented in his official report, "The pluck and daring of such men are to be admired, but the waste of energy, life and money in a useless and probably unsuccessful attempt to reach the pole can only be deplored, as no additional scientific knowledge is likely to be gained by this achievement."[32]

This practical sentiment could well have been part of the reason that Bernier wasn't encouraged to pursue his polar project with government money.

The three men also discovered five new Inuit graves. The bodies had been wrapped in muskox skins and covered with stones. Beside them were snowknives, an old gun, and other items belonging to the deceased. Borden took the gun back to the ship as a souvenir. He lamented that he could not get a skull, though, as the bodies were still too fresh. There is no reflection in either Borden's journal or Low's published report of who these people were or why they were buried there.

The ship then crossed to Cape Herschel on the mainland of Ellesmere. The bay was choked with icebergs and the ship, attempting to pass between two smaller bergs at full speed, struck heavily on a sharp point of rock. The impact on the bow tilted the ship so that its rail was nearly in the water. The ship continued over the rock, striking amidships and finally hammering the stern. Depth soundings were quickly taken and determined that with seventy fathoms all around, the rock they had struck was the peak of a submerged mountain.

It was difficult to assess what damage the ship had sustained. The pumps were put to work but the ship was taking on very little water. This was the incident in which Borden claimed that the sealant of seal oil and coal dust kept the water out. The men were grateful that the walls of the ship's bow were eight feet thick. Once back in a Halifax dry dock, however, it was revealed that the rock had loosened the iron stem plate, which was later torn away butting into heavy ice. As well, seventy-five feet of the keel had been ripped off by the encounter with the rock, and the stern post had been twisted.

Shortly after the incident, Low and some of the crew landed at Cape Herschel and, in a ceremony similar to that performed on Southampton Island in Hudson Bay, read a proclamation taking formal possession of Ellesmere in the name of King Edward VII for the Dominion of Canada.

A flag was raised and saluted. The document was placed in a rock cairn they built on the edge of the cape to notify future foreign exploration parties.

Three days later, on August 15, the ship dropped anchor in Erebus Bay off Beechey Island, made famous as the spot where Franklin's ships *Erebus* and *Terror* had anchored in the winter of 1845–46. The small island had also been a rendezvous point or headquarters for Franklin search parties. Beechey is about a square mile in size. At low tide, a narrow, rocky neck joins it to the southwest end of Devon Island. The southern side of the island has a hill that rises about four hundred feet. The island's surface is covered in small, loose limestone shingle. Despite a few hardy flowers struggling to survive in the spare soil, the island was virtually devoid of vegetation.

As many of the crew as could be spared got into the boats and rowed over to Beechey. The island was a veritable outdoor museum. The crew discovered the remains of Northumberland House, with its low stone wall foundation. It had been built as a supply depot in 1852–53 by Commander

A.P. Low, Geological Survey of Canada, GSC 199681

Men of the Neptune *raising the flag on Cape Herschel, Ellesmere Island, in 1904 to claim it for Canada.*

Pullen of the HMS *North Star*. Pullen was part of Sir Edward Belcher's expedition, the British Admiralty's last effort to locate Franklin. Inside the house, casks of provisions had been broken open by bears.

Scattered about Northumberland House were dozens of empty tins, which had contained rotten food that Franklin had condemned. It was later discovered that the solder used to seal the tins was high in lead content and had dripped down inside. It is now surmised that lead poisoning may have played a part in the demise of Franklin's crew.[33] A pile of leather boot soles was also found near the house, discarded by some relief expedition. A large mahogany lifeboat, its sides battered by ice, had also been left on the beach in the hope that Franklin's expedition survivors would make use of it.

A few hundred yards from Northumberland House, wooden crosses were stuck in the gravely beach, marking the graves of the first three of Franklin's men who perished in the Arctic in 1845. A fourth grave belonged to a member of one of the search parties.[34]

Behind the house, and erected on a rocky terrace, was a wooden cenotaph with a round ball atop it mounted on a platform of cemented limestone. Face downwards on the platform was a large marble slab dedicated to the memory of Franklin and his men by citizens of the United States. Low's men raised the slab to photograph it, then replaced it as they had found it. Low suggested that another government expedition heading to Beechey should bring along cement to fix it in place as originally intended.

Attached to the cenotaph was a tin with a written record from the Norwegian Magnetic Pole Expedition led by Roald Amundsen. It stated that the *Gjøa* had stopped there and picked up provisions left by one of the Scottish whalers, and was proceeding down Peel Sound to get as close as possible to the magnetic pole before the sound froze over. Low took the record, which was eventually forwarded to the Norwegian government.

The crew members picked up little curios to take back with them. Borden took home a piece of wood broken off the mahogany boat, which the *Neptune*'s carpenter made into a picture frame for him. Low took the small cart that had lain near the house as a souvenir. Beechey Island is now designated a site of historic significance. Unfortunately, many of its artifacts have disappeared, taken home by dozens of ships' crews as keepsakes.

The *Neptune* had gone as far west into the Arctic Archipelago as orders permitted. Low felt that age-old temptation of Arctic mariners to attempt the Northwest Passage, though. It had yet to be accomplished. Low was confident that with the right conditions the "staunch powerful steamship" could make it. However, they had sovereignty business to attend to, so turned the ship southward and crossed Lancaster Sound.

The first stop was Prince Leopold Island. As they steamed into the harbour, they spotted an overturned boat with a wooden lean-to against it. A Danish flag flew above it. They blew the ship's whistle but got no response from the makeshift hut onshore. Fearing that this was an encampment of the Norwegian Magnetic Pole Expedition that might be in trouble, a boat was lowered with Dr. Borden, a first-aid kit, and blankets. Fortunately, no one was in dire straits — the site was deserted. The overturned boat turned out to be a boiler from a steam launch left by a Franklin search party. It was surrounded by crates of provisions deposited a few days prior for the *Gjøa* by the Scottish whaler *Windward*. The flag had been raised to signal this to Amundsen's expedition.

The following day, August 17, a boat went ashore and the Dominion flag was hoisted. Copies of the proclamation and the customs regulation were left in the boiler. The expedition then weighed anchor and sailed into nasty weather. It was a heavy sea, and fog froze on the rigging, coating it in a silver hoary frost. The *Neptune* steamed cautiously across the mouths of Prince Regent, Admiralty, and Navy Board Inlets, charting a course for Pond Inlet (known as Mittimatalik) on north Baffin Island.

The men spotted a number of Inuit tents, or tupiks, near Button Point on Bylot Island, north of Pond Inlet. They anchored and Low went ashore. In the thirteen cotton and skin tupiks, Low met a number of women and children and a few sick men. The men had gone off in whaleboats as employees of Scottish whalers in the inlet.

The people were all suffering from internal bleeding and a high fever. Regardless of contagion, they all piled into a whaleboat and went out to visit the ship. Low mentioned that their illness looked like typhoid pneumonia. Dr. Borden makes no note of it in his journal, but describes treating a similarly ill man several days later.

From these people, they learned that two Dundee whaling ships were in Pond Inlet. After the people had returned to their camp, the *Neptune* sailed ten miles up the inlet before anchoring in the shadow of the steep clay cliffs alongside the *Eclipse* and the *Diana* (the same boat that Wakeham had commanded in 1897). Shortly after anchoring, they were visited by the ships' captains, Milne and Adams, as well as Mr. Mutch of the *Albert*, who had established a trading post nearby. Low informed them of the new laws and collected the duties and licence fees. The *Neptune's* officers spent the evening in the pleasant company of these men, listening to tales of whaling life.

The next day, a gale blew up. When it abated they headed down the inlet, where they met up with two more whalers, the *Balaena* and the *Albert*. Low issued licences and collected fees from the captains. On August 27, the *Neptune* left for Cumberland Sound. However, the heavy ice pack forced them eastward almost to Greenland before they found safe passage south again. The men spotted a Norwegian brigantine beset by ice about twenty miles east of Blacklead Island.

The *Neptune* came alongside the sailing vessel and anchored. It was the supply ship for the missions and whaling stations at Blacklead and Kekerten Islands. The ship had been in the vicinity for thirty days, but could get no closer to the islands because of the ice. Not being powered by steam, it could not break through. If the ship was crushed, the stations in the gulf would not get their provisions and all would suffer until the next relief vessel could get in the following summer. Low agreed to take the ship's mail and papers to the stations, but not the provisions. The *Neptune* left the brigantine stuck in the ice, and headed for Blacklead Island.

Reverend Peck and the agent came out to visit the ship where it dropped anchor in the bay. Low and a few men trekked up the summit of the island. From there they had a bird's eye view of the ice-choked north-western part of the gulf all the way to Kekerten Island. In light of the gulf's conditions, Low decided not to attempt to reach Kekerten, but instead head south to Port Burwell.

On September 3, the ship came within four miles of the whaling station at Cape Haven, where its progress was halted by ice. A boat with several Inuit came out to the ship and reported that Captain Jackson, the agent at the post, had set out ten days before for Blacklead Island to procure supplies. The provisions at the station had been virtually exhausted. No supply ship had arrived for the year, no whales had been captured, and the hunt that summer had only yielded a few bear and walrus. Things looked grim for the post.

Leaving these people in a quandary about their provisions, the *Neptune* continued to Port Burwell. The passage was relatively ice free, and it anchored in Port Burwell on September 4. The *Arctic* hadn't arrived yet. The news they received before leaving in July was that the *Arctic* would leave Quebec mid-August, which meant it should arrive in Port Burwell any day. The Low expedition, of course, had no inkling that the ship's departure was delayed a month.

They stayed in the harbour for three days while the crew took on the coal and provisions previously landed by the *Erik* for the police post. Then the ship headed west again through Hudson Strait to Fullerton Harbour.

THROUGH THE STRAIT AND BACK

In Wakeham Bay, they picked up an Inuk who would be their pilot for the rest of the voyage. Five days later, they met the Scottish steamer *Active* as it was heading home. The *Active* belonged to the whaling company that had a station at Repulse Bay. Two brothers, both captains, came aboard and reported on the summer's activities. They had another of Comer's sick men on board.

On Friday, September 16, the *Neptune* entered Fullerton Harbour and anchored. The company was warmly received when almost all the Inuit residents and policemen came out to the ship. Low got caught up on the local news. Staff Sergeant Dee told how he had made a policing expedition to Repulse Bay that summer in a whaleboat with some local Inuit men.

The *Era* had left for more fruitful whaling grounds in Roes Welcome not long after the *Neptune* had departed in July, and had arrived at Repulse Bay, where the August whaling had always been good. Two Scottish whalers lay at anchor there: the steamer *Active* and a sailing ship, the *Ernest William*. While Comer was in Repulse Bay, Staff Sergeant Dee arrived in a whaleboat and passed on the proclamation that Moodie had given Comer, informing the Scottish ships' captains that they were in Canadian waters and were now expected to pay duties. It was the first official patrol that the police had made since arriving in Hudson Bay.

It was not a fruitful summer for any of the whalers. By September 11, Comer decided to return to his old winter quarters at Fullerton. Another of his men was sick and, afraid the man would not make it through the winter, Comer sent him home aboard the *Active*. The *Era*'s crew now numbered fifteen.

Coincidentally, the *Era* arrived and anchored in Fullerton's outer harbour only a few hours after the *Neptune*. Comer came into the harbour in one of his boats to greet Low and the men. He spent the evening aboard the *Neptune* and learned that his sick man, who had gone out on the *Neptune*, had received thirty dollars that Low's crew had collected for him. The money helped the man obtain passage home.

The *Era* let go both anchors the next day in the inner harbour not far from the *Neptune*, while the men of the *Neptune* were busy unloading the supplies for the police post. Comer was pleased to read newspapers that Low had received from the *Erik*. Though the news was no longer new, it was information about life down south that the men missed and now coveted.

Dr. Borden made the rounds visiting the people on shore. He found two of the police officers unfit to remain another year. Constable Conway had severe rheumatism that was aggravated by the cold. Constable Tremaine's gums were bluish and bled on pressure, and his breath was foul; as well, his legs were swollen with black and blue spots. Borden recognized the symptoms of scurvy immediately. Both men came aboard, leaving only Staff Sergeant Dee and Constables Jarvis and Donaldson at Fullerton until the *Arctic* arrived with new reinforcements.

The *Neptune* stayed a week at Fullerton. Comer enjoyed dinner and spent the evenings aboard the steamer like old times. While the *Neptune*'s crew took on ballast and fresh water and got ready to put to sea again, the men of the *Era* began preparing for winter and building their house on deck. The Inuk, Scotty, returned with some other men from deer hunting with thirty deer. The majority of these ended up in the *Neptune*'s larder, which the men were grateful for after eating salt meat for several months. Once again, the locals of Fullerton were supplying the government ship. Comer's gang received two of the deer.

Comer wrote letters home to be put in the steamer's mailbag and mailed in Halifax. Low gave Comer some books, as well as nails, screws, and other small useful things that the steamer could spare now that it was headed homeward. After noon on Sunday, September 25, the *Neptune* weighed anchor on its final voyage east. The men of the *Era* again gave them a rousing send-off with three cheers.

CHAPTER TEN

THE DOMINION GOVERNMENT STEAMER *ARCTIC*

It would always be known as Bernier's ship. Although he had purchased it for the government of Canada, Bernier's name had been associated with a polar expedition for so long that, in the eyes of the public, the ship Bernier sailed north on was his.

The *Arctic* is considered small by today's standards. It was thirty-seven feet wide at the widest mid-section and one hundred and sixty-five feet long, the length of two tractor trailers end to end. It was equipped with special ice propellers, and had a 275-horsepower auxiliary steam engine to assist pushing through ice or when there was no wind. The ship could make seven knots, but rarely travelled faster than four, or a good walking speed. If steam power was used on a windy day, then a fine black powder from the exhaust of the coal-fired boiler covered everything and everyone downwind of the smokestack.

The *Arctic*'s sides and bottom were over forty-eight inches thick. Its hull was curved, so that when squeezed by the pack ice, the ship would rise out of the ice rather than be crushed by it. The *Fram*'s hull was of a similar "coconut-shaped" design.[1] The ship was ice-strengthened by having more ribs, set closer together than the average ship. Its midship section was "a highly complicated assembly of relatively small pieces of timber carefully fitted together."[2] Steel plates over the bow and stern further protected the ship against impact with the ice.

The ship's eighteen iron water tanks held ten thousand gallons of water. Every couple of weeks, the crew undertook the onerous task of filling the tanks. During the summer, the ship would moor up to an ice floe, and water from the thawed salt-free pools on the floe's surface would be pumped into the tanks with two hand pumps. During the winter months, ice from lakes was cut and thawed to fill the tanks. There was no running water on board; no shower, bathtub, or laundry facilities. Laundry was difficult in the High Arctic anyway, as the water froze in the bucket before the clothes could be rinsed. Most of the table and bed linens were filthy, and bedbugs were rampant. The men were issued new underclothes twice a year. Presumably, what they had been wearing until then was discarded or burned.

All of the living quarters, except the captain's cabin, were below the waterline, and there were no portholes. The *Arctic* had steam radiator heat, and its electric lighting was generated by a dynamo. Apparently the lights were no brighter than a candle, so the crew used kerosene lamps that gave off fumes, which had the benefit of helping camouflage the smells on board.[3]

However, in 1904, it was a state-of-the-art vessel and better than any that the crew had sailed on before.

At noon on Saturday, September 17, the *Arctic* was finally ready to cast off its moorings and sail for northern waters. The *Arctic* stood along-side the King's Wharf, with the stone walls of Quebec's upper city high on the cliffs behind.

Bernier's crew of thirty-two men was chosen from Quebec City, Newfoundland, and the Lower St. Lawrence region. A quarter of the crew was French Canadian. Most of them were young and working for less than forty dollars a month. Including the ten RNWMP, made up of non-commissioned officers and constables, plus Commander Moodie, the ship carried a complement of forty-four men.

It was an impressive send-off, befitting a voyage of distinction. The ship's company lined the deck and waved their hats to those onshore who had come to see them off. Fabien Vanasse, the ship's historiographer, wrote,

> The *Arctic* carried its flags aloft on its three masts. The brass band from the Citadelle battery was on the dock serenading our commander. Cheers could be heard from the docks, terraces and ship's bridge as the

honorable Minister of Marine arrived. After Minister
Joseph Raymond Préfontaine inspected the members
of the expedition and underlined, in his speech to the
departing party, the importance of the voyage to the
north 'to enforce the laws of Canada and to affirm its
rights to this territory.'[4]

Despite the recent disappointments and trials, Bernier must have
been exhilarated to stand on the bridge as the ship entered the swell
of the Atlantic. At last he was sailing north through scattered floes of
ice, passing icebergs and pack ice. Often the *Arctic* sliced through large
pans of newer, year-old ice, going over any that got in the way, splitting
them into pieces. It crashed through almost solid ice up to eight feet
thick. Sometimes, bumping against large pans would jolt the boat and
set it off course a few feet. It was reassuring to all on board that the ship
was built for exactly this kind of work.[5] And the captain relished every
minute of it.

Bernier officially held no ill-will toward Superintendent J.D. Moodie.
In reality, though, there was great animosity between the two men. Moodie
was a domineering man, accustomed to giving orders and having them
obeyed. These qualities engendered respect for his position of authority,
but were also the reason he was often disliked. Bernier also viewed Moodie
as having usurped him of his rightful position as commander, and he
bristled at the prospect of playing second fiddle on an expedition he had
worked toward for five years. So, it was not surprising that the two locked
horns from the first.[6]

Also irksome to Bernier was the company that Moodie kept. He had
boarded the *Arctic* with his twenty-year-old son Alec, who was made special constable and was along as his father's secretary. Also accompanying
Moodie on the expedition to Hudson Bay was his wife, Geraldine. Her
presence on board ship is not noted in any official list of the ship's crew.
No doubt Bernier expected her to get off at Pointe-au-Père with the river
pilot. However, she was accompanying them to Fullerton. A woman on
board ship was often considered bad luck by mariners.

MEETING OF SHIPS

The *Neptune* anchored in Port Burwell at noon on October 1. Boats were just being lowered for the men to go ashore when another steamer was announced coming into port. It was the *Arctic*.

The ship came alongside amidst a flurry of excitement. The men of the *Neptune* had all been wondering if they would see the major again. Moodie, now commander of the *Arctic*, came aboard with the ship's officers and was heartily greeted. They carried mail for the *Neptune*, and Low was pleased to receive the "welcome word of recall." Their services in the North would no longer be needed.

Moodie and Bernier were both anxious to reach Fullerton before the harbour froze over, so the *Arctic* weighed anchor later that evening. The crews bid each other farewell and the vessel left after dark on its cruise westward through the strait.[7]

On October 4, the *Neptune* also got underway and steamed out of Port Burwell. It was homeward bound. Passage through Gray Strait was rough and the ship rolled heavily. The trip down the Labrador coast was no better, with the ship wildly pitching and tossing. By the seventh, it was once again south of the treeline. The rough seas drove the ship off course, and two men were needed at the wheel to keep its bow headed into the waves crashing over it. Captain Bartlett admitted that they wanted more ballast. However, the *Neptune* succeeded in pushing through the storms and finally made Halifax on October 12. The ship's company was never so glad to set foot on their own soil.

The *Neptune* became the first Canadian government ship to cruise into Arctic waters. And Low and his men became the first Canadians to land on any of the Arctic islands north of Baffin. The expedition had succeeded in surveying a distance of over 2,040 miles and establishing a semblance of Canadian authority in the North.[8]

FULLERTON HARBOUR

Hudson Strait was free of ice and the *Arctic* made good passage, reaching Fullerton Harbour on October 16. When it was within a few miles of

Fullerton, it ran into some newly formed ice called slob ice, which was floating in and out with the tide. The crew dropped anchor outside the reefs beyond the harbour entrance and waited for a pilot to take them in.

Aboard the *Era*, Captain Comer spotted a steamer to the south "trying to find the entrance to the harbor."[9] Comer suspected that the ship would be his harbour mate for the coming winter, but he had no idea that it was another government steamer under the command of Major Moodie.

The next morning a boat came in from the *Arctic* and went straight to the police post onshore. Shortly afterward, the boat came out to the *Era* with a note from Comer's old adversary. In his usual commandeering style, Moodie asked for natives to come and help pilot the steamer into the harbour. Comer sent a message back that the Inuit were off hunting. He did not volunteer his own services. Fog settled on the bay and the limited visibility made Moodie's row back to the ship a difficult one.

The following morning, with a fresh wind from the northeast, the *Arctic* steamed into the harbour, cutting through the recently formed four-inch-thick ice. The *Arctic* anchored near the *Era*. The schooner respectfully set its colours for the *Arctic*'s crew, but there was no other communication between the ships.

The following day, Moodie requested the use of the schooner's carpenter for a few days to help build a larger house onshore. The three-room building could not accommodate the increased police force of eleven men. Fullerton Harbour was now officially known in police records as headquarters of "M" Division.

Comer allowed his man to help the RNWMP again. How the police would have built a house without the assistance of a proper carpenter is not mentioned. Although, in his 1905 report, Moodie suggests that for future RNWMP posts, "all buildings should be framed before shipment, and each piece marked, ready to be nailed together. The framing is the most difficult and longest part of the work to men not skilled in house building."[10] And no one considered designing buildings to suit the Arctic climate. They were constructed the same way as those built in southern Canada.

The *Era*'s carpenter and the policemen erected a building measuring 30 feet 3 inches by 15 feet 3 inches for the barracks. A room was partitioned off at one end for a non-commissioned officer, but they soon found that it was needed for a trade and quartermaster's store instead. Wood floors were installed in the new barracks, as well as in the smaller quarters built the year before. Linoleum flooring was installed in the small building where the Major and Mrs. Moodie and the high-ranking officers would reside. It soon acquired the title of "*Le Chateau*" by the men on the ship.

The interior walls of both buildings were covered with asbestos paper and oiled canvas as a sort of insulation, but Moodie realized that the only way to keep out the damp and frost was to build a double wall with airspace between. No suggestion was made to bank snow for insulation against the houses, as was common practice with ships frozen in the bay. For the majority of the winter, the curtains in the bedroom were frozen to the floor and a thick collar of ice skirted the room where the walls and floor joined.

In return for the carpenter's services, Moodie sent a barrel of apples, a box of oranges, a bunch of bananas, and four bags of new potatoes over to the schooner — a payment of more value than any monetary one. Comer and his men remarked about eating fruit and vegetables that had been grown that very summer. After receiving the food on October 17, Comer went over to the *Arctic* to thank Moodie and was introduced to his wife, Geraldine. He also met Captain J.E. Bernier.

By October 20, the temperature was 22°F and the ice in the bay was strong enough to walk on from one ship to the other. However, they still needed a boat to get to shore. On the twenty-second, Comer weighed anchor and the *Era* was swung into its winter position with its bow headed north. The *Arctic* did the same.

It was Bernier's first winter aboard a ship frozen in. At last he had the opportunity to put into practice all he had read about in explorers' published accounts, and he took note of Comer's practices as well. There was a lot to prepare for winter, and Bernier kept his crew busy. A deck house was constructed. The anchor was raised and put on shore. The men sawed blocks of ice from the nearby frozen lake and stockpiled them for a supply of drinking water. As well, they piled stones on shore to be used for ballast to replace the weight of the coal and supplies used over the winter. The men also put extra clothes in bags and stored them on shore along with cached food.

On Sunday, October 23, Comer spent the evening with Bernier aboard the *Arctic*, and was "quite well pleased with him."[11] Earlier that day, Bernier had sent Comer one of his "Attacking the Pole" calling cards and his pamphlet, *The Canadian Polar Expedition*, which he'd handed out at his lectures. As well, Bernier gave Comer an electric pocket light to help him read the thermometer in the dark. The men were forging a friendship that would prove invaluable to Bernier.

A few days later, Comer tramped over the ice to the steamer, but regretted his visit. Moodie was just as condescending as before. His feelings about Moodie did not prevent Comer from inviting the company of the *Arctic* to a dance on board the schooner that Saturday, though. The Inuit also came out to the boat for the dance.

Comer's crew brewed a keg of spruce beer each week. Spruce beer, often brewed in northern climes, uses the buds or needles of spruce trees as a substitute for unavailable ingredients like hops. Spruce and pine are a source of vitamin C, so a spin-off benefit of this beer was the prevention of scurvy. Comer provides no details about his brew, but after two years out, his spruce needles would no longer be fresh and would certainly not contain any vitamin C. It was a welcome beverage for its other properties, though.

The birthday of King Edward VII, on November 9, was celebrated as a holiday aboard the steamer. The deck was draped with British and Canadian flags for the dance that evening. However, as Comer was aboard for supper, the health of the president of the United States was toasted after the King's.

On Thursday, November 17, Bernier rigged a windmill to power the dynamo for the ship's electric lighting and heating, which would economize the coal consumption.[12] While Bernier was thus occupied, Major and Mrs. Moodie paid a call on Comer at his residence aboard the *Era*. Their call smoothed Comer's ill feelings. Comer sent over two tierces of molasses, about seventy gallons, in exchange for sugar. He had a private stock in his cabin, but the sugar from the steamer was for his crew. They sweetened their daily ration of lime juice with it.

On Sunday, November 20, Bernier regaled the crew with a lecture about the different voyages made in an attempt to attain the North Pole. It was a subject dear to his heart. His usual passion and enthusiasm, plus the use of lantern slides to illustrate, made it an all-round impressive evening.[13]

The *Arctic* began putting out a newspaper called the *Arctic Weekly*, ably edited by Mr. E. Nagle, electrician and third engineer. It was replete with poetry and the various musings of its contributors. Comer was again one of them. By February, the publisher had run out of steam and stories, though, and the weekly newspaper became a bi-weekly.

As December approached, the days shortened and the temperature plunged. The ice was nearly two feet thick. However, there was not as much snow as usual for that time of year and the men were unable to bank any against the ships. The snow was also soft and not the right type to cut into blocks for igloos, which made life onshore miserable for the Inuit still living in tupiks.

By December 4, the temperature plummeted to -20°F. Major and Mrs. Moodie moved from the ship to the "Chateau" onshore. Although Geraldine shared the small house with the other police officers, it was more private than accommodations aboard the *Arctic*. A phone line was connected from the Chateau to the ship. A trail of tall sticks was also driven into the ice between the steamer and the police post to help people find their way between the two in poor weather. This was nicknamed "*l'Avenue des Dames.*" The title says it all. The single men aboard ship were no doubt glad of the female companionship onshore.

In the autumn of 1904, a woman gave birth to a child whose father was one of the *Neptune*'s crew. The mounted police did more than just protect the local women. Between 1903 and 1910, Comer recorded six children fathered by RNWMP officers. In January 1904, Moodie charged Constable Jarvis with what would now be considered sexual relations with a minor. The girl was only fourteen. Jarvis was supposedly sentenced to three months' hard labour. Pity the women he had relations with, though. In 1905, Jarvis was put on light duty because he was suffering from gonorrhea.[14]

Comer himself had a long-standing relationship with a woman who periodically lived with him aboard ship. The *Arctic*'s historian Fabien Vanasse said her name was She-u-shar-kin-neck, but Comer and the whaling crew called her Shoofly after a popular song. She was one of Ben Arblick's two wives. Arblick worked for Comer for a decade, and was amenable to the arrangement. Bernier was a staunch Catholic, and frowned on intimate relations with the local women. However, his men found ways to sneak away to the local encampment.

OVERWINTERING AT FULLERTON

The New Year of 1905 was brought in with a dance aboard the *Arctic*. The thickness of the ice was thirty-three inches, and the temperature was -23°F. Finally enough snow had fallen to bank against the sides of the ship: a task that had been completed the year before by November 20.

Weather permitting, the men enjoyed daily games of football and baseball, or held foot races and other sports on the ice between the ships and the shore to keep their health and spirits up. On January 26, the policemen and crews of both ships participated in a sporting event. The hundred-yard dash between the ships' captains was the most memorable. Captain Comer beat Captain Bernier. It was all fun, but Comer's victory was not surprising to the cheering crowd or to Comer himself, who wrote, "I came in ahead but as he is some six years older and quite fleshy is not to be wondered at."[15] The two had a rematch race a month later but Bernier still came in second.

The two ice-bound neighbours became good friends. They were like-minded old mariners, and Comer found a more liberal soul in Bernier than he had in the men of the *Neptune*. He shared his knowledge of the Inuit, and inspired in Bernier a great respect for the people. His esteem and admiration for the Inuit grew as he met them on his successive voyages. Bernier also learned much about Arctic ice conditions from Comer. Without this valuable information, Bernier would not have been able to navigate the Bering Sea, and certainly not make it to the Pole. Bernier knew how to navigate ice on the St. Lawrence River or the North Atlantic, but Arctic ice, as he discovered, is different.

The first week of February, Moodie sent off a sledding expedition to deliver the mail to Churchill. Since the previous year's mail had failed to reach its destination, Moodie decided to send his own men to get the job done. The expedition consisted of three sleds, six men, and thirty-two dogs. One sled with two Inuit was forced to return when one of the men fell ill. They had gone with the expedition as far as Chesterfield Inlet.

Alec Moodie, Corporal McArthur, Harry Ford, and Tuperloak, an Inuk familiar with the land they would travel, continued the rest of the way to Churchill. In the mailbag were two hundred personal letters, written by the ships' men, and some official reports. At Churchill, the mail was put aboard a Hudson's Bay Company ship, and eventually arrived in Ottawa. The mailbag got wet on the sea voyage and each water-soaked letter had to be dried out before being delivered.[16]

Not much is mentioned of Mrs. Moodie in Comer's journal and nothing in Moodie's official report. However, Geraldine Moodie was one of the more remarkable people who wintered at Fullerton in 1904–05. Not long after arriving at Fullerton, Geraldine turned fifty. She was not a naive young bride. In fact, she was a grandmother and mother of six. Her daughter, the oldest, was twenty-five. Her youngest, sixteen-year-old Charles, remained behind while Geraldine went north.

Self-portrait of Geraldine Moodie, 1895–96. Geraldine accompanied her husband to Hudson Bay in 1904–05, photographing many of the local people there.

Geraldine Moodie, Parks Canada, PC-696-09

Spending a year in the Arctic was adventurous enough for a young man, but the fact that this middle-aged woman went along demonstrates her strength of character. She had grown up in Toronto and Ottawa. After marrying in 1878, the Moodies headed west. After his commission with the NWMP in 1885, the Moodies lived in Calgary, Medicine Hat, and Lethbridge, Alberta, then at posts in Battleford and Maple Creek, Saskatchewan: all rugged frontier towns newly risen from the Prairie grasslands.

Geraldine was a professional photographer. In 1895, she opened a photographic studio in Battleford, Saskatchewan, becoming the first woman on the Prairies to do so.[17] She later opened a studio in Maple Creek, and another in Medicine Hat. Geraldine photographed frontier life: the large celebrations of the First Nations bands, and the people individually; the uniformed mounted police officers, and their wives and families; as well as the settlers opening up Canada's West. Her photographs of the Cree people in traditional dress, both in her studio and at their encampments, depict their way of life and traditions that were disappearing. Geraldine was aware of the historical significance of the photos she took and carefully copyrighted them.

Considering her frontier spirit and interest in other cultures, it is not surprising that Geraldine was keen to spend a year at Fullerton Harbour. Moodie no doubt had told her about the Inuit living there when he returned from his trip aboard the *Neptune*. With her husband as expedition commander, she and her camera easily took passage aboard the *Arctic*. At Fullerton, Geraldine wasted no time setting up a small photographic studio, initially on board the *Arctic* and then at her house on shore.

Photography had gained popularity by 1904 and cameras were more portable, though the plate-glass negatives were still cumbersome and heavy. Bernier was also an avid photographer, and his photos of shipboard life and the local scenery, while those of an amateur, are also of historical significance. Comer was a decent photographer as well. He even borrowed Bernier's camera and plates on condition that Bernier keep half of his plate negatives.[18]

Geraldine's photographs are not the candid shots that Comer or Bernier took. Her subjects are carefully posed, with a canvas backdrop in front of which the women, children, and men stood or sat. As well, she used artificial studio-type lighting. She became acquainted with the local Inuit, forming relationships and friendships with the women that are apparent, since they appear relaxed and comfortable in her photographs. Her photos capture the dignity and essence of each person.

Three Inuit women photographed by Geraldine Moodie in her studio at Fullerton Harbour, 1904–05.

Geraldine Moodie, Library and Archives Canada, C-089352

The women posed for her in their *amautis*, the parkas designed with a hood big enough to carry a baby or young child inside on the mother's back. As well, the women wore their *attigis*, the under-layer skin tops, which they had meticulously decorated with intricate beadwork. Parkas called *qulittaqs*, with the fur side out, were worn over top.[19]

Despite Geraldine's obvious skill and professional experience, she was not recognized as the expedition's official photographer. Frank MacKean held that position, much to the irritation of Major Moodie. When the expedition was being organized, W.J. Topley, the renowned Ottawa photographer, suggested Professor J.A. Lajeunesse, but patronage won out, and the Department of Marine and Fisheries hired Frank Douglas MacKean, a friend of Liberal MP William Ross.

MacKean was paid forty dollars a month to be ship's artist. He did take some striking photographic portraits inside igloos, but his forte was landscape painting. His paintings were displayed in the saloon. MacKean's works of art no longer exist, and his few surviving negatives are part of Captain Bernier's collection. Geraldine's photographs, however, are now held in collections at the RCMP Museum in Regina, the Library and Archives of Canada, and the British Museum, as well as in private collections.[20]

Geraldine Moodie, Library and Archives Canada, PA-147945

Men of the 1904–05 expedition to Hudson Bay sitting on the snow banked up beside the Arctic, on May 12, 1905. Moodie is front and centre; Bernier is seated to the left of Moodie.

One of her photos is of the *Arctic*'s crew taken in May 1905. The men sit in front of the ship as if on bleachers, with three rows of men elevated one behind the other. They are actually sitting on the snow banked around the ship. Moodie is front and centre. Even seated he is a large man. Everyone is dressed in warm caribou and winter gear. Moodie is wearing a policeman's cap. His long moustache droops on either side of his mouth. He looks directly at the camera and his eyes are pale and steely. Bernier sits to Moodie's right, typically looking off to the side, but his attitude conveys the animosity between the two men.

At the beginning of March, the ice in Fullerton Harbour was fifty-eight inches thick. A snowstorm blew up on March 2 that made visibility so poor that two of the *Era*'s sailors had difficulty getting back to the vessel after a dance aboard the *Arctic*. One man found his way to the ship, but missed the gangway and tried to get in through a window. The carpenter got lost entirely and ended up on a nearby island. When he realized he was lost, he dug himself a hole in the snow and stayed there until morning. Though there was a line of sticks to guide the men between the *Arctic* and the police post on shore, for some reason there was no such marked route between the two ships.

Dr. W.S. Flood, like Borden before him, treated Comer's men. Fortunately there were no serious illnesses or deaths aboard either ship that year. However, playing football on the ice had its hazards. In mid-March, the *Era*'s carpenter broke his leg above the ankle while kicking the ball around. Dr. Flood was away on a trip to Walrus Island, so Staff-Sergeant Hayne skillfully set the fracture.

The carpenter was transferred back to the *Era*, where he convalesced in steerage as comfortably as possible. The doctor returned the following day and came over to visit the injured man with Hayne. Even though Flood had returned, Hayne continued to check in daily on the carpenter's broken leg.

Hayne was obviously a caring man with skills beyond that of a routine policeman. The men who came to typify the mounted police in the North were like Hayne, who responded to a variety of extraordinary circumstances that they would not be expected to deal with in the south.

Friday, March 17, St. Patrick's Day, was declared a holiday by the British-born Moodie. It was celebrated with a football match in the afternoon and a dance in the evening, topped off with an issue of rum all round for the men and champagne for the officers. Bernier and the Québécois sailors happily joined in the toasts.

The following day, four Inuit arrived by dogsled from Chesterfield Inlet to trade. One man carried a letter addressed to the commander of ships at Cape Fullerton. It was from Roald Amundsen of the Norwegian magnetic pole expedition. His ship *Gjøa* had sailed through Peel Sound and Franklin Strait, then down James Ross and Rae Straits, and had anchored for the winter on King William Island, northwest of Hudson Bay.

The Norwegians might have been able to navigate the most southerly Northwest Passage that year, as Amundsen noted that ice conditions were favourable. However, Amundsen had gained financial support for his expedition by purporting that its primary purpose was to determine the location of the north magnetic pole. So he and his men halted their progress partway through the Passage to conduct their related studies. They set up camp on southern King William Island at latitude 68°38'N, longitude 96°W, and erected an observatory to study how the magnetic field changed with time and caused the magnetic pole's position to change. He calculated that the north magnetic pole had moved thirty miles north of where James Ross had first located it in 1831.

Amundsen met the Netsilik Inuit who had an encampment close by and learned valuable survival skills from them. He was an eager student and learned how to build igloos, drive dog teams, adhere to the Inuit diet, and wear skin clothing, thus fully adapting to the Arctic environment. He later successfully used these skills on his march to the South Pole.

Artungelar, an Inuit guide, had left the *Gjøa* on November 28, 1904, with a companion and four dogs. In the four months since he had left, Artungelar had run into trouble on his journey. Three of the dogs had died and he had shattered his hand when his gun had accidentally discharged a few days before arriving at Fullerton. However, within a week he was able to begin his return journey to the *Gjøa*, his hand heavily bandaged.

Amundsen's letter reported that all seven men on board were well. He also requested eight dogs. Moodie asked Comer if he could purchase dogs from him. Comer told Moodie to buy five dogs from the Inuit who worked for the schooner and send them from himself (the Canadian government). Comer would send his own gift of five dogs to Amundsen. Moodie "bought" dogs for Amundsen from the local men, giving each of them pieces of clothing: overalls; a pair of pants; a shirt, handkerchief, or cap; or a two-quart tin pail. Comer scornfully reported that the whole lot did not even equal the value of a single dog. The representative of the Canadian government was treating the Inuit as unfairly as the whalers he complained of in his reports.

Artungelar left on March 26 with ten dogs and letters from Moodie, Comer, and Bernier. Bernier included newspaper clippings in his mail, which Amundsen later thanked him for profusely.[21] Artungelar made the return trip in half the time, arriving at King William Island on May 20, 1905.

Amundsen's expedition continued through Simpson Strait, Queen Maud Gulf, Dease Strait, and Coronation Gulf, spending the winter of 1905 near Herschel Island. In 1906, the *Gjøa* made the final stage of the voyage, through the Beaufort Sea and out the Bering Strait to the Pacific Ocean, becoming the first ship ever to complete the fabled Northwest Passage.

Artungelar delivered a request to the ships from Amundsen for sled dogs in March 1905. He returned to Amundsen with dogs, newspaper clippings, and letters from Moodie, Comer, and Bernier. Artungelar shattered his right hand on the way to Fullerton.

Amundsen later claimed the other polar prize of the South Pole, making a dash for it with dog-pulled sleds. He raised the Norwegian flag at the Earth's southern axis on December 14, 1911, beating the British team, led by Robert Scott, by thirty-five days. Scott's men hauled the sledges over the Antarctic's ice and snow themselves. Amazingly, after a century of polar travel, the British still did not incorporate any of the valuable Inuit techniques or modes of transportation, such as dogsleds. If they had, Scott might have had a winning chance at claiming the Pole.

SPRING AND SUMMER 1905

By April, the weather had warmed sufficiently so that part of the snow banked around the vessels was removed. The ice in the bay had reached a thickness of seventy-two inches. On April 10, Alec Moodie and the three other men who had taken the mail to Churchill returned. The trip there took thirty-three days, with a nine-day layover in Churchill, then twenty-three days to return. The men had completed an impressive 1,100-mile journey.

On May 16, Comer had the temporary deck house taken down. He sold the lumber — all two thousand feet of it — to Moodie for fifty dollars. Moodie used the wood to build a storehouse on shore near the other two buildings. The policemen managed to construct the building without the assistance of the *Era*'s carpenter, who was still recuperating from his broken leg.

On June 7, Comer and his men departed on their whale hunt. Before leaving, Comer paid Dr. Flood $78.68 for his medical services. He paid the medical bills in muskox skins. As these were already declared by Comer, they weren't considered illegal and were more prized to Flood than cash. Comer also paid Hayne for attending to the carpenter's broken leg. The 1905 whaling expedition was more successful than the previous season's, as they captured two whales.

By the third week of June, the ice had thinned enough that the men of the *Arctic* were able to cut through it to let an anchor down. This was a precaution. The harbour ice still held the ship in its frozen grip, but when it melted, the ship would move freely with the tide. The anchor kept it positioned in the bay.

Before the French-Canadian celebration of Saint-Jean-Baptiste Day, Bernier approached Moodie about organizing a *grande fête* for it. June 24 would conveniently fall on a Saturday, and so the celebrations would not interrupt a regular work day. But Moodie informed Bernier that the only holiday was the King's birthday, having conveniently forgotten the St. Patrick's Day celebration.

And so, June 24 came and went without any public festivity. This was a real slight, considering that a quarter of the crew was francophone. Not surprisingly, complaints later arose that Moodie had discriminated harshly against the French Canadians. Some crew members even felt he punished them more severely than others. Bernier had little respect for Moodie, and upon his return south did not censor criticism, telling a *Montreal Star* reporter on October 10, "I don't like to speak disparagingly of anyone, but I must say that Major Moody [sic] was an impossible man to work with."

Dominion Day, July 1, was not observed as a holiday either, as the men — crew, police, and Inuit — commenced to break up the ice to enable the *Arctic* to leave the harbour. They worked for three days sawing and cutting, poling pieces away to clear a channel. All was in readiness for the tide on July 5, and at 1:15 p.m. the *Arctic* sailed out of Fullerton Harbour. The three Moodies were aboard ship, as well as several policemen. Sergeant Hayne was left in charge of the reduced detachment.

Tragedy struck the police post that afternoon. Shortly after the *Arctic* left, two of the policemen took a canvas canoe across a nearby lake. Constables Joseph Russell and Andrew Stothert paddled out among ice chunks floating not far from the shore. As they approached one, Russell stood up in the canoe. He lost his balance and fell overboard. In trying to get back into the boat he capsized it and both men ended up thrashing about in the icy water. Neither were strong swimmers and only Stothert made it to shore. Constable Russell's body was recovered three hours later. He was buried on nearby Grub Island with his fellow officers and members of the community in attendance. The twenty-four-year-old Russell had signed on with the police for seventy-five cents a day.[22]

It had been arranged before they left the previous September that the *Arctic* would rendezvous with a relief ship at Erik Cove, Cape Wolstenholme, on July 25, 1905. The supply ship would be carrying coal and supplies for the police post. Moodie, foreseeing they had time before the appointed meeting to go to Churchill to pick up the mail, directed the *Arctic* south along the coastline.

Ice halted its progress, and on July 8 the ship was rendered powerless when both propeller blades were sheared off by the ice. Tackle was rigged and the broken propeller hoisted up. It took the crew over twelve hours to fit a new propeller. Fortunately they had two spares, as the first one they tried didn't fit properly. With ice still prohibiting the way and no open water to the south or the west, Moodie abandoned the idea of getting to Churchill.

The *Arctic* then shaped a course across Hudson Bay. At noon on July 16, they arrived at Cape Wolstenholme, just east of Digges Island at the entrance to Hudson Strait. They dropped anchor in Erik Cove an hour later. When Moodie had visited Comptroller White the summer before, he had suggested locations for more police posts on Hudson Bay and along the Hudson Strait, so he anticipated that the supply ship would also bring up a load of lumber for this purpose. He thought a post near Cape Wolstenholme would be ideal, and scouted for a good location. About forty miles east of Digges Island, they spotted a protected harbour that Comer had told them about, and steamed slowly into its entrance.

Four men in kayaks came over to their anchorage from the nearby island. They reported that the ice had left the harbour on June 1. The harbour wasn't on any chart, so the flag was run up and a big ceremony held on board. The men proudly used their rifles to underscore the fact that they had taken possession.

Fabien Vanasse recorded the July 20 ceremony. The Canadian Navy flag was raised on deck and Commander Moodie, in full uniform, "declared that henceforward the bay would bear the name of Préfontaine Bay in honour of Raymond Préfontaine, Minister of Marine and Fisheries, that the immense cape with the towering and graceful features would henceforth be named Cape Laurier in honour of Sir Wilfrid Laurier, Prime Minister of Canada.... The commander's pronouncement was followed by a hearty round of cheers to honour these illustrious patrons after which the ceremony ended."[23] As well, the island at the entrance to the harbour was officially named White Island after the RNWMP comptroller.

The men were unaware that Low had visited the fiord the previous year and already taken possession. Not only that, but it had been visited by the famous coureur de bois Pierre Radisson in the seventeenth century. After Moodie's ceremony, all boats were used to land supplies for the new post. On the twenty-third, Corporal Nicholson, constables Jarvis and MacMillan, and interpreter Ford went ashore to look after the recently landed stores. The *Arctic* steamed out of the harbour and headed back to Erik Cove to meet the supply ship.

When the supply ship didn't arrive by July 26, Moodie left a note for the ship's captain with the Inuit there, and the *Arctic* headed back to Préfontaine Bay. Five days later, with still no sign of the supply steamer, the *Arctic* returned to Erik Cove. They lay at anchor all the next day, waiting, and on August 2 built a cairn on shore with a letter in it stating where the *Arctic* had gone. As well, they set a buoy just offshore with a notice painted on it to look in the cairn. Then they headed back to Préfontaine Bay, but found no sign of the supply ship.

Moodie decided they should make for Port Burwell to see if there was any news there of the ship. They put a sheet of asbestos lumber on the site where they wanted the police post buildings erected and painted instructions on the sheet so that the supply ship would see it and unload the lumber there. After the fog lifted the afternoon of August 13, the men weighed anchor and the ship headed east to the Labrador Peninsula under steam and canvas.

The *Arctic* arrived at Port Burwell on the fifteenth, and anchored alongside a steamer. It wasn't the supply ship, but the *Scylla*, flagship of Commodore Paget, with Governor Sir William McGregor of Newfoundland on board. They spent a few relaxed days beside the ship. One evening there was a smoking concert and supper aboard the *Scylla*, and Captain Bernier gave his lecture on "How to Reach the North Pole."

On the nineteenth, a Newfoundland Fishery Protection boat arrived at Port Burwell and informed Moodie that the *Neptune* had left Halifax on July 11 with supplies for them. Moodie had intended to cruise Cumberland Sound as the *Neptune* had done the summer before, but with this news he decided to stay in the strait until they met up with the *Neptune*. The morning of August 23, the *Arctic* headed west through the strait to Préfontaine Bay. However, they encountered heavy ice and bergs being driven down from the north side of the strait. Concerned that the ice might force them into Ungava Bay, they turned back to Port Burwell.

The captain and two engineers reported problems with the windlass. The windlass was turned by hand to adjust the length of the anchor cable and used to "weigh" anchor when the ship was being moved. The fires in the boiler were put out to conserve coal while the engineers and carpenters worked on it. The windlass was still shored up with timber when the *Diana* arrived at Port Burwell at the end of August.

Crossman, the *Diana's* chief engineer, who had been engineer in Wakeham's day, also examined the windlass and gave Moodie the same diagnosis as the *Arctic's* crew. As the prognosis was not good, Moodie decided to go to Chateau Bay, Labrador, where he could wire for instructions on how to proceed. Moodie's decision to go to Chateau came only after hearing Crossman's opinion; he had given little weight to Bernier's very experienced one.

The *Arctic* managed to weigh anchor. After encountering a heavy sea through Gray Strait on September 4, it headed south along the Labrador coast for Nachvak. At the Hudson's Bay Company post, interpreter Harry Ford disembarked. The ship met the steamer *Kite* on its way south to the Straits of Belle Isle. Its captain reported that the *Neptune* was loaded and waiting in St. John's harbour for orders to sail.

Joe Lane and his family at Port Burwell, 1905. Lane was the interpreter on Moodie's expedition in 1904–05. James Lane was the interpreter on Gordon's expeditions twenty years earlier, so it is likely that Joe was his son.

They arrived at Chateau Bay at 4:30 p.m. on September 9. Moodie immediately went ashore and wired Deputy Minister Gourdeau about their situation and asked for instructions. They were to await the *Neptune*. On September 16, the *Neptune* finally arrived and supplies were transferred. The *Arctic* had spent close to two months waiting to meet its supply ship.

White's original orders to Moodie had been to explore and patrol, "Hudson Bay, Hudson Strait, Davis Strait, Baffin's Bay, Smith Sound, Kennedy Channel, Lancaster Sound, and other bays and channels on the west coast of Hudson Bay, Davis Strait or Baffin's Bay."[24] In waiting for the supply ship, Moodie had let the opportunity to explore those waters pass. He had left the *Neptune* the summer before to head south, just as Low headed north to explore the Arctic islands. He had neglected his duty to patrol those waters then and now.

On September 23, orders came that the *Arctic* was to carry on to Quebec City for repairs. It was too late in the year to make a northern cruise once the ship was repaired. Their three-year mission had been cut short. The *Arctic* had been diverted from its North Pole purpose to patrol the northern waters, and it hadn't even crossed the Arctic Circle.

BACK TO FULLERTON

Moodie, his son Alec, and the five police officers who had made the journey aboard the *Arctic* all transferred to the *Neptune*, which carried supplies for the Hudson's Bay Company post at Churchill, as well as for Fullerton. Geraldine would continue south with the *Arctic*. The *Neptune* began its cruise up the Labrador coast on September 24. Harry Ford was taken on board again at Nachvak before the ship continued northward to the strait.

The *Neptune* encountered poor weather the entire way. It met heavy ice and large bergs in the strait. The crew did not stop at Préfontaine Bay to set up a new police post, as Moodie had envisioned, but continued straight across Hudson Bay.

The ship entered Hudson Bay on October 4. It made fair progress until it struck heavily on reefs at 4:15 in the morning. By their positioning at latitude 60°20'N, longitude 86°50'W, Captain Bartlett calculated that they were almost in the centre of Hudson Bay. The ship pounded heavily over the reefs. It was dark and snow squalls had come up, so Bartlett held the ship in position until dawn, when he could see what they were up against. At first light, the men saw the seas breaking on reefs all around them. The captain found a narrow channel and took them out of the reefs. The weather worsened with heavy snow squalls and sleet. With the compass now unreliable, the ship kept in sight of the coast. One seaman and two policemen kept watch all night.

The vessel was taking on water at the bow where it was staved in near the keel, and the men were forced to keep the pumps going constantly. Things worsened when the seas and wind got more tempestuous. Waves washed over the forward end of the bridge and curled over the chartroom, crashing onto the main deck where the two whaleboats swinging on the davits were smashed to pieces. The main boom was broken from the goose-neck, which attaches the boom to the mast, allowing it to swing sideways. It was swept overboard with both poop ladders, and harness casks were ripped from their lashings. The men jettisoned the deck load to lighten the ship. They worried that if they didn't, the deck load could break loose and smash the cabin skylight, resulting in the ship flooding.

The rough weather continued, and the ship was viciously battered by the storms. Moodie decided to head to Fullerton Harbour first, as they were closer to it than Churchill. The *Neptune* made Fullerton on October 12. Ford and the five police officers disembarked with the supplies. Moodie wished them a pleasant winter and remained aboard the *Neptune* as it carried on down to Churchill with supplies for the Hudson's Bay Company.

The unloading of supplies at Churchill was made treacherous by yet another vicious sea. Sheets of ice carried away both anchors and ninety fathoms of chain. Captain Bartlett held the ship's position with steam power. The risk of remaining longer in the river was great, and Bartlett decided to leave, though not all the stores had been landed.

The *Neptune* struggled back across a turbulent Hudson Bay. Still taking on water, it managed a perilous journey through heavy seas and reached the entrance to Hudson Strait on October 28. Snow and ice accompanied it through the strait. The ship finally limped into the port at St. John's on November 8. It had been the worst seas Captain Bartlett had ever seen.

* * *

The *Arctic* had a far less dangerous voyage, however. After shoving off from the *Neptune*, it continued its southward journey to the Gulf of St. Lawrence and upriver, anchoring at the King's Wharf, at Quebec, in early October 1905. The *Arctic* had proven its worth in northern Canadian waters and would soon take on this task again.

CHAPTER ELEVEN

A QUESTION OF SUPPLY

When Bernier arrived in Quebec, he found a letter waiting for him. It was from Fridtjof Nansen. Nansen had heard Bernier intended to sail through "Bering Straits and to make a drift across the North Polar Basin." Nansen wrote, "This is the one expedition I have advocated, and which I have been looking forward for, because in my opinion, such an expedition well conducted would give us a material scientif [*sic*] observations compared with which those of other arctic expeditions in the future would be of little importance."[1]

This was all the captain needed to fire up his enthusiasm for a North Pole expedition once more, and he launched another publicity campaign. Bernier began petitioning for funds throughout the winter of 1905, but this time the new governor general, Lord Grey, refused him support. Interest on high was waning for his mission. As well, parliamentarians were concerned with his most recent expedition.

On May 15, 1906, MPs in the House of Commons went over the Committee of Supply's report on "Maintenance and repairs to government steamers and ice-breakers, including steamer '*Arctic*,' $375,000." The Conservative Opposition focused on the supplies loaded on the *Arctic* in 1904. The government had paid $118,582.60 to supply and outfit the ship for a three-year cruise, but the ship had returned in a year. The Opposition wanted to know why and what had happened to all the supplies.

The Conservatives queried every expense on the expedition supply list, from $54.90 paid for ten checkerboards to the $22,000 spent on clothing for the men. The necessity of the amount of items procured was also questioned, such as the purchase of 8,500 cigars and 1,200 gallons of lime juice.

The Opposition voiced three serious accusations: more goods had been purchased than were necessary for the expedition, these goods had been purchased at extravagant prices, and more goods had been purchased than would go aboard the vessel. But most serious was the overarching suggestion that this was "done for the purpose of giving a rake-off to somebody."[2]

The following day, Laurier announced to the House his government's determination to appoint a special committee to investigate the Opposition's charges. A committee was struck, on May 18, made up of six Liberals and four Conservatives. Its mandate was to determine if the public's money had been properly spent or if it had been a "rake-off." Key people were asked to testify and the inquiry commenced on June 6, 1906.

Among those testifying before the commission were Captain Bernier, J.V. Gregory (agent of the Department of Marine and Fisheries in Quebec), Major Moodie, Steward C.H. Duchesney, Purser Wingate Weeks, Dr. Flood, and Lieutenant-Colonel White of the RNWMP, all of whom had something to do with the supplies purchased and loaded on the *Arctic* in 1904.

On June 28, the committee's report was presented to the House of Commons. The debate over it was vigorously sustained without interruption from the opening of the House in the morning, through the evening, until its adjournment at 2:00 a.m.

The Honourable Louis-Philippe Brodeur, minister of the Department of Marine and Fisheries, noted that Conservative leader Robert L. Borden had unfairly launched his attack after Raymond Préfontaine, whose department had overseen the supplying of the steamer, was dead.[3] Brodeur compared the cost of recent Arctic expeditions and showed that the Canadian expedition cost less than either the German or English expeditions, and, furthermore, the most expensive of the Canadian expeditions sent out had been under the Conservative government.

Brodeur explained that there had been four Canadian government expeditions sent to the North before 1904. The cost per man on the *Arctic* for provisions was $1.03, but on the *Neptune*'s trip north in 1886 the cost was $1.30. That expedition was organized by Mr. George Foster, then Conservative minister of Marine and Fisheries.[4]

The next day, "*Arctic* Report Carried by House" appeared in the *Globe*. The June 29 news story reported that the Opposition, in the end, had no case:

> It had been abundantly proved that the boat could hold all the supplies purchased. Captain Bernier was a thoroughly honest man, and he saw the goods go on the *Arctic*. Mr. Macpherson contended that the insinuation that there was a "rake-off" was utterly without foundation, as were the suggestions that some of the goods were taken off the boat again, for the reason that most of the goods were of a character fit only for use in northern regions. With regard to the whiskey and cigars put on board, men who knew the hardships of such a trip would not object to a few comforts being placed aboard.

The *Arctic* had returned after only a year because of damage to equipment, and two thirds of its three-year supplies were still on board. The accounts of what had been purchased and used tallied with the original order and proved that every dollar of goods purchased went on board the vessel. The government was entirely above board in supplying the ship.[5]

THE 1906 *ARCTIC* EXPEDITION

Before the scandal erupted about the *Arctic*'s supplies in the spring of 1906, the Department of Marine and Fisheries began planning another expedition to patrol Arctic waters, and this time they chose Bernier as commander.

Bernier was now fifty-four years old, and a run at the Pole was becoming physically less of an option for him. He reassessed his career and decided that patrolling the Arctic for the government was "work of greater importance than any attempts to reach the Pole so far as Canada was concerned."[6] By the time the House voted to accept the committee's report on the 1904 supplies for the *Arctic*, preparations were already well underway for that summer's expedition to the Arctic Archipelago.

On July 13, 1906, the eve of the *Arctic*'s second northern expedition, Parliament amended the *Fisheries Act*, asserting, "Hudson Bay is a wholly territorial water of Canada and therefore the licence of fifty dollars per annum will be chargeable on all vessels ... British or foreign."[7]

This amendment was a little late in coming. By 1906, the number of vessels in Hudson Bay, Baffin Bay, and Davis Strait had drastically declined, mainly because the whaling industry was vanishing from the Eastern Arctic. The demand for whalebone was reduced, and electricity had begun to replace the need for whale oil used in lamps. But largely, a century of uncontrolled whaling had harvested virtually the entire whale population.[8] The federal government had literally missed the boat in collecting licence fees. Had it begun doing so when Lieutenant Gordon had encouraged it twenty years earlier, it would have enriched the coffers by thousands of dollars. Nonetheless, the Dominion government was now ready to administer the Arctic.

Bernier, at last commander of his own Arctic expedition, was also appointed fishery officer, giving him authority to issue licences and collect fees from whalers and act as justice of the peace. This time, Bernier was not required to patrol Hudson Bay. The RNWMP under Moodie's aegis was being as well monitored as resources allowed. A second post was being established at Churchill that summer. The more northerly waters were not monitored by Canadian authorities, so Bernier was sent there.

His 1906 cruise orders issued by Deputy Minister Gourdeau required him to proceed north, call at Port Burwell, check out the ice conditions in Hudson Strait, then stop in at the whaling stations on Cumberland Inlet. From there the expedition was to enter Lancaster Sound and make for "Pond's Inlet," and attempt to push west as far as possible. "All lands on either hand should be visited. All the old depots should be examined. A look in should be had as far as conditions will permit, at the various sounds and straits leading north and south from Melville Bay and Bank's Strait." His orders clearly stated, "It will be your duty to formally annex all new lands at which you may call, leaving proclamations in cairns at all points of call."[9] Sovereignty was his mission.

Because there was no means of contacting the outside world, expeditions left written records about their activities and details about where they were going inside cairns, erected on islands or along the shoreline and visible from the sea. In these rock-pile mailboxes, generations of explorers left documents outlining their main northern points of call and where they intended to land next. Bernier was ordered to do the same, "so that in case of any accident your movements could be traced by a relief ship which would be sent next season."[10]

The *Arctic* was outfitted and repaired at the government shipyard at Sorel, about 125 miles upriver from Quebec City at the confluence of the St. Lawrence and Richelieu rivers. It was loaded with 530 tons of coal. A small collection of sheep were also stowed on board in pens. Taking fresh meat along was a healthier alternative to barrels of salted beef and pork.

By July 14, the ship was ready to sail. They cast off their moorings and anchored in the St. Lawrence River off Sorel to adjust the ship's compass. When all was ready, they weighed anchor and set sail for Quebec City.

It was 12:45 a.m. the next morning when they anchored at the government wharf at Quebec. Within half an hour, the Norwegian steamer *Elina* crossed their bow. The pilot had miscalculated the ships' positions in the dark and the *Elina* passed too close to the *Arctic*, snapping its bowsprit and jib-boom and breaking the gear attached to it. The mishap delayed the expedition's departure two weeks while the *Arctic* underwent the necessary repairs.

Bernier makes a very matter-of-fact mention of the incident in his report, but one can imagine him cursing and chomping at the bit to get underway.

With a crew of thirty-two men and nine officers, including ship's doctor, historian, customs house officer, and purser, the *Arctic* had a full complement. Though the government chose the men who would be officers of the expedition, Bernier had a say in hiring the crew. These men were experienced, competent matelots. Nearly half were from the Southshore region of the St. Lawrence, men like Bernier who had come from a long line of mariners. Some were even from his hometown of L'Islet-sur-Mer.

Only five of the men had been with Bernier the year before. Chief engineer John Van Koenig had been second engineer. Jules Morin, who had been quartermaster in 1904–05, was now second mate. Fabien Vanasse was again the official expedition historian. Wingate Weeks was hired again as purser. And Paul Levasseur was promoted from waiter to chief steward.

Young Levasseur's father was Major Nazaire Levasseur, the president of the Quebec Geographical Society, who had been Bernier's staunchest supporter in his pursuit for financial backing for a North Pole expedition. Bringing Levasseur's son on his northern expeditions was the least Bernier could do to thank him.

This time, the government hired an official photographer, George Lancefield. One seaman who was often at odds with Lancefield was John Simpson, the twenty-four-year-old assistant customs officer. Simpson kept a diary with details of the year's voyage, including the petty squabbles and minutiae left out of the official report. Simpson as customs clerk was hired by the government, and Bernier took a strong dislike to him. The feeling was mutual, and Simpson's diary details the little run-ins he had with the captain.

On Saturday, July 28, the *Arctic* was once again fit for sea. It was a fine, cloudless day. Deputy Minister Gourdeau was on board for the official send-off. Captain Bernier stood on the bridge. He gave orders, and the crew cast off from the King's Wharf at 11:00 a.m. The following morning, the captain and Dr. Joseph Raoul Pepin made an inspection of the ship "to look into the general sanitary condition of the vessel."[11] All was found in order.

The pilot was landed at Pointe-au-Père at 2:30 p.m. and the ship lay at anchor, awaiting instructions from the Department of Marine and Fisheries. None arrived. At seven the next evening, after receiving mail for the crew, they hove anchor and proceeded to Chateau Bay, Labrador. Here they received final orders on August 3. The men wrote letters home and the mailbag was sent ashore. This was their last opportunity to send correspondence to family and friends for a year.

The next day, with a strong breeze from the southwest, they set fore and aft sails and headed north toward Greenland to avoid the path of the icebergs floating southward. On August 11, they crossed the Arctic Circle — a momentous event for Bernier.

All were awed by the fiords and the enormous icebergs they passed as the ship ran alongside the magnificent Greenland coast. Just beyond

Disko Island, the captain shaped a course north by northwest. The *Arctic* entered an ice-strewn Davis Strait. Bernier remained on deck twenty-four hours while the ship was steered between the treacherous bergs. On the fifteenth, at 74°42′N and 63°W, they were forced by the fog-reduced visibility to make fast to an ice floe. The crew filled the fresh-water tanks from the pool of water on the floe's surface. The ship then proceeded west across Baffin Bay to Lancaster Sound.

After passing Bylot Island, the ship entered Navy Board Inlet and headed east around the south side of Bylot into Eclipse Sound, pursuing a course for Albert Harbour, the location of a known Scottish whaling station. The men dropped anchor on August 19, just offshore from the whaling station. Mr. James Cameron, representative of the post and the Dundee sloop *Albert* (after which Albert Harbour was named), and five Inuit came out to the ship in a whaleboat. Cameron mentioned the excellent salmon fishing not far from there, and a number of the ship's company headed to Salmon River to set their nets.

The next day, the ship anchored at Pond Inlet.[12] The men were welcomed by the Tununirmiut (the North Baffin Inuit) community who came aboard to greet them. Bernier got five or six bear skins and some

Whaling station at Pond Inlet, September 1906. Bernier is to the right of the barrels. Bernier renamed this station "Berniera" after purchasing the property in 1910.

fox pelts. He hired two Inuk there — Miqqusaaq and Miqutui — and paid their wives with provisions for six months while the men took their place on board as guides and interpreters. The Inuit names were difficult for the southerners to pronounce. They were written phonetically as Macashaw and Macatowee. However, their names were further bastardized, as the crew nicknamed them Monkeyshaw and Cameo.

Bernier learned from Cameron that the whaling ships had not yet managed to get through the middle pack ice to Pond Inlet and were still in Lancaster Sound. So he left the notices of the new law with regard to whaling licences for Cameron to give to the whaler captains when they arrived. That evening, they sailed back up Navy Board Inlet to Lancaster Sound. Bernier was now ready to perform his duty, annexing each of the islands they came across.

ANNEXING THE ISLANDS

It was drizzling on August 21 when they arrived off the western coast of Bylot Island. Bernier and fifteen of his men took the steam launch ashore to claim the 5,100-square-mile island. Bernier named the landing spot Canada Point. Here they built a cairn, lugging stones to pile around a larger stone. They raised a flag and Bernier read his proclamation.

> This island, Bylot Island, was graciously given to the Dominion of Canada, by the Imperial Government in the year 1880, and being ordered to take possession of it in the name of Canada, know all men that on this day the Canadian Government Steamer *Arctic*, anchored here, and I planted the Canadian flag and took possession of Bylot Island in the name of Canada. We built a cairn to commemorate and locate this point, which we named Canada Point, after, and in honour of the first steamer belonging to the Canadian Navy.
>
> Being foggy no latitude was obtained. On the chart this point is located in Long. 80.50 west and 73.22 north Latitude.

From here the *Arctic* will proceed onward through Navy Board inlet, to the westward into Admiralty inlet, and from there westward to Port Leopold, where we will leave a record of our future work.

Witnessed thereof under my hand this 21st day of August, 1906 A.D., in the fifth year of the reign of His Most Gracious Majesty King Edward VII.

J.E. Bernier, Commanding Officer, by Royal Commission.[13]

Five men's names were added below Bernier's: Fabien Vanasse, the historiographer; Joseph Raoul Pepin, the doctor; James Duncan, the customs officer; Wingate Weeks, the purser; and George Lancefield, the photographer. The entire landing party posed for a picture around the cairn and flag.

Men claiming Baffin Island at Canada Point, August 21, 1906. Captain Bernier is second from left with the white cap. The man seated to the left of the cairn is chiselling the name "Arctic," after the ship, into the large rock.

George R. Lancefield, Library and Archives Canada, PA-139394

Lancefield's photo shows the men in their dark wool navy-issue coats with lines of brass buttons down the front and caps on their heads. A couple of men sit on the gravelly beach in front of the cairn. One fellow sits directly in front of the big rock with one hand holding a chisel; the other is poised with a hammer, carving the name *Arctic* into the rock. One man has a shovel; another, Fabien Vanasse, rests his hand on the butt of a rifle. The men stand stiffly, unsmiling, befitting the auspicious task they are carrying out.

The men returned to the ship at 3:00 p.m. and carried on with their mission, steaming into Lancaster Sound that night.

Bernier's proclamation was more ostentatious than the ones made by Low in 1904. The proclamation at Canada Point is typical of those that followed, with the name of the island and the direction they were headed being the only differences. For each annexation, there was a ceremony. The crew built a cairn of rocks or cast one out of cement if no rocks were readily available. Then a flag was raised, a proclamation read, the document sealed in a tin or jar and left in the cairn, and a photograph taken for posterity. The island was then officially claimed.

Next, the expedition anchored at Prince Leopold Island. After breakfast, men landed and found the *Gjøa* cache in a bad state. This was the same supply depot left for Amundsen that Low had inspected in 1904. Bernier found the old ship's boiler with Low's proclamation inside it that claimed North Somerset Island and all adjoining islands. Bernier had no need to claim Leopold again, so just had the flag raised on the peak of the shed and a photograph taken of it.

Also in the boiler was a 1904 notice signed by J.D. Moodie that a detachment of mounted police had been sent into Hudson Bay to maintain law and order. The notice went on to say that duty would be charged and collected from ships in waters lying north of Hudson Bay by a Canadian cruiser annually visiting the waters. The note finished ominously, "Any violation of the laws of Canada will be dealt with by an officer of the police accompanying such a cruiser."[14] The *Arctic* was the only Canadian government ship cruising the waters north of Hudson Bay. No policeman was on board.

The men returned to the ship. Fog descended, but the expedition proceeded west to take possession of Prince of Wales Island. It was soon stopped by an immense icefield. Even a lookout on the crow's nest could see no end to the ice ahead. So, the ship headed north to Griffith Island instead, arriving August 24. The men landed, built a cairn, and named the point of land they stood on the "Honourable Richard R. Dobell Point," after the deceased Liberal member for Quebec West who had supported Bernier's work. After the annexation ceremony, the men promptly returned to the steamer. They headed for Sherringham Point on Cornwallis Island, not far north of Griffith. They landed and claimed the second island that day.

Bernier refers to the flag they raised as the Canadian flag, but Canada was without its own flag. The Red Ensign or the British Union Jack were considered the country's flags at the time. Bernier alternated between the two in the choice of banner raised over the cairns.

The last days of August were spent landing on and claiming as many islands as they could. They took possession of Cockburn Point, Bathurst Island, and all the islands adjacent to it. Here, they found three copies of records in sealed metal boxes left by the British explorers M'Clintock, Belcher, and Bradford while searching for Franklin in 1851. Bernier made it a point to collect all the records left by the explorers. These were brought back for the Victoria Memorial Museum in Ottawa.

After claiming Byam Martin Island, they charted a course west to Melville Island. They landed on a tip of land, naming it Arctic Point after their ship. They left a record taking possession of Melville, Eglinton, and Prince Patrick Islands, and all adjoining islands thereof, although no one set foot on the latter two.

They were now close to the entrance to the most northern Northwest Passage route. Bernier noted that the ice was not much heavier than it had been when they first entered Lancaster Sound. They could see openings in the ice all along the coast of the island, giving the impression that passage through it was possible. However, Bernier wrote, "As we had to return to issue licenses to the whalers, we decided to go to Pond's Bay."[15]

They headed east with sails unfurled, taking advantage of the wind. They kept to the south side of Lancaster Sound so as to annex the islands they passed. They landed on a southern point of Lowther Island in Barrow Straits and named it Gourdeau Point in honour of the deputy minister of Marine and Fisheries.

They reached Russell Island at 9:00 p.m. on August 30. The sun didn't set in this high latitude that time of year, and the men carried out their task of claiming the island as if it was the middle of the afternoon. Ice thwarted their efforts to make Prince of Wales Island. They decided to lay up in Resolute Bay, Cornwallis Island, but ice and fog drifted into the bay and they were obliged to weigh anchor. The next morning they shaped a course for Erebus Bay across the Wellington Channel.

They encountered more drifting ice en route, but dropped anchor off Beechey Island at two o'clock in the morning of September 2. After Sunday service, the men went ashore. It didn't take long to explore the small island. They found among the usual historic relics the proclamation that A.P. Low had left two summers before.

They located the large marble slab inscribed as a tribute to Franklin and his men from the citizens of the United States. Low had suggested that another expedition visiting the area raise the slab and affix it as originally intended. Bernier was charged with carrying out the job. He noted, "We started the work on September 3. Monday we landed three-fourths of the crew with six barrels of cement for this work. We set the tablet in this cement in an upright position."[16]

John Simpson was given the task of painting the grave markers of the men buried in the frozen ground beneath the shale. He carefully painted each man's name on his marker. The other crew members set about gathering as many relics as they could, and discovered the notices left in the cairn built by the HMS *North Star* in 1853. Bernier left his own report of the *Arctic*'s movements in the same cairn. The men also moved the yacht *Mary* to higher ground, so it would not be "destroyed by the sea" and still be of service in the event of a shipwreck in the area. Fog descended on the island as they worked, and the men were glad to get back to the ship to change into warm dry clothes and enjoy a hearty supper.

On Tuesday, September 4, at 4:00 a.m., they left Erebus Bay, sailing east, then across Lancaster Sound towards Admiralty Inlet, on the northwest corner of Baffin Island. That afternoon, they cruised carefully into the inlet to avoid the dangerous reefs. Magnificent reddish cliffs rose six hundred feet on either side; a marked difference from the flat islands they had recently landed on. The *Arctic* sailed south through the inlet to Adams Sound. Second officer Jules Morin was put in charge of a small party that was sent into Arctic Bay to see if there were any Inuit living there.

Customs officer James Duncan and his assistant Simpson organized supplies for a depot to be left at the head of the inlet. However, when word came from the scouting party that no Inuit were living at Arctic Bay, Bernier decided not to set up a depot, but return to winter at Pond Inlet, where a settlement already existed.

As they steamed north out of Admiralty Inlet, Bernier named all points of land, or small bodies of water, they spotted that were not already noted on the charts. The majority he named after his patrons: Berlinguet Bay and Baillargee Inlet after the president and past president of the Quebec Geographical Society; Vanasse Bay after the historiographer; Moffet Inlet after the editor of the Ottawa newspaper *Le Temps*; Brodeur Peninsula after the minister of Marine and Fisheries; and Levasseur Inlet after his greatest supporter. Some of these places still carry these names.

Close to the end of the inlet they saw a polar bear swimming near the ship. Six shots were fired before it was killed, then hauled aboard. The bear was strung up by the neck to the rigging. With his paws pulled wide and mouth hanging open, it looked every bit the ferocious beast it was. A photograph was taken for posterity. (This photo was later cropped and the bear pasted on the Christmas dinner menu.) It was the first polar bear killed by members of the expedition, and was considered one of the more exciting events of the cruise.

A WINTER AT POND INLET

Saturday, September 8, was a fine, calm, clear day and the *Arctic* shaped a course eastward to Pond Inlet, entering Navy Board Inlet that night.

Regular Sunday church service was held the next morning at 10:00 a.m. By noon, they had spotted the highlands of Albert Harbour at the eastern end of the sound. Albert Harbour was a favourite spot for whalers to overwinter, as it was protected. Bernier also saw it as an ideal place to overwinter. They dropped anchor in the bay at 5:30 p.m. near the Igarjuak whaling station on the southern shore, with its stunning backdrop of Mount Herodier and a deep valley. Igarjuak is named "the big cooking place" by the Inuit because the shape of the land looks like a fireplace.

Cameron, from the whaling and trading station, immediately came out to the ship and dined with the captain and his officers. The whaling fleet, he reported, was due to arrive any day. One ship had been in but had gone out. The rest were apparently caught in the ice. Bernier decided to prepare their winter quarters while they awaited the whaling ships' arrival.

The tanks were filled with fresh water from a brook near their anchorage. The men began to build a cover over the main deck with the lumber they had brought north for this purpose. The steam engine would not be used for propelling the boat that winter and the funnel's space was required for more room on deck, so the ship's funnel was dismantled. Stoves would be brought up on deck at the end of November to keep this covered area warm for the men during the winter months.

While some of the men were roofing over the deck, others worked in the hold making room to stow the sails. Twenty-eight tons of coal was moved from the after hold to the bunkers, and the chief officer and his men took on stone for ballast. The cook slaughtered the last of the sheep brought from Quebec and hung it in the rigging to keep it out of the way of the dogs that Bernier had purchased for sledging trips that winter.

Bernier, Duncan, and Lancefield went ashore and met Captain James Mutch, who lived at the station with Cameron. Mutch had built the shore station there for the Robert Kinnes & Sons Ltd. trading company of Scotland in 1903. Bernier collected fees from Mutch, issued a licence, and conducted customs and fisheries business with him. Mutch, who had been whaling in the Eastern Arctic for twenty years, was fluent in Inuktitut. He often acted as translator for Bernier that winter of 1906–07.

On Sunday, September 30, the Scottish whaling steamer *Eclipse* came into the harbour. The *Eclipse* was owned by the Dundee company that Mutch represented. Mutch had already paid the fifty-dollar fee for it on behalf of the company. Cameron would return to Scotland with the *Eclipse*, while Mutch would stay to man the station.

On Sunday, October 1, Bernier and customs officer Duncan went aboard the *Eclipse* and met Captain Milne to discuss customs and fisheries. Milne offered to send mail from Bernier's men back to Canada once he arrived in Scotland. The men all wrote letters home, and the bag of mail was taken on board the Scottish steamer that night. It was a roundabout way to deliver letters, but they would arrive months before the writer. When the *Eclipse* sailed for Scotland on October 3, 1906, light ice was floating in the harbour.

On November 9, 1906, the King's birthday, the crew fired a royal salute on shore and took "possession of Baffin Land and all adjacent islands and dependencies adjacent to it, in the name of the Dominion of Canada."[17] Basically, it was a repeat of Wakeham's 1897 ceremony, but at a more northerly locale. The photograph of forty unsmiling sailors and Inuit looks anything but celebratory. The sailors, still wearing melton coats and caps, not warmer skin parkas, sit on a snowy hump. A flagstaff with a limp flag sticks up at the back of this white mound. Captain Bernier stands at the back, closest to the flag, wearing his white captain's cap and an open overcoat.

At the beginning of December, meal hours changed. Breakfast was served at 9:30 a.m., dinner at 3:00 p.m., and a night lunch at 7:30 p.m. All were getting used to shorter days and a sedentary life.

George R. Lancefield, Library and Archives Canada, PA-165672

Bernier, his crew, and a group of Inuit claiming Baffin Island for Canada at Pond Inlet, November 9, 1906. Captain Bernier is at the centre back, looking toward the flag pole.

Bernier was not forgotten down south, though. An advertisement for Simpson's department store in the *Toronto Daily Star* on December 6, 1906, announced,

Santa Claus Meets Capt. Bernier

Whalebone Island, Polar Canada, December 5th.

"Had dinner with Captain Bernier aboard the Gaus. Invited him to visit me at the North Pole next year. The captain busy painting the islands of the Arctic Circle Canadian red. Sending mail and parcels south with me."

Life aboard a ship frozen in ice was tough and often boring. Men did not have the same tasks that would have kept them occupied at sea, so Bernier did his best to keep them active. He distributed traps so they could go out on the land and trap foxes and rabbits. This gave the men something to do, and encouraged exercise in the fresh air. However, as in any situation where people live in close quarters for long periods of time, personalities clashed and petty squabbles erupted.

On December 18, the crew was put to work getting the ship ready for Christmas. The ship was cleaned and flags hung for the occasion. Simpson noted the disgruntled employees: "Crew cleaning up. Captain had them washing decks; men all angry as they did not consider it was fair to ask them to do so at 26 below zero."[18]

There was an Inuit community nearby, and Bernier made a point to include them in invitations when there were celebrations aboard the *Arctic*. Christmas was a big event and the locals were invited to dine and dance. Bernier was fun-loving, and the Inuit affectionately called him Kapitaikallak — the stout little captain.

Christmas was celebrated in style; 160 Inuit came aboard and enjoyed the dancing until 11:00 p.m. Some of the crew enjoyed a few too many libations, as Simpson notes in his diary: "The 2nd and 3rd engineers both drunk, 2nd very. The 2nd mate, Chasse, Bob Lessard and Paul Mercier also drunk, but no one did anything out of the way."[19]

Simpson's diary contains many accounts of the crew's less than exemplary behaviour, though. He and the majority of the men found companionship with the local women. No pregnancies or cases of venereal disease were documented, but likely the same scenarios existed at Pond Inlet as at Fullerton Harbour, and children were born after the men left town on the ship.

On January 3, Simpson wrote, "Just heard that the Captain was not going to allow any more women on board as some abused the privilege."[20] This is noted after Lancefield was caught with a woman in his room. The men found ways, though, to visit the women in their own tupiks or igloos.

Bernier had posted a notice on November 23, 1906: "Seeing that the ice is now getting dangerous, nobody is allowed to leave the ship without permission and without a companion. Every one must be on board the ship at 8 p.m. sharp, and report to the watchman."[21] However, in early 1907, an incident occurred that was a harsh reminder of how essential the rule was about not leaving the ship alone.

On January 14, able seaman James Ryan had been granted permission to walk on the ice around the ship for exercise that morning. But when roll call was taken at four o'clock that afternoon, Ryan was not on board. It was dark at this point, and two men were dispatched with lanterns to the village on shore. They reported back that Ryan had been to the village alone but had left for the ship at 3:30. He had invariably lost his way on the ice. Bernier ordered search parties to fan out in all directions.

At 11:00 p.m., Ryan was found by Joseph Goulet and Napoléon Chassé about three miles northeast of the ship. He had been wandering on the ice for over seven hours. He was literally half frozen. His hands, ears, nose, and cheeks were severely frostbitten. One of his eyes was even frozen and "he was nearly blind." Dr. Pepin worked hard to save the young man's eyesight. His recovery took three months.[22]

The only tragedy to cloud an otherwise relatively uneventful winter was the death of Frederick Brockenhauser. The ship's oiler suffered a heart attack before 7:00 a.m. on February 11, 1907.[23] His body was laid out in the north mess room all day. After service, he was put in his coffin on deck and left all night. The funeral service at ten o'clock the next morning was as close to a southern one as possible. Bernier says in his report that Brockenhauser "was buried with all the services of burial possible, and due honour."[24] It was attended by all expedition members and a large number of Inuit. His grave was covered with stones and a large cross with an epitaph erected on it. A pall of depression settled over the entire company.

On March 31, Easter Monday, Bernier had a competition to guess the width of Pond Inlet from the Baffin shore to Bylot Island. Joseph Lessard, the quartermaster, had the closest guess with 35,324 feet. The actual distance measured was 35,684 feet. The winner of the competition received a box of cigars.

The ice in the harbour was now sixty inches thick. Bernier marvelled that the ice was so smooth; he thought an automobile could drive for hundreds of miles on it.

Several sledging expeditions were carried out by different company members in April and May. These expeditions were a change from the monotony of life aboard ship. At the beginning of June, Duncan and Simpson headed to Button Point on Bylot Island to intercept the whaling fleet. Captain Mutch had two whaleboats dragged over the ice to the island by dog team so that he'd be ready to hunt from the floe edge.

Duncan and Simpson collected customs duties and fees for the fifty-dollar whaling licences from whalers *Diana*, *Eclipse*, *Balaena*, and *Morning*. They also received a bag of mail for the *Arctic* men. Their mail had come from southern Canada via Dundee, Scotland — the opposite route to the mail they'd sent home with the *Eclipse* in September.

By June 18, the air was warmer and the deck house was dismantled. On June 27, the *Arctic* finally floated free of its icy bonds. The insulating snow banked around the ship had melted a month before. Though the ice was softening around the ship, it was still fifty-eight inches thick in the bay.

CONTINUING TO ANNEX THE ISLANDS

By the third week of July, the temperature had warmed so much that the harbour ice dissolved into broken, slushy pans. Bernier went up a hill to look at the ice floe. The *Arctic* was still anchored in the midst of ice. Though all was in readiness to break clear of it, it would be several more days before any attempt would be successful.

On July 27, one year after leaving Quebec, the engineers were given orders to get up steam. They left Albert Harbour at 11:30 a.m. but had only made ten miles in four hours. Heavy ice forced them to lay to. Nonetheless, after being locked in ice for ten months, the entire ship's company was glad to be moving again.

On the thirty-first, the ice opened up and the ship headed northwest for Jones Sound. The next day they were making good headway, but with the heavy swell, quite a few men were seasick. They had lost their sea legs over the winter in their sedentary accommodations, and it would take some time before they became accustomed to the roll and movement of the ship again.

As they neared Jones Sound, the view from the crow's nest was of "an immense mantle" of year-old ice covering the sound. Bernier decided to turn back and head east to Coburg Island. On August 2, Captain Bernier, Chief Officer Hayes, Second Officer Morin, and photographer Lancefield landed on Coburg Island, planted the flag, and claimed it. Then they headed south, back into Lancaster Sound to Prince Leopold Island, where they retrieved some of the supplies cached there the summer before.

From there they could see that Barrow Strait to their west was choked with ice and there was no passage in that direction. Bernier decided to head north again and shaped a course for North Devon Island. On the morning of Monday, August 12, they entered Jones Sound. What a difference ten days had made. The sound was free of ice toward Cone Island off the south-eastern end of Ellesmere Island.

They anchored off Cone Island, and at 6:00 a.m., Bernier sent Chief Officer Hayes over to the island to raise the flag and leave a proclamation of possession. By 8:00 a.m., Hayes was back on board the *Arctic* with a couple of documents in hand that had been left by Otto Sverdrup.

As Jones Sound was still solidly frozen to the west, they proceeded eastward along the Ellesmere coast, which Bernier referred to as North Lincoln Land. That afternoon they landed at a point on southeast Ellesmere, at latitude 76°19'N, longitude 81°24'W, which Bernier christened King Edward VII Point. Bernier sent two officers ashore. The men built a cairn of stones, planted the flag, and left a container with a proclamation in it. The proclamation, signed by Bernier, Hayes, Morin, and Weeks, gave notice that they had taken possession of "North Lincoln, Grinnell Land,

Ellesmere Land, Arthur Land, Heiberg Land, Ammund Ringnes Land, Ellef Ringnes Land, King Christian Land, formerly named Finlay Land; North Cornwall, Graham Land, Buckingham Island, Table Island, and all adjacent islands as forming part of the Dominion of Canada."[25]

It was a bold proclamation. The only one of these islands that any of their party actually landed on was North Lincoln, Ellesmere Island, and only two men had done so. Bernier was claiming all the islands that Sverdrup and his men had so painstakingly explored and mapped, without ever setting foot on any of them.

When Sverdrup got wind of this in the fall of 1907, he wrote to the Norwegian Foreign Office demanding to know how the Sverdrup Islands would be saved for Norway. He was informed that nothing could be done until the Canadian government formally challenged the claim that Sverdrup had published in the last paragraph of his book *New Land*.[26] The Canadian government made no open challenge to Sverdrup's claim.

After the proclamation at North Lincoln, rum was issued all round in celebration. The expedition then headed southeast. Though leads were opening up in the ice, the crew encountered numerous snow squalls. The ice on the sea was melting even as the air was starting to cool. They made Cumberland Sound on August 26, but it was choked with ice.

They got within four miles of Kekerten Island and spent the night frozen in the ice. On August 28, they steamed into the harbour at Kekerten, and Hayes was sent over to check in with the station agent, Mr. Milne, to inquire into the state of fishing and other local conditions. Hayes soon returned to the ship with the news that Milne had died on August 13, and his death seemed suspicious. Bernier decided to hold an inquiry into the deaths of both Milne and Davidson, the agent before him who had also died suddenly two years previous.

The following morning, two boats were lowered with the doctor and several officers to hold inquests into the station agents' deaths. The men examined the buildings and opened Milne's coffin. They returned aboard at 3:00 p.m. Bernier notes in his report that "the results were both satisfactory, as we have discovered the cause of death in both cases."[27] The agents had committed suicide.

The *Arctic* called in at Blacklead Island but found the station agent had left the year before. The Inuit they met there had no information about the fisheries or other conditions either. The expedition departed for Port Burwell, arriving on September 2. The men happily spent a month on dry land with the Moravian missionaries and the Inuit community.

Bernier felt that Port Burwell was an ideal spot for a proper harbour and government customs house. He and his men began to do the groundwork for such a site, taking soundings and inspecting and charting the bay. They marked a location for a future lighthouse with a stone cairn. They cleared stones from a bar in the bay that was interfering with navigation and used the stones for ballast aboard ship. They also marked spots for day beacons on the outer and inner harbours.

On Wednesday, October 2, with the work there completed, Bernier gave the order to raise steam. That afternoon the *Arctic* steamed into the outer harbour, but was obliged to drop both anchors because of the strong southerly wind. Snow was falling and the hills were covered in a thin coat of cold white. Three days later, they hove anchor and headed into Hudson Strait.

The Arctic *at Port Burwell, 1907.*

George R. Lancefield, Library and Archives Canada, PA-096482

It was blowing a gale, and almost the entire company was seasick. They were making a course for Resolution Island, on the north side of the strait, to take soundings, but the miserable weather and the fact that only seventy-five tons of coal remained on board forced a change of plans. It was time to steer a course southward down the Labrador coast.

On Saturday, October 12, the *Arctic* came alongside a Newfoundland whaler, *Port Saunders*, which was tied fast to a whale. Bernier noted that it was the fifth whale that the ship had taken in a week, with each whale yielding between seven and eight hundred dollars.[28]

Bernier and three others boarded the ship. They returned to the *Arctic* with a newspaper telling of the Quebec Bridge disaster. A lot had transpired in the fifteen months they'd been gone. The news that meant the most to Bernier, though, was that Roald Amundsen and his men aboard the *Gjøa* had made the Northwest Passage. The Pole was still unconquered.

On October 17, they made Pointe-au-Père, where they received newspapers and took the pilot aboard for their journey up the St. Lawrence River. At 7:00 a.m. on October 19, the ship anchored one and a half lengths of cable from the King's Wharf below Quebec City. The officers and crew were paid the balance of their wages and discharged. Bernier visited his wife in Lévis, and then headed to Ottawa to make his report to the government.

CHAPTER TWELVE

CRUISE OF THE *ARCTIC*, 1908–09

On February 20, 1907, while Bernier was stuck in the ice in Pond Inlet, one of his supporters, Senator Pascal Poirier, put forth a motion: "That it be resolved that the Senate is of the opinion that the time has come for Canada to make a formal declaration of possession of the lands and islands situated in the north of the Dominion, and extending to the north pole."[1]

Poirier stated that all the islands and waters within the longitudinal lines from 141 to 60 degrees west up to the Pole were Canadian territory and no foreigner had a right to hoist a flag on any of it.[2] Claiming the region within this longitudinal pie-shape emanating from the Pole, as described by Poirier, was a logical way to denote Canada's boundaries. It was known as the sector theory. However, it did not receive support in the Senate, and never reached the House of Commons.

Although the Canadian government did not approve the sector theory, the government of Tsarist Russia did. In 1917, it asserted that all islands (including those not yet discovered) between its mainland and the North Pole were claimed by Russia.[3] However, despite the lack of support for Poirier's sector theory, maps of Canada began showing its eastern and western borders following the longitudinal lines in a large triangle that intersected at the North Pole.

Bernier wholeheartedly agreed with Poirier that Canada should publicly assert its title to the Arctic Archipelago. But Laurier favoured a quiet establishment of government presence before making any proclamations.

Minister of the Interior Sifton also didn't want to arouse suspicions about government actions in the North.[4]

Despite this, the public was keenly aware of Bernier's northern expeditions. On Friday, May 22, 1908, the *Toronto Daily Star* ran a little blurb about his upcoming summer expedition. "Captain Bernier will continue his good work of planting the British flag on the islands of the Arctic Circle. It seems a pity that a dye works couldn't be started on the shores of Hudson Bay, which, draining into all those northern seas, would gradually give them the right, red color."

The public stood proudly behind him.

Bernier also had a knack for self-promotion. A full front page story, "Another Northern Cruise for Captain Bernier," ran in the *Quebec Daily Telegraph* on June 13, 1908, saying Bernier "expected to annex the balance of land in the far north" on his expedition that summer.

Quebec City was wreathed in banners and flags in July 1908 when Bernier and his crew were preparing to depart. It was celebrating its three-hundredth anniversary, commemorating Samuel de Champlain's historic landing on its shores and establishing a settlement there. Foreign ships from around the world arrived in port for the celebrations. The Prince of Wales (later King George V) was there aboard the HMS *Indomitable*.

The *Arctic* lay at the King's Wharf, ready for departure at the end of July. Two British naval officers came aboard the *Arctic* and informed Bernier that His Royal Highness wished an audience with him. Bernier, Canada's illustrious explorer, was escorted aboard the *Indomitable*, where he told the prince his plans to take possession of the islands of the Arctic Archipelago that had been discovered by British explorers.[5]

Newspaper reports claimed thousands of people crowded the wharves to see the *Arctic* off. The expedition consisted of forty-three men. Thirty-one men made up the crew, with seven officers. Eight of the men had been on the 1906–07 voyage, including Second Mate O.J. Morin, Chief Engineer John Van Koenig, and Fabien Vanasse, who returned as historiographer. The Honourable Louis-Philippe Brodeur, minister of Marine and Fisheries, and Rear-Admiral Charles Edmund Kingsmill, director of the department's Marine Service, were on board to wish the members of the expedition well. Each gave a speech, expressing his confidence in the men and their mission, and wished them all a prosperous and successful cruise.

The *Arctic* left to incredible fanfare at 1:30 p.m. on July 28. It saluted as it steamed between the British, American, and French ships. All the vessels in sight returned the salute as it passed between them down the length of the harbour. It was a moving moment for the men on the *Arctic*.

"The magnificent band of the H.M.S. *Indomitable*, the Prince's flagship, played 'Auld Lang Syne,' and we were thrilled by the kindly spirit suggested in selection of music by the men who were serving under the same flag, which our little ship was starting out to again plant upon the heights of the far northern lands. The band of each ship broke into music as we came abreast, and we spontaneously joined in a chorus of cheers," wrote Bernier in his autobiography.[6]

They had fair weather for their trip down the St. Lawrence. Two days later they landed the pilot at Pointe-au-Père and picked up a bag of mail and parcels that families and friends had sent the expedition members. The ship entered the Gulf of St. Lawrence on August 1, and steamed up the Labrador coast. Bernier handed out heavy clothing to the men and noted that most of the ones new to Arctic travel were not properly dressed for extreme cold weather.

They sighted Greenland, "clothed with snow and ice and the valleys filled with glaciers."[7] The ship wound its way up the breathtaking coast. On August 19, at 5:30 p.m., the crew dropped anchor in the harbour at Etah on high northwest Greenland, which had become the base camp for American North Pole expeditions. Both Dr. Frederick Cook and Lieutenant Robert Peary were staging attempts at the Pole from this point. When the *Arctic* arrived, the *Erik*, under the command of Captain Sam Bartlett, was anchored in the harbour. Peary had just left the day before, aboard the *Roosevelt*, for more northerly waters. Cook had got a year's head start, beginning his North Pole trek with two Inuit companions in 1907.

Bernier noted that Peary had a large quantity of stores, including coal, on the shore. Peary had left his bo's'n John Murphy and cabin boy Billy Pritchard to guard his cache for the winter. Bernier's men landed provisions for Cook and left them under the care of New York multi-millionaire Harry Payne Whitney. The thirty-four-year-old was at Etah with two other sportsmen, hunting for Arctic big game trophies.

Bernier noted in his report that "an effort was made to procure two teams of dogs, but the men in charge of Commander Peary's stores would not sell the dogs on any account."[8] An article later appeared in the *Toronto Daily Star* titled, "Bernier Gave Aid to Cook but Peary's Men Were Ugly." It said, "Bernier left supplies sent by Mrs. Cook at Etah, Greenland, in care of Harry Whitney, August 20, 1908. Bernier asked for Eskimos and dogs and was refused by Murphy."

While at Etah, captains Bernier and Bartlett visited each other aboard their respective ships. Bartlett offered to take the *Arctic*'s mailbag and promised to telegraph their progress when he reached Newfoundland. The expedition members all dashed off letters to families and friends, and appreciated the opportunity to send word home.

INTO CANADIAN ARCTIC WATERS

On the twentieth, the *Arctic* left Etah and sailed west across Baffin Bay. The next day, it headed south around Devon Island and entered Lancaster Sound, destined for Beechey Island. It dropped anchor there on August 24, "in 13 fathoms of water abreast of Sir John Franklin's memorial tablet."[9] At 10:00 a.m. the crew landed four boatloads of supplies and built a cache to house them. They also included a record of their next destination. They made magnetic observations and gathered geological specimens. It was not the sightseeing stopover it was two summers before. By 4:00 p.m. they were ready to leave Erebus Bay. They hove anchor and proceeded to Griffith Island, but their progress was soon stopped by pack ice.

The next day the wind changed direction, driving the ice into Lancaster Sound. They could then sail westward. Bernier was on a mission. His task was to claim all the islands of the Arctic that he had not yet claimed.

On the evening of August 26, they sighted Melville Island, the enormous island of over sixteen thousand square miles. The next morning they were running alongside Melville Island and passed Cape Bounty, so named because of the £5,000 reward offered to the commander who took his ship to the longitude of 110°W, the farthest point west reached by a British expedition. William Edward Parry received this honour in 1820, and collected the reward.[10]

The *Arctic* passed Winter Harbour, where Parry's two ships, *Hecla* and *Griper*, had spent the winter of 1819–20. At Cape Providence, the *Arctic* was now at the entrance to the sixty-mile-wide M'Clure Strait, which connects Viscount Melville Sound to the Beaufort Sea. It is the most northerly of the Northwest Passage routes.

Scouting the strait from the crow's nest, the lookouts reported it to be free of ice to the west as far as they could see. But to the south heavy Arctic ice was visible. Bernier's official report includes a photograph of M'Clure Strait taken from the crow's nest that shows open water yawning endlessly before them.

Had his orders been to traverse the Northwest Passage, Bernier was confident he could have done it, but as he did not have official permission, he turned back.[11] The expedition stopped to set up a rough cache on Cape Providence on the southwestern arm of Melville Island. The cache would offer supplies for emergencies or in the event they undertook any overland explorations. Then they turned back to settle into a harbour for the winter.

Bernier mentioned that he had kept his eye open for an ideal wintering spot as they travelled along the coast. However, being an Arctic buff, there could be no other place for him to spend the winter frozen in than Parry's old quarters. It was no coincidence that when they turned back it was to head for Winter Harbour.

At seven o'clock on the morning of August 28, the *Arctic* anchored outside the entrance to the harbour. Two boats were lowered to take soundings before the ship entered. The *Arctic* safely steamed into an ice-free Winter Harbour and anchored in seven fathoms of water. When Parry had arrived almost a century before, the bay was already frozen over and his men had to cut a channel in the ice for two miles in order for the ships to advance into it. The *Arctic*'s anchorage was 74°47'N latitude and 110°48'W longitude. No one had been that far northwest in over fifty years.

From where the *Arctic* was anchored, the men could see Parry's Rock on a rocky ridge above the shore. Parry's Rock is a sandstone block the size of a house. It stands alone, shoved up on a rise of rugged, barren land by a receding ice shelf ten thousand years ago. The rock overlooks the secluded bay and broad gravel beach. There is nothing within a mile radius that rivals it in size and it can be seen from any point in the bay.[12] It is the sandstone sentinel of Winter Harbour.

Bernier "immediately visited the historical Parry rock for records," noting the inscription of the names of Parry's ships, *Hecla* and *Griper*, were as readable as the day they were carved into the side of the enormous boulder by the ships' physician eighty-nine years previous.[13] Leopold M'Clintock also had the name of his ship, *Intrepid*, engraved in the sandstone in 1852.[14]

The following day, the lifeboats were stowed safely onshore so if a disaster befell the ship during the winter, the men would have a means of leaving the harbour when the ice did.

On August 30, the gasoline-powered motor launch headed off to Dealy Island, east of Winter Harbour, where Captain Henry Kellett had left a large depot in 1854 during his Franklin search. Bernier found Kellett's roofless stone-walled house there. Inside were thick oak barrels of supplies and provisions with enough food for sixty-six men to last 266 days. Bernier's men took the dimensions of the house to repair the roof later.

Kellett had also built a cairn on a high point on the island, and Bernier found his records in it. The men returned to the *Arctic* with the records, two of M'Clintock's sledges, and a couple of muskets, which no longer worked. Bernier replaced the guns with Ross rifles and one thousand rounds of ammunition.

On September 1, the men began covering over the ship's deck from stem to stern with inch-and-a-half tongue-and-grooved first-class lumber. It was enough to cut the wind and offer a somewhat warmer shelter. In the deep of winter, when the outside air temperature was forty below zero, the temperature on deck was only twenty-five below, with no wind. The crew also piled stones for ballast on the shore to replace the consumed coal and stores.

A hunting party was dispatched to a herd of muskoxen spotted to the west. Sixteen animals were killed. Two were skinned and brought back to the boat that day. The rest were brought on board over the next few days. The job of moving the animals to the ship was extraordinarily difficult because the men had to tromp through thick, muddy, softened permafrost, dragging the beasts from where they were killed inland to the shore. The carcasses were then put onto the small boats and rowed out to the ship.

Muskox proved to be the main source of meat that winter. Bernier was surprised at the beasts' lack of fear of the hunters. The animals continued grazing while the men easily got within shooting range. All the wildlife Bernier's men encountered were so unfamiliar with humans that they weren't timid or wary. Geologist J.G. MacMillan succeeded in killing three eider ducks with a hammer in his hand.

The muskoxen were hung in the rigging, and the two pigs that had made the journey north on the ship from Quebec were also slaughtered. The temperature was below zero and the carcasses kept well in this natural refrigerator. The rule was that fresh meat would be served twice a week. The other days they would eat salt meat.

As the British explorers who had visited Melville Island had included the locations of their cairns in their published reports, Bernier had a good idea where to find them. He recovered documents left by Commander Parry in 1820, by M'Clintock in 1852–54, and by Kellett in 1854.

The meteorologist, Walter Erastus Weddell Jackson, set up an observatory on Melville Island about three thousand feet from the shore. He measured the barometric pressure, wind velocity, temperature, magnetic observations, and precipitation. From the beginning of the voyage he had conducted a number of measurements from an instrument shelter he had placed three and a half feet above the ship's upper deck. He also attached an anemometer and wind vane to the mainmast one hundred and ten feet above the sea to measure the force of the wind.

By mid-September, M'Clure Strait was still ice free, but three-inch-thick ice had formed in the bay and around the ship. The ice was not thick enough to support a person, but two days later the ice was several inches thicker, enough to hold the ship in its icy grasp. The *Arctic* was now frozen in for the winter.

Bernier ran a tight ship. He set down the ship's rules and regulations. The men were to be in bed by 10:00 p.m. with lights out by 10:30 p.m. The quartermasters took turns as watchmen. One watched until midnight, the other until 6:00 a.m., when the cook got up to make breakfast for the ship's company. It was important, now that they were beset and stationary for the winter, to keep the men busy. The captain sold the men a hundred fox traps. A great rivalry developed between the men, and the competitive ones caught a lot of foxes.

The men were given a half-day holiday on Saturdays to wash their clothes and bedding. Without a washing machine, the washboard got a good workout. Despite the captain's orders, the sheer drudgery of washing everything by hand meant that not all the bedclothes were washed weekly and probably not all the men's clothes either. Woollen pants, jackets, and sweaters rarely got a wash. Underwear and shirts were the most laundered items.

At the end of every week the captain and the doctor made a full inspection of the vessel. The ship was found to be very tight and all quarters were warm and comfortable. With the boiler running only enough to keep the ship warm, about seventeen hundred pounds of coal was consumed per week, as opposed to two thousand pounds per day when the ship was moving under steam.

By mid-October, the ice was thick enough to haul sledges of provisions to the shore, where a snow-house cache was built. They now had a series of supply depots built from Pond Inlet to Winter Harbour, which would be essential should the ship be destroyed by fire or crushed in the ice.

Enough snow had fallen that the men began banking it around the ship. The men dragged snow from the land on sledges when all the snow near the ship had been used for the wall.

On October 19 the sun set at 3:00 p.m., leaving them in twilight for two hours before the moon rose for the rest of the day and night. Up to this date, water could still be seen in M'Clure Strait. After the twenty-third, it became a sea of ice. The days shortened quickly, and on November 5, the sun set for the last time until spring.

On November 9, the King's birthday, the ship was decorated with flags. Bernier wrote, "We were not favoured with sunlight to give the best effect to the variety of colour displayed from our rigging, but the light from the full moon, with her more highly burnished face than is seen in the south and reigning through the day, furnished sufficient light to distinguish the colours."[15] At noon the men fired a twenty-one-gun salute with their rifles.

The ship's company began experimenting with three sled designs for their upcoming spring sledging expeditions. They built sleds of their own design; sleds based on those used by men aboard the *Investigator* and the *Resolute*; and sleds, or *qamutiks*, based on Inuit design. They experimented with different materials for runners: steel, bone, un-iced and iced. The short, heavy one, based on a design similar to Inuit sleds, not surprisingly, pulled easier than the others at temperatures lower than fifteen degrees below zero. Bernier assessed the men for their suitability for sledging expeditions and made a list of who would make up the sledging parties.

On the shortest day of the year, the temperature sank to -40°F and the ice was forty-two inches thick in the bay. Despite the intense cold, the ship was decorated for Christmas. The saloon and men's quarters were decorated with flags, and a large photograph of the minister of Marine and Fisheries was hung on the mainmast. No doubt his image was cursed by the odd expedition member, though. The temperature continued to fall, reaching fifty-five below zero on December 29. This was recorded as the coldest day of their entire trip.

New Year's was a bigger celebration than Christmas. Dinner was served at 3:00 p.m. Glasses were raised to the prime minister, the minister of Marine and Fisheries, and friends back home. On January 2, the two cows that were brought from Quebec for the milk they would provide were slaughtered. The experiment had failed. The animals consumed forty-two bales of hay and thirty bags of cornmeal in five and a half months, but yielded a minimal amount of milk for the effort. Each cow weighed 671 pounds dressed and the meat was enjoyed by all.[16]

The sun rose on February 18 at 9:40 a.m. and shone until 2:20 p.m. The ice was now seventy-seven inches thick. Despite the sun, the temperature remained below -40°F.

On February 20, 1909, meteorologist Jackson placed a staff on top of Parry's Rock for a tidal benchmark. A flat metal beaver, very much like the one on Bernier's 1898 calling cards, was attached to the staff. On one side of the beaver is engraved "ARCTIC" and on its tail "1909." Only Bernier would have stuck such an animal on Parry's Rock.

At the end of March, two sledging parties, totalling eleven men, journeyed across M'Clure Strait to Banks and Victoria Islands to annex them. They returned to the ship the next day, "finding, the sleighs required altering, and that the packages of biscuit which had been opened were found unfit to send with a party on so perilous a journey."[17] The parties set out again on April 6. A third exploring party of meteorologist Jackson and geologist MacMillan set off for Cape Bounty the same day.

All three exploring parties hauled the sleds themselves since no dogs had been purchased for the expedition. Their attempt to procure dogs at Etah had failed, and there was no contingency to get them elsewhere. Bernier merely followed in the footsteps of the British explorers and put the men in the traces instead. The trek across M'Clure Strait was extremely arduous. Without snowshoes, the men dragging the sleds sank with every step in deep snow that wouldn't bear their weight. The cold and high winds also impeded their progress.

On April 20, Green returned to the ship with three men who had frostbitten feet and could not proceed to Banks Island. Just as Bernier had omitted taking dogs with them, he, or whoever was in charge of clothing the men, had failed to procure proper fur skin boots, or *kamiks*, made by Inuit. These were far warmer than the southern-style leather boots the men wore. The three frostbitten men fortunately recovered without losing any toes, and set out again on the first of May.

On May 2, the sun did not set below the horizon. Provisions left on the ice were now brought on board because the surface of the ice was beginning to melt under the twenty-four-hour sunshine. On May 8, five of the men who had gone with Morin returned to the ship and reported all well. Morin, Pike, and Chassé had carried on to Banks and Victoria Islands to annex them. Bernier sent the five men back to meet Morin's returning party to help haul the sleds.

The eight men arrived back at the ship two days later. Banks and Victoria Islands had successfully been annexed, and records of the expeditions' activities left at Cape Russell on the northeast tip of Banks. A party of three others under Green's leadership had gone to Bay of Mercy on Banks Island and wouldn't return for several weeks. On May 17, Morin left on another trip to Banks Island with three others in the hopes of meeting up with Green's party on their return. Van Koenig and Lessard accompanied the travellers as far as Cape Providence, where they would stay and take observations of the climate and ice movements in the strait.

Green and his two companions returned to the ship on June 11. They had made it to Bay of Mercy, where M'Clure and his men had spent two harrowing winters trapped in the ice aboard the *Investigator* before being rescued. M'Clure claimed to have left a cache with enough supplies for sixty-six men and had anchored the ship in such a position that it would be stranded upon a shoal, and so would last there. But evidence of M'Clure's two miserable winters had vanished. Green failed to discover any cache or documents left by M'Clure. The *Investigator* was nowhere to be found either, having sunk in the bay.[18] Green and his men were the first southerners to visit Bay of Mercy since M'Clure and his men abandoned ship fifty-six years before.

By mid-June, water lay on top of the ice in the bay, though the ice was still too thick for the ship to move. Bernier gave orders to put ashes on the ice in the path the ship would take, which would assist the sun in speeding up the melting process.

Morin and his party returned on June 24. The last few days of their journey back to the ship were spent trudging knee deep through the frigid water that now lay on top of the ice. Both Morin and Green's sledging parties had endured a lack of food, as bears had destroyed the caches they had built prior to their trips.

A Sweeping Proclamation

Dominion Day, July 1, 1909, was an auspicious one. All the flags were flying, and Bernier wrote in his report that "the day itself was all that could be desired."[19] That afternoon, thirty-four men and a baby muskox left the ship, trooped a mile across the slushy but still frozen bay, and scrambled up the gravely beach to Parry's Rock for the most important annexation ceremony yet. Captain Bernier led the procession.

The officers were dressed in shirts and ties with their double line of brass buttons down the front of their peacoats. Bernier wore his captain's cap and navy blue coat, with its three gold stripes on the sleeve cuffs. One man carried a Union Jack; another, the Red Ensign; a third, a heavy camera and tripod; and Chief Engineer John Van Koenig carried the neatly wrapped bronze plaque he had spent the winter engraving.

When the men were assembled before Parry's Rock, a place was cut into its sloping side into which the slab would be laid. The plaque was two and a half feet long, a foot wide, and an inch thick. The captain made a moving speech, saying they had annexed a number of islands one by one and that they now claimed all islands and territory for Canada.

With ceremony, Bernier unveiled the plaque that Van Koenig held, and it was bolted to the rock. The men gave three cheers in honour of the prime minister and the minister of Marine and Fisheries.[20]

The crew then assembled in two awkward lines in front of Parry's Rock, with the newly fastened plaque behind them. The flag-bearers stood on either side of it with flags unfurled. The baby muskox stood in front, licking Bernier's hand. Their photograph was taken and the men dispersed to enjoy their holiday, "picking wildflowers, which grew in abundance, and securing objects of interest."[21]

On the top left-hand corner of the plaque is an ornate carving of the Red Ensign Canadian flag emblazoned with the Union Jack and the Dominion coat of arms. Below the flag is a relief of the *Arctic* steadfast in the ice. On the right-hand side of the plaque the description reads: "This Memorial, is Erected today to Commemorate, the taking possession for the 'DOMINION OF CANADA' of the whole 'ARCTIC ARCHIPELAGO,' lying to the north of America from long. 60°w. to 141°w. up to latitude 90°n. Winter Hbr. Melville Island, *CGS Arctic*. July 1st 1909. J.E. Bernier. Commander."[22]

The plaque spelled out the same pie-shaped sector that Poirier had promoted in the Senate.

Bernier and his sweeping proclamation at Parry's Rock on Melville Island, Dominion Day, July 1, 1909.

One of the crew members, Claude Vigneau, described the day in his journal:

> Thursday, July 1st 1909. It is a big day for us all today. We set the flags up at 8 a.m. Cool wind from the N.W. It is cloudy. At 2 p.m. we went to Parry's Rock. The captain made a speech. He had pictures taken of us. We brought the baby muskox along. After the ceremony, six of us went to write our names on another rock, 20 steps from Parry's Rock. We got there at 4:30 p.m. On our rock, are the names of C. Vigneau, W. LeBel, A. Bourget, R. Goulet, G. Gosselin and W. Vaillancourt, 1909. Le capitaine treated us tonight. Everybody is gathered in the "salon" — songs and piano.[23]

It was the captain's finest hour. He did not have government authorization for such a sweeping proclamation, but had performed it of his own accord, confident that the importance of his actions would be recognized and praised by politicians in Ottawa.

The rest of July was spent preparing to leave winter quarters. The snow had melted from the land. The ice in M'Clure Strait was reduced to four feet in thickness, the water on top of it helping melt the ice beneath. However, in the more protected Winter Harbour, the ice still measured five feet. All they could do was wait.

On July 30, the men cut a channel in the ice. Three days later, they began to break the ice with the ship and made headway towards the entrance of the harbour. The next day Bernier went up on the hills to place some final records and scout the status of the ice in the strait. A large crack had appeared and the ice was moving. At 2:00 p.m., the ice in the bay broke up and, raising the anchors, the *Arctic* steamed out of the harbour.

Its progress was halted by moving ice in the strait, and the ship retreated and moored back in the inner harbour. Moving ice constantly threatened the ship, forcing the men to keep up steam and move around the harbour. At midnight on August 12, 1909, leads opened in the harbour ice. The *Arctic* was at last released from its icy winter quarters, and steamed east into M'Clure Strait.

AN ARCTIC PATROL

The expedition resumed its patrol work.

It headed northeast around Melville to Bathurst Island before the extensive polar ice pack forced it south. On August 26, the *Arctic* was beset by ice off Griffith Island, but was released two days later. The ice was noticeably heavier than it had been the year previous. Bernier commented how exactly one year before, they had entered an ice-free Winter Harbour while M'Clure Strait was seemingly free of ice.

Sailing through open water, they experienced the first rolls of the ship in a year. The sun had begun to set just below the horizon for a short time, creating a brief twilight, though there were still twenty-four hours of daylight. They made for Navy Board Inlet, and by September 1 were passing Canada Point on Bylot Island. They anchored in Albert Harbour, visited the post, and found that the Dundee whaler *Morning* had brought them mail. It had travelled from Canada to Scotland and back.

On September 3, the *Arctic* continued its southward journey, entering a large bay in Clyde River on eastern Baffin Island two days later. They anchored at the bottom of the bay beside the whaling schooner *Jeanie*, captained by Sam Bartlett. It had been sent to pick up Harry Whitney from his hunting expedition at Etah to bring him back to New York. However, once on board, Whitney redirected the ship to Baffin to continue hunting. At 1:00 p.m., Whitney, Bartlett, and a passenger, Royal Fuller, came aboard the *Arctic*, where they were cordially welcomed and spent three hours.

Bernier issued his first hunting permit to Whitney. Bernier informed Whitney that as he had a motor whaleboat on board, he required a fishery licence. "I accordingly issued the license and received the fee. We exchanged a quarter of musk ox meat for some magazines furnished by Mr. Whitney."[24]

In light of Major Moodie's 1904 ban on hunting and trading muskox, it is ironic that Bernier, a representative of the government, traded muskox meat with Whitney for magazines.

In Whitney's book *Hunting With Eskimos*, published in 1910, he mentions his encounter with the Canadian fishery officer:

I was a poacher, therefore, in the eyes of Canada, though I had known nothing of this far-reaching law until Captain Bernier informed me of its existence. Never have I willingly poached, and so in exchange for fifty dollars I received the requisite license from the Captain, permitting me to hunt, chase, kill and obtain anything from hares or trout to bears or whales; and to exchange, barter and trade with the said and aforesaid natives of the wide and limitless Arctic dominions of Canada with a free and law-abiding hand.[25]

This tongue-in-cheek comment shows how virtually irrelevant the licensing system was. It was neither well-publicized nor properly controlled. Fifty dollars to the millionaire was a negligible amount, at any rate. Implicit in Whitney's account, though, is the acceptance that he was hunting on Canadian soil. However, if one of the vessel's captains decided not to pay for a licence, Bernier could really do nothing about it. Fortunately, his authority was respected and he never encountered such a dilemma.

The men on the *Arctic* first heard the news that Cook and Peary had each claimed to have reached the North Pole when they met the *Morning* at Igarjuak. At that time, Cook, having the earlier claim, was initially recognized as the conqueror of the Pole. It was likely the main topic of conversation with Whitney and Bartlett, as both knew the two polar explorers. Bartlett's nephew, Bob, was captain of Peary's ship *Roosevelt*.

Once again, Captain Bartlett offered to take letters from the *Arctic* south. First Officer George Braithwaite took the opportunity to send word home to his wife. She notified the paper when she received it at the end of September. In a special dispatch to the *Toronto Daily Star* on September 29, a photo of the *Arctic* with its bare masts and rigging rising from a snowy embankment highlighted the announcement that "Capt. Bernier Returning, Will Arrive in Few Weeks." The article said, "It is probable Capt. Bernier hoisted the Union Jack at places passed over by Cook on his dash to the Pole."

The *Arctic* carried on its patrol, following the Baffin coastline with the intention of encountering other whalers. Off the coast of the Cumberland Peninsula, Bernier handed out another licence to Captain Cooney of the

St. Hilda from Southampton, England. The *Arctic* arrived at Port Burwell, anchoring on September 15. The crew took on ballast and left three days later. Following orders to sail into Hudson Strait, the expedition made a course for Ashe Inlet on Big Island on the north side.

On September 20, they dropped anchor at Ashe Inlet. The station built by Gordon's men in 1884 had been reduced to a few walls and upright supports, although when Wakeham had stopped there in 1897, the building had still been in fair shape. However, it had been erected as a temporary structure and had not weathered the harsh winters. Bernier and four others climbed the highest hill to Tyrrell's Bluff, the stone beacon built by Gordon in 1886. From this vantage point, Bernier saw a Hudson Strait entirely free of ice. Bernier's men built two wooden beacons to further assist mariners entering the inlet.

On September 24, they passed out of the harbour. As there was a light wind from the southwest, they set all sails and headed east, making the Button Islands on the night of the twenty-fifth. Continuing south along the Labrador coast, they passed through the Strait of Belle Isle in fine weather.

On October 3, the *Arctic* stopped at Pointe-au-Père, near Rimouski, to pick up the river pilot to help navigate up the St. Lawrence. Welcome letters and papers from families and friends were awaiting the ship's company. Here, Bernier sent Dr. Cook a congratulatory telegram: "Felicitation on your success. Regards to family."[26] He must have harboured a certain amount of envy, having had the ambition to claim the Pole himself.

The ship carried on up the St. Lawrence River and passed several ships going the opposite way. These vessels recognized the *Arctic* and saluted the expedition with signals and whistles. Word had gone before them that they were approaching Quebec City. On Tuesday, October 5, the *Arctic* was welcomed home by a great crowd on the King's Wharf.

JOURNEY'S END

People swarmed the docks, eager to greet and celebrate the return of the valiant matelots who had braved extraordinary conditions to raise the flag of the Dominion on the northern islands.

Reporters from across the country were anxious to get Bernier's reaction to the news about the Pole being conquered. "The Americans have the honour of locating the Pole. I wish it had been a Canadian instead, and would have liked to be afforded the opportunity," Bernier told the press.[27]

Bernier went on to Ottawa to make his report to the government. On October 16, fresh from his expedition, he delivered a lecture at the Canadian Club that was enthusiastically well-attended by local dignitaries, including the Right Honourable Sir Wilfrid Laurier.

As Bernier rose to make his speech, the audience responded with ringing cheers and gave him a handkerchief salute led by Prime Minister Laurier. Bernier had a keen audience. When he said, "My little trip was to confirm what had been done, and I have secured for Canada the whole of the Arctic Archipelago, in detail and wholesale," the audience erupted with cheers and laughter.[28]

Bernier's speech touched on the various aspects of his voyage, including the wildlife on Melville Island and handing out licences to foreigners like Harry Whitney. Bernier had brought several objects of interest to show the men present. One was the record left by Sir Edward Parry, another was a pole used by Sir John Franklin, and the third was a reproduction of the bronze plaque that had been fastened to Parry's Rock. This reproduction ended up on display in Messrs. Rosenthal's jewellery store window on Sparks Street, a block from the Parliament buildings.

As well as the historical artifacts that Bernier brought south with him, he also brought the muskox calf they had found on Melville Island. The expedition's naturalist, Frank Hennessey, had made a small drawing of it, titled "The Daughter of Melville." Bernier thought that the Experimental Farm in Ottawa would take the Daughter of Melville to study, but they declined. The Holt Renfrew Company temporarily kept it at its zoological garden at Montmorency Falls Park outside Quebec City until the Bronx Zoo in New York City bought the muskox from Bernier in November 1909.[29]

The *New York Times* reported that it was the only animal of its kind in captivity in the United States. "The Zoo officials have not quite decided on the diet for the new arrival, but for a while hay will be his chief food. It is not known what the musk oxen really find to keep life in their bodies in the Far North, where in the Winter months the ground is covered many feet deep with snow."[30] The dilemma was resolved and the zoo eventually became home to many muskoxen.

Bernier enjoyed the fame his flag-raising expeditions brought him. His was a household name, worth something to Canadians, and so it was sought by companies to promote their products. On November 24, an advertisement appeared in the *Toronto Daily Star* for the Canada Metal Co. Ltd. A letter from Bernier was contained in the quarter-page advertisement commending the company's metal to people. It said, "I made use of your Harris Metal in making the memorial slab left on Melville Island, when taking possession of the 'Arctic Archipelago.'"

Bernier embarked on a lecture tour, starting at Massey Hall in Toronto on December 2, 1909. His lecture, replete with lantern slides of his three Arctic trips, was titled "Our New Dominions in the Arctic Archipelago," and was hailed as the most important lecture engagement of the season. "The narrative and illustrations will be a thrilling account of romance and adventure," said the lecture's advertisement.[31]

This time Bernier wasn't drumming up interest in a bid for the Pole, but riding the wave of excitement that Cook and Peary had generated. He was a Canadian Arctic celebrity in his own right at the summit of his glory.

CHAPTER THIRTEEN

To the Northwest Passage, 1910

After Bernier's address to the Canadian Club in October 1909, Prime Minister Laurier rose and said, "The Government is determined to keep a patrol of the northern seas. Islands there that have been thought barren are a wealth for us and our children. Capt. Bernier's mission will be to resume his work and come back when he thinks he has accomplished it. He shall not be fettered by this or that. He shall go to the Pole or beyond it if he desires."[1]

When the *Arctic* weighed anchor on July 7, 1910, on its fourth official voyage, Bernier again stood on the bridge as commander. He would patrol the same waters he had cruised the year before, but this time Bernier had received permission to attempt the Northwest Passage via M'Clure Strait. His official instructions for the two-year voyage were "to patrol Davis strait, Baffin bay, Lancaster sound, Barrow strait, Melville sound, McClure strait, and Beaufort sea to Herschel island, thence through Behring strait to Vancouver or Victoria, B.C."[2]

Deputy Minister of Marine and Fisheries Alexander Johnston's instructions were clear: attempting the Passage was left to Bernier's judgment in ascertaining the ice conditions and taking into account the danger to the ship and its company.[3]

A July 26, 1910, article in the *Globe* shows the magnitude of the instructions: "With the government steamer *Arctic*, provisioned for a two years cruise Captain Bernier is now en route to Canadian Polar waters, with the government's permission, to attempt the Northwest Passage and bring his vessel around to Victoria, BC. A feat which was unsuccessfully attempted by Parry, Ross, Franklin and other polar navigators from the past century."

Bernier had lost the chance of attaining the North Pole, but the Northwest Passage offered him a glorious place in marine history.

On July 7, all was in readiness for the Arctic voyage. Spirits were high, especially after the success of the previous year's trip. The Honourable L.P. Brodeur, minister of Marine and Fisheries, could not be present at the sailing, so the Honourable Joseph E. Caron, the Quebec provincial minister of agriculture, made the farewell speech. A crowd of two hundred, the crew's families and other locals, were on the dock to wave them off. Flags of other ships in the harbour were hoisted in honour of the event and their steam whistles saluted the *Arctic* as it passed by. It was not the royal fanfare of 1908, but worthy of a northern expedition.

Many of the thirty-eight men on board were back for their fourth northern trip with Bernier, including O.J. Morin, who was promoted to first officer. Two newcomers, Second Officer Robert Janes from Newfoundland and Third Officer Edward Macdonald from Prince Edward Island, were unilingual anglophones, minorities on a ship with over three-quarters of the crew francophone.

Macdonald signed on for the two-year journey on June 30, 1910, and joined the ship six days later. He had gone to sea at twelve, and later served as a soldier in the Boer War in South Africa. He was a hard character, a proponent of corporal punishment and a traditional hierarchical structure aboard ship. His five-hundred-page diary recounts his fifteen-month experience on the *Arctic*.

Macdonald's first impression of the crew on July 5 is not positive. He wrote, "As I was coming on board tonight I stumbled over three or four of the crew lying drunk near the gangway. It is my private opinion that they are a bum lot of sailors and not the kind of men that are required on an expedition like this."[4]

The ship weighed anchor two days later. Weather was fair with a west wind and the ship's square sails were hoisted. The men filled the tanks with fresh water before they got too far down the St. Lawrence to where it would become salty. Between Quebec City and Pointe-au-Père, Dr. Joseph Etienne Bolduc, the ship's doctor, carried out an inspection of the crew.

The *Arctic* arrived at Pointe-au-Père the next day, received final orders, and took aboard mail and stores. The vessel continued downriver to the Gulf of St. Lawrence.

The expedition's route north to Baffin Island included the usual detour via Greenland. The ship entered Lancaster Sound, then headed south through Navy Board Inlet to call at Pond Inlet, arriving on July 30. Ice was still thick in the harbour and the ship was forced to anchor outside of it. The first officer and three others were sent to the whaling station. Morin returned to the vessel with five Inuit who reported that the whalers *Morning* and *Diana* had called in at the station but had left.

The next day, the *Arctic* got underway but only made a mile before a solid pan of ice stopped it. On August 3, the ship slipped through the moving ice into Albert Harbour and dropped anchor in 320 fathoms of water. The next day, men landed with lumber and constructed a small building to cache three months of supplies for emergency use.

Floating slabs of ice, moving in and out with the tide, forced a week's delay in the ship's departure. Usually by August the ice had receded from Pond Inlet and Albert Harbour. However, it was apparent that the ice was late melting that year. While they waited at Albert Harbour for the ice to clear out, the crew went to Salmon River and caught close to five hundred fish. Bernier collected fishery licence fees from Captain Milne, of the *Diana*, and asked him to forward the ship's mail to Ottawa.

On August 12, Bernier bought thirty-eight huskies and hired two Inuit men as guides, Macatowee and Macashaw. These were the two men who had joined Bernier on his 1906–07 voyage.

The *Arctic* weighed anchor and proceeded around the east side of Bylot Island. It stopped at Possession Bay on northern Bylot, and Bernier located a cairn made by Sir John Ross's men. The cairn was in disarray. Broken bottles were strewn about, but a stove with the date of 1848 engraved on it was still intact. Bernier had no success locating Ross's records, but left his own on the peak of one of the hills surrounding the bay.

The ship pushed through Lancaster Sound with difficulty. The ice was exceedingly heavier than the year before and progress was slow. It cautiously put into an ice-filled Erebus Bay at Beechey Island. The men landed and added more provisions to the cache they had made the previous year. Second Officer Robert Janes found an 1850 record left by Ross, which

Bernier safely stowed in his cabin. It was another artifact for the Victoria Memorial Museum in Ottawa.

The ship got underway again, but its progress was impeded by ice. At times, the vessel was beset, but soon freed when the wind changed direction, blowing the ice away. As it passed Cornwallis Island on August 24, conditions worsened. The compass was useless now, so the ship was steered along the coastline. By Monday, August 29, little water was visible ahead. However, the next day a lead opened and the ship made it as far west as Dealy Island off Melville Island.

The expedition stopped to inspect Kellett's storehouse, which Bernier's men had repaired the year before. They took the boat that Kellett had left there on board. It showed the fifty-seven years it had weathered on Dealy, and was so deteriorated that it was of no use, so was replaced by one of the *Arctic*'s boats. Kellett's boat became another artifact for the museum.

The expedition arrived at the previous year's wintering spot on August 31. The ship's entry into Winter Harbour was aided by the stone beacons erected in 1909, saving the men the effort of taking soundings. Bernier instructed the men to build another cache, which would aid their survival in the event they ran into trouble attempting the Passage.

The cache was a shed, twelve by sixteen feet, with a plain board-and-batten exterior and a window on each side. The crew left a gun, ammunition, a barrel of coal, tins of flour, biscuits, pemmican, Bovril, sugar, coffee, tobacco, and other useful supplies inside.[5] This would be a veritable treasure trove to Vilhjalmur Stefansson and his small expedition when they crossed Melville Island six years later.

Before leaving Winter Harbour, Bernier attached a tin case with his record, laying out his navigation plans, to the staff on Parry's Rock. On September 2, the *Arctic* got underway. Thirty miles south of Cape Providence, it met a dense wall of jumbled ice, stretching to the south as far as they could see. M'Clure Strait was blocked with a solid mass of impenetrable ice. The ship could go no further. This came as no surprise, considering the difficulty of their passage to this point.

At noon, Bernier sent Second Officer Janes aloft. He reported the ice floe was fifty to sixty feet thick with hills on it as high as any berg, and extended westward as far as he could see. "I gave up hope of crossing McClure Strait. We had reached the farthest point in this direction of any vessel."[6]

Bernier had read enough Arctic history and accounts of explorers whose vessels were crushed to know the danger of old ice to wooden ships. It was foolhardy to attempt the Northwest Passage. Admitting defeat must have been an enormous disappointment to Bernier. Without this accomplishment, his work in the archipelago was reduced to that of patrol officer. His last chance for glory faded as they turned back.

Third Officer Macdonald's September 2 account is critical of Bernier's decision at M'Clure Strait. He wrote, "At 9 p.m. ice very heavy. Commander thinks it is impossible to force a passage. Turned back heading eastward. I do not know much about ice conditions in the North but I think we should have tried a little harder before turning back."[7]

Macdonald was a novice when it came to Arctic travel. It was his first time encountering heavy ice, and he did not go up to the crow's nest to see the unbroken ice floe that Janes reported, so his comments are not well-informed.

Of the Northwest Passages, Bernier thought that M'Clure Strait, the most northern route, was the most direct route to the Bering Sea. He was correct, but, historically, it is rarely free of ice. It was an anomaly that this Passage had appeared to be mostly open water the year before. Undoubtedly, 1909 was one of the few summers in centuries that it was so. For the majority of the nineteenth and twentieth centuries, a heavy concentration of ice solidly plugged M'Clure Strait. It is highly unlikely that Bernier could have made it in 1910 in his little wooden ship.[8] Amundsen had made the Northwest Passage by traversing the most southerly route, which is the route most commonly used today.

RETREAT

Defeated by the wall of old ice, the *Arctic* worked its way east to Byam Martin Island, weaving in and out of leads in the ice, crossing Viscount Melville Sound, first north then south in an effort to avoid the large pans. By September 8, it headed to Cornwallis Island, and met continuous snow squalls. The crew was assigned the harrowing task of removing ice from the rigging and sails.

Bernier decided to winter in Arctic Bay off Admiralty Inlet on northwest Baffin, where he had visited in 1906. He chose the sheltered bay at latitude 73°2'N, near the entrance to Adams Sound, which branches eastward from Admiralty Inlet. With his love of Arctic marine history, the harbour's name may have recommended itself to him as well.

Commander Parry first entered Admiralty Inlet in 1819 on his search for the Northwest Passage, but, as it was choked with ice, he turned back without fully charting it. Captain Willie Adams of the whaling vessel *Arctic* explored and mapped the inlet and region in 1872. Arctic Bay was named after his ship and Adams Sound was named after its captain.

Arctic Bay is protected by surrounding high, rugged red hills and an eighteen-hundred-foot-high mountain on its east side. This mountain was known by the people residing at Arctic Bay as Ingniksaaluk. However, Bernier christened it King George V Mountain after the new king, who had ascended to the throne in May 1910. The King had been the Prince of Wales in 1908 who had bid Bernier an auspicious farewell from Quebec City.

On Saturday, September 10, Bernier took the ship into Arctic Bay and anchored in twenty-five fathoms of water, a quarter of a mile off the bay's west shore. When Bernier visited the bay in 1906 there had been no inhabitants there, though the area, known as Ikpiarjuk, had long been a site occupied by Inuit migrating from the west. That summer of 1910 an Inuit encampment was established onshore.[9] The ship was soon welcomed by eighteen men, women, and children who came out to greet it. On the thirteenth, Bernier went ashore to meet with Chief Nasso and have a census taken of the small population.

Bernier had learned his lesson the year before about the importance of having dogs for sledging expeditions. The thirty-eight dogs purchased at Igarjuak had spent a miserable month on deck as the ship attempted its westward passage. The deck was washed down every morning, but the smell from the dogs was overwhelming. Macdonald complained in his diary in July, "I could not do all my watch on the bridge last night without coming down occasionally to get some fresh air."[10] On September 15, the dogs were landed on shore. Once the bay froze over, the dogs were tethered on the sea ice nearer the ship. It was a more comfortable arrangement for men and dogs.

Bernier began carrying out duties befitting a government expedition: exploring for economic minerals in the region and surveying the uncharted coastlines. The first of several expeditions were sent off to explore the bay and area. Second Officer Janes led a small party into the surrounding countryside for a fifteen-day trek. The captain, Dr. Bolduc, and a few others headed off to explore nearby Victor Bay. The temperature was 27°F.

While the parties were absent, First Officer Morin was in charge of the ship and oversaw the preliminary construction of the deck covering. Some of the men transferred stores and boats to the land for emergency purposes. Chief Engineer Van Koenig emptied one boiler and kept steam in the other for heating the ship. J.T.E. Lavoie, the ship's meteorologist and surveyor, set up a cement pillar on shore to take observations.

By September 23, the land was bare of snow. Ice in the bay was thickening, but Adams Sound and Admiralty Inlet were still ice-free. Six days later, the ice around the *Arctic* was four inches thick. There was no danger of the ship moving from this position until the next summer, so the anchor was raised and put on the gangway. The men could now walk safely on the ice, go ashore, and visit the people living in the tupiks. Visits were made in the opposite direction over the ice too, with many locals attending Sunday religious services.

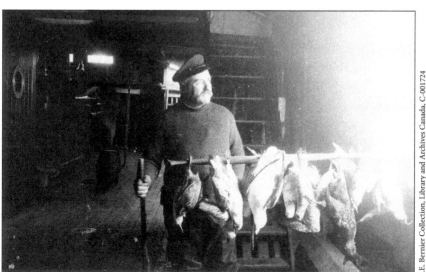

Captain Bernier with a catch of ducks aboard the Arctic, *Albert Harbour, 1906.*

In early October, the men cut ice blocks from a small nearby lake to melt for drinking water. Over two days, the men cut and stacked two hundred tons of ice. It was exceedingly difficult work. After cutting the ice and removing it from the lake, the ice blocks had to be lowered down the side of a mountain and then hauled to the ship on sleds. The lack of snow on the ground made this difficult. The men soon contrived a funicular-type contraption for lowering the ice down the mountain that would pull an empty sled up as the loaded one went down. Dr. Bolduc analyzed water from a melted block and pronounced it to be of the purest quality.

At the end of October, ice blocks were stacked around the ship as a wind buffer. Once snow fell, it would be packed into the space between this ice wall and the ship for insulation. Everything was now in readiness for winter.

WINTERING IN ARCTIC BAY

Second Officer Robert Janes and Arthur English, the mineralogist, returned from an excursion to the bottom of Adams Sound with a chunk of rock that had flecks of copper in it. The men believed the rock was evidence that the region offered potential mineral wealth. So, the men made a second prospecting trip.

A more ambitious expedition was sent out on October 10 to survey land along the coast of Prince Regent Inlet and down towards Fury and Hecla Strait, which separates the southwest end of Baffin from Melville Peninsula on the mainland. This party, led by J.T.E. Lavoie, included First Officer Morin, assistant steward Joseph Mathé, and two Inuit guides, Monkashaw and Koudnou. Lavoie would make surveys and report on the geological formations they saw.

The men headed south along the east coast to the end of Admiralty Inlet. Here, Morin parted company with the others and returned to the ship. Lavoie, Mathé, Monkashaw, and Koudnou crossed to the western cape of Baffin Island, which Bernier had named Brodeur Peninsula in 1906, to the coast of Prince Regent Inlet. Snow now blanketed the landscape and the men were able to cover good ground by dogsled. The four men returned to the ship on November 17. In the thirty-six days they were away, they covered five hundred and fifty miles.

A number of other smaller prospecting parties sent out around the region came back with rocks stained with rust, or with flecks of copper, gold, silver, or quartz. The amateur prospectors labelled bags of specimens with whatever metal or mineral they assumed the rocks contained. There were no tools aboard the *Arctic* to accurately analyze the minerals, so the specimens had to be transported south for a Department of Mines mineralogist to confirm what they actually were. Thus, the ship's hold was loaded with large amounts of apparently valuable rock.

Unfortunately, the *Arctic*'s prospectors were mistaken in their mineral analysis. In Arctic Bay the men discovered shale they thought contained oil. Mineralogist Arthur English concurred that it was potentially valuable. The men loaded ten tons of this rock into the ship's hold. When the shale was examined at the Department of Mines, "no percentage of oil" was found contained in it. The rock's only value was as ballast.

The sun went below the horizon on November 9, and did not appear again for ninety-one days. November 9 had been kept as a holiday in honour of King Edward VII, but since his death that spring, the day was no different than any other.

Keeping the crew occupied in the dark winter days was a challenge. Bernier arranged concerts in the saloon and lent his phonograph, or played the piano while the men sang English, French, and Inuit songs, depending on the singer. Just as he had with the 1908–09 expedition, Bernier encouraged the men to take exercise and fresh air by setting traps. The men took him up on this, but Bernier undoubtedly benefitted, as he owned the traps. The men gave him half the furs they caught in exchange for using his traps.

Macdonald and ship's historian Fabien Vanasse both reported the number of times the Inuit visited the ship to trade. On April 13, Macdonald wrote, "A large party of Esquimaux arrived at the ship this afternoon from Ponds Inlet. I have been thinking for some time that this is more like a fur trading voyage than anything I can compare it to." Later, Macdonald noted, "Skins seem to be the principle thing on board and everybody seems to be after them. If one of our puppies die he soon loses his skin. I overheard one of the stewards remarking a few days ago 'if one of the crew would happen to die it is very likely he would be skinned too.'"[11]

Despite the activities Bernier organized to occupy his men, the *Arctic* was a small space in which to live, eat, and sleep for a group of young, energetic men. Sometimes tempers flared and occasionally a fist fight broke out. On January 15, Macdonald recorded "a free fight in the galley this morning about 6 a.m," between the chief cook and the second cook.[12] By the end of the trip, Macdonald wrote that the cooks had a fist fight about once a month, which had to be broken up by one of the officers. Yet, as he saw it, neither one was severely punished.

Macdonald felt that Bernier was soft on discipline. His own form of punishment, he wrote, included a "flaying pin."[13] Bernier settled for dire warnings. The men were brought before him for any wrongdoing with an opportunity to explain themselves. Macdonald noted that Bernier's method was all bark and no bite. However, Bernier's methods went a long way to ensuring his crew was not disgruntled. Being trapped in the ice for nine to ten months, it was necessary that bad feelings weren't allowed to fester between the men. Comer had put men in irons in Fullerton Harbour, and Bernier knew that that technique did not gain him any respect. Bernier's methods worked, though, as many of his crew sailed under him for fifteen years.

Saturday afternoons the men had a half-day holiday. After "divine service" on Sundays, the men had the rest of the day off. Flags were raised, which signalled to the Inuit that they could visit for dinner.

These visits were often reciprocated by members of the crew after lights out. Bernier frowned on this and forbade the men to go. Macdonald wrote, "Some of the men have been going to the Esquimaux village in the night directly against the orders of the captain for the purpose of trading no doubt. The Captain found some of them out today and had them brought before him in his office and gave them a very severe talking to and promised six months imprisonment to the next one disobeying his orders."[14]

Despite the threat of six months' imprisonment for disobeying orders, the transgressors continued to visit the "village," and likely not for trading purposes. Descendants of the children of sailors from the *Arctic* still live in Igloolik, Pond Inlet, Arctic Bay, and Iqaluit today.

As well as building stone cairns on the islands they stopped at, Bernier, the devout Catholic, also erected crosses. While they were in Arctic Bay, he had a large square-timbered cross raised on the long, rocky spit that juts into the entrance of the bay, separating it from Adams Sound. Bernier felt this cross would guide future vessels in deep water. Affixed to it was a small lead plaque roughly inscribed with "Holy Cross," the name *Arctic*, and the date in April 1911 when it was erected. Hereafter, Bernier referred to the spit as Holy Cross Point.

By the first week of December the embankment around the ship was nine feet high, seven feet wide, and twenty feet longer than the ship. The men had collected most of the snow from the nearby hillside to build it, as not much snow had fallen, and it had been quickly scraped off the ice for the ship's insulation. About six inches of snow lay on the land. The total amount of snow that fell the entire time the ship was frozen in was eleven and a half inches. With this snow wall for insulation, the living quarters' temperature comfortably ranged from 60°F to 70°F.

Lavoie recorded the daily weather using two mercury and two spirit Fahrenheit thermometers, as well as two standard barometers obtained from the Toronto Observatory. The lowest temperature that winter was 55.2°F below zero. July 7, 1911, was the warmest day, with the temperature reaching 53.4°F. Lavoie noted that the mercury froze nine times in the thermometer. He also measured the thickness of the ice. It was thirty-two inches thick by the end of January, reaching its maximum thickness of fifty-six inches on May 20.

On December 12, Second Officer Janes was sent overland with a bag of mail to Pond Inlet, one hundred and fifty miles north. He left in the company of three Inuit with three *qamutiks*, or dogsleds, each carrying about five hundred pounds. Two of the men were from Pond, so were returning to their families. The third Inuk would return to Arctic Bay to give notice of Janes' safe arrival. Their progress was slow because the snow was thin on the land, making it difficult for the dogs to pull the sleds.

They arrived at Pond Inlet ten days later to discover that the Inuit community there was starving. Seals had been scarce. Janes was dumbfounded that despite their destitute condition, no one had broken into the government cache of supplies that Bernier had stored there. Janes opened the cache and gave the people food to help them survive the winter.

Janes' was a one-way trip. He remained at Pond Inlet over the winter, carrying out some prospecting and investigating the trading and fishing prospects in the region. He was picked up by the ship when it called at Pond Inlet on its homeward journey in August.

One of the most impressive cross-country expeditions of the 1910–11 voyage was carried out by J.T.E. Lavoie. On March 15 at 8:30 a.m., Lavoie left the ship in the company of the Inuk guide Koudnou and another Inuit couple, Pioumictou and his wife. They were joined by two other Inuit men going on a bear-hunting expedition. Several other families joined them along the route. At one point the caravan they travelled with was made up of five *qamutiks*, fifty-six dogs, seven men, six women, and three children. Lavoie and his companions headed to Prince Regent Inlet, and he continued his survey of the region down to Fury and Hecla Strait.

The official 1910–11 government report of the voyage was compiled from Bernier's log by a government civil servant who had no experience of life aboard ship, let alone life in the Arctic. Though it is written in the third person, the writer's biases and the prejudices of the day come through. However, Appendix No. 2 is Lavoie's report, which is taken directly from his diary and told in his unaffected, matter-of-fact way. Lavoie's impression of life on the land and the people he travelled with is clearly documented.

> As I had acquired experience in my expedition of last fall, I had decided to run this one on an entirely different principle and adopted the Eskimo ways of travelling, clothing, sleeping, etc. Being used to this country they cannot but be more practical than we in these matters. Therefore, on leaving the "*Arctic*" I had discarded all European clothes and dressed in a double skin suit…. Every night we built an igloo (snow hut) of blocks of snow. Although it took us an hour every night, it was preferable to pitching a tent, and more comfortable, as it kept the wind out…. I got used from the first to eat raw meat, either caribou, bear or seal; I got so used to it that I found as much delight as the natives in sitting on the ice immediately after a seal had been killed, to eat its liver with blubber before it had lost its animal heat."[15]

The British Navy had failed to do this. It insisted on doing things in its own superior fashion — to the detriment of many expeditions. Numerous Arctic and Antarctic expeditions were carried out by men who were not as open-minded as Lavoie and perished for their obstinacy.

Lavoie's diary reads like an adventure book. He suffered snow blindness, was stalked by polar bears, and endured a number of deprivations. A month into their trip they were literally buried in their igloo by a violent snowstorm. They had to dig out the dogs several times over the course of the storm so they wouldn't smother under the snow. To get out they had to crawl out the top of their igloo, as the entrance way, *qamutiks*, and dog harnesses were buried under five feet of snow.

Lavoie surveyed the east coast of Prince Regent Inlet down to the Gulf of Boothia. He named various headland points along the way for people on the expedition: Morin Point, Van Koenig Point, Macdonald Cape, and Janes Cape. He named the large bay halfway down the peninsula Bernier Bay, in honour of his commander. Easter Cape got its moniker because they were there at Easter time. Lavoie also named several minor landmarks after his two brothers, and one of his sisters who passed away.

On April 29, at Fury and Hecla Strait, he left a document in a cairn. Lavoie decided to continue south to survey Foxe Channel, then cross Baffin to Cumberland Sound, where he would meet the *Arctic* at the Anglican missionary station. He intended to send Pioumictou back to let Captain Bernier know his plans, and carry on with Koudnou. However, Koudnou could not be persuaded to accompany him. He would be absent from Arctic Bay for a year by the time he returned, and he worried about his wife and child managing without him. So they headed north to the ship.

On May 6, they camped at the bottom of Admiralty Inlet. Lavoie noticed he hadn't corked the tin can containing a gallon of gasoline. Unthinkingly, he grabbed the can and put it between his knees to screw the lid on. The nearby stove ignited the fumes. The can blew up in his hands, sending shards of metal flying. Lavoie's face and hands were severely burned. Fortunately, his caribou clothing protected his body or he would have burned to death.

His suffering was intense. He later wrote, "Water was continually running from my sores, producing a burning itchy sensation. Large pieces of burnt skin and flesh fell from my face. I felt feverish and at times cold and unable to eat. I could not even swallow condensed milk. Pioumictou's wife looked after me as a mother."[16]

Lavoie was unable to move for the next two days. On the eighth, they broke camp and headed back to the ship. Every day Pioumictou's wife fed him like a small child, and her attentions helped him gain strength. She licked Lavoie's eyes and eyelids, as an animal would lick its young, but her method was an incredible cure.[17] It prevented his blindness. His companions gave him clothing and wrapped him in a blanket while travelling on the *qamutik*. They reached the *Arctic* at 3:00 a.m. on Thursday, May 11. His face was so badly disfigured by the burn that the watchman failed to recognize him climbing the gangway.

The doctor was immediately awakened to give him medical attention. Captain Bernier attended him day and night for a week until Lavoie was able to get up and around as usual. Dr. Bolduc admitted that the Inuit woman's treatment saved Lavoie's life.

Macdonald wrote of the incident, "Mr. Lavoie's face is in a very bad state. His whiskers and mustache are all burned off and his face is one mass of scabs. I would not have known him when I seen him first if I had not heard he had arrived on board. He will carry many of the marks all the days of his life."[18]

The writer of the official expedition report obviously did not read Lavoie's account of the accident included in the appendix, as he wrote, "Mr. Lavoie reported that he had met with an accident through the explosion of a lamp and was slightly injured, causing him to return to the ship a few days earlier than he had intended."[19]

Lavoie and his party had been away for fifty-seven days and covered 939 miles. His had been an incredible odyssey.

The days were lengthening and the ice and snow melting. The ice was still four feet thick around the ship, though. The men began preparing to leave the bay. The ship was caulked and repainted. The hold was emptied onto the ice, then the stores were repacked on top of the ballast and a complete inventory of it all was taken.

By June, wildlife was returning to Arctic Bay. The sea ice was becoming porous and the men spread ashes before the ship's stern to speed up its melting. They also cut a channel in front of the ship for it to move through.

However, with the rest of the bay and Admiralty Inlet choked with ice, the ship was not going anywhere.

July 7 marked the one-year anniversary of the *Arctic*'s departure from Quebec City. The anchor, which had been hauled up in the fall, was let go in eighteen fathoms of water. The dogs were taken back on board and put in a pen for the voyage. All was in anticipation of leaving the harbour.

On the ninth, the villagers came out to the *Arctic* to bid farewell. That afternoon the ship broke free of the ice. The anchor's chain was let out to sixty fathoms. The *Arctic* was ready to depart at a moment's notice. Bernier climbed to the top of King George V Mountain to have a look. There was no water in sight. Adams Sound had not broken up yet. Admiralty Inlet was still thick with ice too. It would be some time before the *Arctic* could leave the bay.

Ten days later, there was still no movement of the ice in the inlet whatsoever. The ship made its first effort to steam out of its anchorage toward Adams Sound, but was halted five miles out of the bay. On July 21, the ship made some progress north through Admiralty Inlet but was soon

The Arctic *in ice.*

Richard Finnie, Library and Archives Canada, PA-207174

beset by ice. The ship began to drift backwards in a southward direction, and remained at the mercy of the moving ice. Five days later, it was once again abreast of Adams Sound. They were back where they started.

Finally, on July 29, the engineer "got up steam" and, with the men pushing the ice away from the boat with boat hooks, they managed to finally break clear of Admiralty Inlet. They steered the ship around the top of Baffin Island, only to find Navy Board Inlet still choked with ice. Officers were on watch day and night. It was another week before the expedition reached Albert Harbour and dropped anchor. Second Officer Janes immediately came aboard.

From here, a number of exploring parties were sent out. Lavoie had recovered enough to join Morin's exploring party to Milne Inlet in the steam launch to do some prospecting. Bernier and Van Koenig set out to visit a place near Salmon River where Janes had spotted coal. They hiked up a nearby mountain and found narwhal bones at 1,250 feet and a tree trunk lying on its side at 1,750 feet elevation. They cut a chunk out of it to bring back to scientists in Ottawa.

By August 16, all explorations were completed and the captain decided to traverse the narrow Fury and Hecla Strait, which was the quickest route to Hudson Strait — if it was passable.[20] Throughout the winter Bernier had consulted a number of Inuit who had travelled along that coastline for their assessment of the ice conditions. These men had an expansive knowledge of the region in question, and were able to outline on paper the coasts and channel. Their knowledge had been both acquired first-hand and passed down for generations.

They told him that no two seasons were alike. Some years it would be entirely closed by ice. Wakeham had noted the massive old ice discharging from Foxe Channel into Hudson Bay in 1897. This route had long proven treacherous for wooden vessels.

Bernier was game to try it. And the *Arctic* headed to Prince Regent Inlet, and got as far south as Cape Kater. Observations from the crow's nest offered no encouragement. A solid mass of ice prevented their progress. Bernier consulted Lavoie, who had first-hand knowledge of the region, having travelled the coast that spring. Lavoie agreed that the strait was absolutely impassable. They would have to return to Quebec by the usual route, up and along the Baffin Island coast.

Third Mate Macdonald wrote in his diary on August 17, 1911, "The captain thinks it is impossible to get to Fury and Hecla Strait as the Gulf of Boothia seems to be full of ice, and turned around and proceeded north again. It does not take much ice to frighten the captain when he does not want to go any place."

Despite what Macdonald thought, Bernier knew what he was doing. The *Arctic* turned its bow north and, with the advantage of a south southeast wind, passed out of the heavy ice. The ship called in at Pond Inlet, but didn't stay long, and carried on along the coast of Baffin.

On August 31, they reached the entrance to Cumberland Sound. A course was steered for Kekerten Island. On September 2, Captain Bernier, wearing his fishery officer hat, went ashore to visit the whaling stations and issue licences. He was accompanied by Lavoie, the appointed customs officer, and collected duties on traded merchandise, such as furs. The vessel then sailed for Blacklead Island, where the men carried out the same duties, as well as delivered books to the Inuit who were living there. These books had been translated into Inuktitut by Reverend Peck, who had moved to Toronto.

The *Arctic* continued on its southward voyage, stopping at Port Burwell to issue licences to a whaling vessel. The ship stayed at Port Burwell five days before casting off on September 12. The weather was fine, "clear enough to permit the Officers to count the Button islands; the number is thirty-seven."[21] The rest of the journey down the Labrador coast and up the St. Lawrence was uneventful.

At fifteen minutes after midnight on Monday, September 25, 1911, the *Arctic* dropped anchor in the harbour of Quebec City, having travelled over ten thousand miles, covering a total of four thousand miles on sledging trips alone.[22] The ship had returned safely without damage, other than the usual wear and tear expected from sailing in ice-strewn Arctic waters.

THE *ARCTIC*'S RETURN

Four days before the *Arctic*'s return, on September 21, 1911, the Liberals were defeated in the federal election. With them went Bernier's political support.

Bernier had claimed all the islands for Canada, so it looked like he would now be relegated to the role of fishery officer. He was much too ambitious a man for such a job. Anticipating this, he had begun to make plans for his departure from government service before he had embarked on this last northern voyage.

In May 1910, Bernier had been granted a tract of 960 acres of land, for one dollar, in the area south of Pond Inlet near Albert Harbour. He modestly named his property *Berniera*. He also bought the house and outbuildings that had made up the whaling station owned by the Dundee whaling firm of Robert Kinnes & Sons. A year later, he purchased thirty acres at Button Point, on Bylot Island, and another sixty acres at the mouth of the Salmon River. This effectively made him the first official landowner on North Baffin Island.

Bernier was a shrewd businessman who had made successful financial business ventures early in his maritime career. Now he would be in the fur-trading business. However, he still needed a ship to get to Baffin Island. Being captain of a government ship was his best means of achieving that, although that option was soon jeopardized.

After the *Arctic*'s return in September 1911, there were complaints that Bernier had traded extensively with the Inuit. Assistant Steward Joseph-Eugène Mathé told a Quebec newspaper that Bernier had traded government goods for personal gain. He was accused of trading items from the very government caches that he had set up on previous voyages.

Mathé sent formal letters of complaint to the minister of Marine and Fisheries, the minister of the interior, and the minister of justice. He was supported by O.J. Morin, Bernier's first officer and right-hand man on the last two voyages. This is surprising, but the details behind Morin's dissatisfaction with Bernier are not clear. Robert Janes also had bitter complaints against the captain, claiming he had not been properly paid for work he had done for Bernier during his stint in Pond Inlet.[23]

Another whistleblower was the historiographer Fabien Vanasse, who had been with Bernier on all four of his Arctic expeditions. His diary accounts are filled with biting comments about the captain and other crew members, which calls into question his role as objective documenter. He was one of those who reported that Bernier had pilfered the caches belonging to the federal government, and made big profits with the furs.

In spite of the whiff of scandal this held, Bernier still had supporters in Parliament. On March 18, 1912, the Honourable Rodolphe Lemieux, Liberal member for Gaspé, stood in the House: "Perhaps I may be permitted to say here that the government ought to recognize the work done by Captain Bernier in the far north. The Captain ought to receive through the recommendation of this minister the recognition generally given to an old officer of the Crown."[24]

Despite such support, an inquiry was held into the allegations in April 1912. In the end, Bernier was exonerated. There was nothing in his contract that prohibited him from trading with the Inuit for his own gain.[25] However, he was not reinstated as captain of the *Arctic*. His days as a representative of the government had come to an end.[26] And so had his free ticket north.

Bernier's achievements had been impressive, though. He had spent three winters in the Arctic, travelled over thirty thousand miles, and enforced government authority and jurisdiction by collecting customs duties and issuing hunting and fishing licences.[27] Most importantly, he had helped secure Canada's claim to the entire Arctic by annexing all the islands for the Dominion.

AFTERWORD

THE HUDSON BAY SURVEYS

No government patrol was sent to the Arctic Archipelago in the summer of 1912. The *Arctic* did go north that summer, however, but without Bernier at the helm. The ship only went as far as Hudson Strait as part of a four-month expedition for the Hydrographic Survey of Canada. The *Arctic* was required for the third and final year of surveying the Hudson waters in support, once again, of building a railway to Hudson Bay.

While Bernier was claiming the Arctic islands for Canada, the government was considering more economic uses of its North. In 1909, the idea of a Hudson Bay shipping route to European markets was revived. Once again, the project looked like it had the potential to succeed and received approval from the Dominion government.

Hydrographic surveys were ordered of the harbours at Nelson and Churchill the summer of 1910 to report on them "as desirable termini for railways, or rather whether or not they can be made ports to be used with safety by ocean-going vessels."[1] These surveys would ultimately determine which would be the better harbour. The decision, apparently, had not been properly settled by the expeditions carried out for this purpose by Gordon and Wakeham.

During the summers of 1910, 1911, and 1912, hydrographic surveys were conducted of the harbours at Churchill and the Nelson River. As well, a magnetic survey was to be conducted of Hudson Strait and Hudson Bay in the summer of 1911. For this job the government purchased the schooner *Burleigh*. Thirty-one-year-old W.E.W. Jackson, of the Toronto

Observatory, was in command of this particular expedition. Jackson had been the meteorologist on Bernier's 1908–09 trip.

The Hudson waters had long foiled navigators by making their compasses unreliable. Lieutenant Andrew Gordon had noted the issue in his 1886 final report: "The last, and indeed the most serious, difficulty that I anticipate is in the faulty working of the compasses."[2] Gordon detailed that iron ships, which would be the shipping vessels used to traverse the Hudson Bay route, were most at risk for compass deviation. Thus the necessity of making a more accurate magnetic survey of Hudson Bay and Strait would give ships' captains an advantage of knowing how to make allowance for the deviation of the compasses.

Jackson's magnetic survey aboard the *Burleigh* progressed no farther than Hudson Strait under its own power. The *Burleigh*'s "auxiliary gasolene [sic] engine installed for manoeuvering during observations at sea" was not sufficient to propel it any great distance.[3] Without a steam engine, the *Burleigh* had to be towed by the main survey ship, *Minto*, up to Hudson Strait. It was cut adrift from the *Minto* at the mouth of the strait shortly after the ships arrived on July 27.

The *Burleigh* was damaged by the frequent buffeting in the ice of Hudson Strait, and by July 30 was leaking so badly that the ship was forced to return south. The *Burleigh* limped back to Halifax, arriving September 7. The magnetic work was deferred for another year.

The following summer of 1912, the steamer *Arctic*, no longer required for use in High Arctic waters, replaced the *Burleigh*, and Jackson was again in charge of the magnetic surveys.[4] This was his second voyage aboard the *Arctic*. Captain Joseph Couillard was captain of the *Arctic* that summer. Only two crew members had sailed aboard the *Arctic* before: Paul Tremblay, waiter on the 1910–11 expedition crew list, was the second mate, and John Van Koenig was still the *Arctic*'s chief engineer. No one knew the workings of the ship's engines and boilers better.

Jackson successfully carried out the magnetic survey of Hudson Strait and Hudson Bay that summer. No doubt the use of a steamer built for work in Arctic waters was of huge benefit to the project. Jackson was able to report on magnetic observations along the route from the Atlantic to Churchill and Nelson. His were the first significant magnetic observations since those made by Gordon in the 1880s.

After the 1912 voyage to Hudson Bay, the *Arctic* was used as lightship No. 20 on the Lower Traverse of the St. Lawrence River. Government-operated lightships were manned mobile lighthouses. The ship's mizzen-mast was replaced with a tower that had a powerful Fresnel-lens searchlight on it. Lightships were anchored in dangerous waters to aid marine traffic navigation and provide additional guidance into port.[5] It was a less than glorious retirement for a ship that had seen more exciting northern service.

THE HUDSON BAY RAILWAY

Construction of the Hudson Bay Railway was a long, drawn-out affair, with efforts thwarted by economic, political, and geographic issues.

Despite the recommendations of the official expedition reports, the Hudson Bay Railway Company favoured the more southerly port at the mouth of the Nelson River, as it was a physically shorter distance from Winnipeg, which meant cheaper railroad construction. When the lines between The Pas and Churchill and The Pas and the mouth of the Nelson River were surveyed in 1908, Nelson was several million dollars cheaper to build. It was, therefore, chosen as the location for the port on Hudson Bay.[6]

Work began on the Hudson Bay line to Port Nelson, but the geography proved a major difficulty to overcome. Construction over frozen muskeg and permafrost posed daunting challenges. A considerable amount of work was carried out both on the railroad to and the port of Nelson. At one point, over seven hundred men were living and working in Nelson. Once Canada entered the First World War in 1914, government financial backing for the railway dwindled, and construction ceased in 1917.

In 1926, the new Mackenzie King government vowed to complete the Hudson Bay Railway. In 1927, Churchill was definitively decided on as the port of destination, and the final length of track was laid on March 29, 1929. That September, the first shipment of wheat travelled the iron road. The total cost of the railway exceeded forty-five million dollars.[7]

The Hudson Bay Railway never proved to be as lucrative as expected. The short shipping season was a handicap. Churchill, Canada's only Arctic seaport, was owned and operated by the federal government until 1997, when the American company OmniTRAX bought the money-losing port for seven dollars, then took over the Hudson Bay Railway. Ships that now dock at the port of Churchill are up to 956 feet long and have a displacement of seventy thousand tons, a size incomprehensible to the men who commanded wooden steamships through Hudson Strait and across the bay more than a century ago.[8]

The current shipping season is from mid-July until the beginning of November, only a few weeks longer than Gordon and Wakeham had recommended.

The Expedition Men

After Bernier's final government expedition in 1911, no efforts were made to explore, map, or administer the Arctic islands until a major expedition to the Western Arctic was mounted by Vilhjalmur Stefansson from 1913 to 1918.

Without a doubt, those first men who ventured into the Arctic on Dominion government expeditions are to be lauded for their trailblazing efforts and contribution to our knowledge of the Canadian Subarctic and Arctic. Many who participated in and led the Dominion government's northern expeditions went on to have illustrious careers.

After the expeditions, the Hudson Strait observers and station men returned to their various cities and jobs. They were an outstanding group of young men, considering they had volunteered to spend a year in utter isolation in a foreign land away from all amenities. They were men of science who were up for adventure. Many of them were pioneers in their profession who went on to make their own contributions to Canadian society.

William Ashe, observer at Ashe Inlet, had been sub-assistant astronomer on the International Boundary Commission in 1872. He replaced his father as director of the Quebec Observatory in 1886.

Herbert Burwell went to Vancouver in 1887. He joined the civil engineering firm of Gardener and Hermon, which oversaw the city's water supply. Burwell was personally in charge of Capilano Creek and built the intake and settling basins. His name was bestowed on a second geographical location in 1927 when Mount Burwell, on the east side of Lynn Creek, north of Vancouver, was named in his honour.

Robert Stupart became director of the Meteorological Service. He was instrumental in the expansion of the service across western and northern Canada. He was knighted for his work in 1916.

James Tyrrell and his brother, Joseph, completed an epic 3,200-mile canoe and snowshoe trek across the barren lands of the Northwest Territories from Lake Athabasca to Hudson Bay via the Dubawnt and Thelon Rivers in 1893. In 1900, Tyrrell led a Dominion Lands Survey expedition through this same Keewatin District of the NWT.

Robert Bell was appointed acting director of the Geological Survey of Canada from 1901 to 1906. Bell then held the position of chief geologist until he resigned from the survey in 1908. Under his leadership, however, increasing attention was paid to the mineral potential of the country.

William Wakeham was commissioned to lead a number of high-level fisheries studies for the government. The larger bay west of Stupart Bay was named Wakeham Bay after his 1897 expedition. Wakeham reached a level of distinction in having nine geographical features from Hudson Strait to the Gaspé named in his honour.

Albert Peter Low became director of the Geological Survey of Canada in 1906. In 1907, he became the first deputy minister of the Department of Mines.

George Albert Young, Low's assistant on the 1897 expedition, was an economic and structural geologist. He became chief geologist of the Geological Survey of Canada in 1924.

Walter Erastus Weddell Jackson became assistant director of the Meteorological Service, and was involved in the planning for the Second International Polar Year in 1932.

However, of all the men who led government expeditions to the Arctic, Joseph-Elzéar Bernier is the most famous. He was a household name and his exploits were widely known. The geographical societies of Quebec, Canada, and Britain conferred on him due recognition for his work. Bernier was proud to put the initials F.R.G.S. after his name — Fellow of the Royal Geographic Society — a title bestowed upon such eminent explorers as Parry and M'Clintock.

Both Bernier and the *Arctic* were called into service during the summer months from 1922 to 1925 on the Eastern Arctic Patrol, a joint RCMP/ Department of the Interior expedition to Canada's High Eastern Arctic. In 1925, Bernier was seventy-one years old. It was the last voyage for both the captain and his ship. Bernier went into semi-retirement afterward, but continued to give slideshow lectures on his work in the North.

The *Arctic* was sold for scrap. However, the Gulf Iron and Wrecking Company did not succeed in completely "breaking up" the ship. Its complex hull structure was too labour-intensive to dismantle and, with the possibility of extensive dry rot, was not worth the cost of salvaging. It was towed to the south shore of the St. Lawrence River, where it was left wallowing on its side.

Ironically, the floating cemetery where the *Arctic* was abandoned was in sight of Bernier's house in Lévis. Bernier was devastated to see the hulk of his *Arctic* rotting on the sandbar. The ship encapsulated his lifelong ambition to explore the Arctic, and his love for the North and the country he served so patriotically.

The veteran Côte de Sud sea captain rated a half-page obituary in the *Montreal Daily Star* after his death in 1934. "The 82-year-old explorer put up a valiant fight against death, clinging tenaciously to life for days when physicians expected him to die any minute." Even his death took on legendary proportions in the obituaries. However, the scope of what he and others did for Canada in visiting the Arctic to study, map, and claim the islands is worthy of legend.

END NOTES

Please visit *http://shadowofthepole.com* to view the complete end notes accompanying this work.

ACKNOWLEDGEMENTS

"Write the story you find" was one of my journalism professor's mottos. The amazing thing, though, is that the story you find is rarely a story that stands alone. It is connected to other stories, other events, other people. Researching one story leads to many other equally fascinating stories that, when told together, form a history.

Likewise, researching and writing this book evolved through encounters with many interconnected people. In 2003, Louise Morin, Captain Bernier's grandniece, gave me his calling card, which ultimately inspired me to tell his story. Since then I have met numerous Arctic experts, both in person and by email or phone, who offered new and additional information. Knowledgeable staff at Library and Archives Canada willingly helped me find obscure files, forgotten journals, and unpublished reports. Jean Mattheson at the Archives' photo division and Martin Legault at the Natural Resources Canada library kindly tracked down incredible old photographs and maps that help bring the expeditions and their companies to life.

Heartfelt thanks to family and friends who were not only supportive, but enthusiastic about a history of early Canadian Arctic expeditions. In particular, my American friend, Patra Beaulieu, spotted all the words that should be spelled the Canadian way. Sara Bannerman blazed the publishing trail before me and shared pointers. My former professors, Lois Sweet and Catherine McKercher, not only taught me to "write the story I found," but were also helpful in directing my path to a publisher.

A very special thank you to Melissa Pitts, director of UBC Press, for believing this book fills a hole in Arctic history. Her advice and that of the peer review group were tremendously helpful in crafting a manuscript for a wide range of readers.

The terrific folks at Dundurn, particularly Margaret Bryant, Shannon Whibbs, Caitlyn Stewart, Cheryl Hawley, and Allison Hirst, expertly guided me through the publication process. Publicist Jim Hatch enlightened me on the benefits of social media as promotion. And I am most grateful to my marvellous editor, Jenny Govier, whose meticulous editing I fully admire and aspire to.

Above all, I am eternally grateful to the two remarkable women whose encouragement and enthusiasm carried me from the first page to the last. My mother, Janet Osborne, and my J-Skool companion Cathy Allison were my first readers, and their insightful comments helped to shape this book. Their constant interest, excitement, and support for my research and writing journey and every single step of this process kept me buoyed. Without the indefatigable support of these two women I would not have succeeded in writing this book.

I also want to thank my father, the first voyageur I knew, and my daughter Gemma, who is following in his footsteps.

SELECTED BIBLIOGRAPHY

BOOKS

Appleton, Thomas E. *Usque Ad Mare: A History of the Canadian Coast Guard and Marine Services.* Ottawa: The Queen's Printer, Department of Transport, 1968.

Barr, William. *The Expeditions of the First International Polar Year, 1882–83.* Calgary: Arctic Institute of North America, 2008.

Beattie, Owen, and John Geiger. *Frozen in Time: The Fate of the Franklin Expedition.* Vancouver: Greystone Books, 1992.

Bernier, Joseph E. *Master Mariner and Arctic Explorer: A Narrative of Sixty Years at Sea from the Logs and Yarns of Captain J.E. Bernier, F.R.G.S., F.R.E.S.* Ottawa: Le Droit, 1939.

Berton, Pierre. *The Arctic Grail: The Quest for the North West Passage and the North Pole, 1818–1909.* Toronto: McClelland and Stewart, 1988.

_____. *Klondike: The Last Great Gold Rush, 1896–1899.* Toronto: Anchor Canada, 1972.

Blake, E. Vale, and Captain George E. Tyson. *Arctic Experiences: Aboard the Doomed* Polaris *Expedition and Six Months Adrift on an Ice-Floe.* New York: Harper and Brothers, 1874; New York: Cooper Square Press, 2002. Page references are to the 2002 edition.

Brown, Robert Craig. *Canada's National Policy, 1883–1900: A Study in American Relations.* Princeton: Princeton University Press, 1964.

Coates, Kenneth S., and William R. Morrison. *Interpreting Canada's North: Selected Readings.* Toronto: Copp Clark Pitman, 1989.

Cooke, Alan, and Clive Holland. *The Exploration of Northern Canada, 500 to 1920: A Chronology.* Toronto: The Arctic History Press, 1978.

Diubaldo, Richard. *Stefansson and the Canadian Arctic.* Montreal: McGill-Queen's University Press, 1978.

Dorion-Robitaille, Yolande. *Captain J.E. Bernier's Contribution to Canadian Sovereignty in the Arctic.* Ottawa: Department of Indian and Northern Affairs, 1978.

Fairley, T.C. *Sverdrup's Arctic Adventures.* London: Longman's Green and Co. Ltd., 1959.

Fleming, Fergus. *Barrow's Boys.* New York: Atlantic Monthly Press, 1998.

Fogelson, Nancy. *Arctic Exploration & International Relations, 1900–1932.* Fairbanks: University of Alaska Press, 1992.

Grant, Shelagh D. *Arctic Justice: On Trial for Murder, Pond Inlet, 1923.* Montreal: McGill-Queen's University Press, 2002.

Hall, D.J. *Clifford Sifton, Volume Two: A Lonely Eminence, 1901–1929.* Vancouver: University of British Columbia Press, 1985.

Harley Eber, Dorothy. *When the Whalers Were Up North: Inuit Memories from the Eastern Arctic.* Montreal: McGill-Queen's University Press, 1989.

Henson, Matthew A. *A Negro at the North Pole.* New York: Frederick A. Stokes Company Publishers, 1912.

Hoehling, Adolph A. *The* Jeannette *Expedition.* New York: Abelard-Schuman, 1967.

Knuckle, Robert. *In the Line of Duty: The Honour Role of the RCMP Since 1873.* Renfrew, ON: General Store Publishing, 1994.

MacEwan, Grant. *The Battle for the Bay.* Saskatoon: Western Producer Book Service, 1975.

Madden, Ryan. "Alaska Boundary Dispute." In *Encyclopedia of the United States of America: Past and Present,* edited by Donald W. Whisenhunt, Supplement Volume 1. Gulf Breeze, FL: Academic International Press, 1995.

Mancini Billson, Janet, and Kyra Mancini. *Inuit Women: Their Powerful Spirit in a Century of Change.* Lanham, MD: Rowman & Littlefield Publishers, 2007.

Markham, Captain Albert Hastings. *The Great Frozen Sea.* London: C. Kegan Paul & Co., 1880.

_____. "Through Hudson Strait and Bay: A Naval Officer's Holiday Trip." In *Good Words For 1888*, Vol. 29, edited by Donald McLeod, 23–28, 116–23, 187–94, 256–64. London: Isbister and Company Ltd., 1888.

Morrison, William R. "Eagle over the Arctic: Americans in the Canadian North, 1867–1985." In Coates, *Interpreting Canada's North*, 169–84.

_____. *Showing the Flag: The Mounted Police and Canadian Sovereignty in the North, 1894–1925*. Vancouver: University of British Columbia Press, 1985.

Nansen, Dr. Fridtjof. *Farthest North: The Incredible Three-Year Voyage to the Frozen Latitudes of the North*. New York: Random House Modern Library Paperback Edition, 1999.

Nares, Captain Sir G.S. *Narrative of a Voyage to the Polar Sea During 1875–76 in H.M. Ships "Alert" and "Discovery."* London: Sampson Low, Marston, Searle, & Rivington, 1878.

Petrone, Penny, ed. *Northern Voices: Inuit Writing in English*. Toronto: University of Toronto Press, 1988.

Phillips, R.A.J. *Canada's North*. Toronto: Macmillan of Canada, 1967.

Ross, W. Gillies, ed. *An Arctic Whaling Diary: The Journal of Captain George Comer in Hudson Bay, 1903–1905*. Toronto: University of Toronto Press, 1984.

Ross, W. Gillies. "Whaling, Inuit, and the Arctic Islands." In Coates, *Interpreting Canada's North*, 235–51.

Saint-Pierre, Marjolaine. *Joseph-Elzéar Bernier: Capitaine et coureur des mers, 1852–1934*. Sillery, QC: Septentrion, 2004.

Schley, W.F., and J.R. Soley. *The Rescue of Greely*. New York: Charles Scribner's Sons, 1885.

Tremblay, Gilberte. *Bernier capitaine à 17 ans*. Ottawa: Lemeac, 1972.

Tuttle, Charles R. *Our North Land: A Full Account of the Canadian North-West and Hudson's Bay Route; Together with a Narrative of the Experiences of the Hudson's Bay Expedition of 1884*. Toronto: C. Blackett Robinson, 1885.

Tyson, George Emory. *The Cruise of the* Florence; *or, extracts from the Journal of the Preliminary Arctic Expedition of 1877–'78*. Washington, DC: James J. Chapman, Publisher, 1879.

Vodden, Christy. *No Stone Unturned: The First 150 Years of the Geological Survey of Canada*. Ottawa: Minister of Supply and Services, 1992.

White, Donny. *In Search of Geraldine Moodie*. Regina: Canadian Plains Research Center, University Of Regina, 1998.

Whitney, Harry Payne. *Hunting with the Eskimos*. Toronto: Cole Publishing, 1910.

Zaslow, Morris. *The Opening of the Canadian North, 1870–1914*. Toronto: McClelland and Stewart, 1971.

_____. *Reading the Rocks: The Story of the Geological Survey of Canada, 1842–1972*. Toronto: Macmillan Company of Canada, in association with the Department of Energy Mines and Resources and Information Canada, Ottawa, 1975.

ARTICLES

Anderson, William. P. "The Hudson-Bay Expedition of 1884," *Science* 5, no. 110 (March 13, 1885): 214.

Ashe, William A. "The Hudson Bay Route," *Science* 10, no. 223 (July 22, 1887): 47.

Baird, P.D. "Planting the Flag North," *Canadian Geographical Review* 83, no. 3 (September 1971): 74–83.

Burant, Jim, Mary Psutka, Joy Williams, and Claude Minotto. "To Photograph the Arctic Frontier, Part VI," *the archivist* 5, no. 1 (January–February 1978): 1–5.

Finnie, Richard S. "Farewell Voyages: Bernier and the *Arctic*," *The Beaver*, Summer 1974, 44–54.

_____. "Bernier and the *Arctic*," *Explorers Journal*, September 1975, 130–39.

Harley Eber, Dorothy. "A Feminine Focus on the Last Frontier," *Arctic Circle*, Spring 1994.

Jampoler, Andrew C.A. "Disaster at Lady Franklin Bay," *Naval History Magazine* 24, no. 4 (August 2010).

Logan, Robert A. "Staking Canada's Arctic Claim," *Sentinel*, November–December 1970.

Luedecke, Cornelia. "The First International Polar Year (1882–83): A Big Science Experiment with Small Science Equipment," *Proceedings of the International Commission on History of Meteorology* 1, no.1 (2004): 55–64.

Mimeault, Mario. "A Dundee Ship in Canada's Arctic: SS *Diana* and William Wakeham's Expedition of 1897," *The Northern Mariner* 8, no. 3 (July 1998).

Thomas, Morley K. "A Brief History of Meteorological Services in Canada, Part 1: 1839–1930," *Atmosphere* 9, no. 1 (1971).

Todd, Alden. "Adolphus Washington Greely (1844–1935)," *Arctic* 38, no. 2 (June 1985): 150–51.

THESES AND GOVERNMENT REPORTS

Bell, Robert. "Summary Report of the Operations of the Geological Survey of Canada," submitted December 31, 1885, as part of the *Annual Report of the Department of the Interior of 1885.*

Bernier, Joseph E. *Report on the Dominion Government Expedition to Arctic Islands and the Hudson Strait on Board the C.G.S. "Arctic," 1906–1907.* Ottawa: C.H. Parmelee, Printer to the King's Most Excellent Majesty, 1909.

_____. *Report on the Dominion Government Expedition to Arctic Islands and the Hudson Strait on Board the D.G.S. "Arctic," 1908–09.* Ottawa: Government Printing Bureau, 1910.

_____. *Report on the Dominion Government Expedition to Northern Waters and Arctic Archipelago of the D.G.S. "Arctic" in 1910, Under Command of J.E. Bernier.* Ottawa: Government Printing Bureau, 1912.

Bovey, J.A. "The Attitudes and Policies of the Federal Government Towards Canada's Northern Territories, 1870–1930." MA history thesis, University of British Columbia, 1967.

Gordon, Andrew R. *Report of the Hudson Bay Expedition under the Command of Lieut. A.R. Gordon, R.N., 1884.*

_____. *Report of the Second Hudson's Bay Expedition Under the Command of Lieut. A.R. Gordon, R.N., 1885.*

_____. *Report of the Hudson's Bay Expedition of 1886, Under the Command of Lieut. A.R. Gordon, R.N., 1887.*

King, W.F. Confidential document, *Report Upon the Title of Canada to the Islands North of the Mainland of Canada.* Ottawa, January 23, 1904.

Low, A.P. *Report on the Dominion Government Expedition to Hudson Bay and the Arctic Islands Aboard the D.G.S. Neptune, 1903-1904.* Ottawa: Government Printing Bureau, 1906.

_____. "Report for the Geological Survey Department," *Sessional Papers* No. 13A, Volume II, Third session of the Eighth Parliament of the Dominion of Canada, Session 1898. Ottawa: S.E. Dawson, Printer to the Queen's Most Excellent Majesty, 1899.

McDonald, Brian J. "Summary of Transits of the Northwest Passage, 1903 to 2002." Department of Fisheries and Oceans, Central and Arctic Region, January 2003.

Minotto, Claude. "Frontière Arctique du Canada: Les expéditions de Joseph Elzéar Bernier, 1895-1925." MA history thesis, McGill University, 1975.

Moodie, John D. "Report of Superintendent J.D. Moodie on Service in Hudson Bay, Per SS *Neptune*, 1903-04," *Sessional Paper*, No. 28, A. 1905.

_____. "Report of Superintendent J.D. Moodie on Service in Hudson Bay (Per SS *Arctic*, 1904-05)," *Sessional Paper*, No. 28, A. 1906.

Taylor, Andrew. *Geographical Discovery & Exploration in the Queen Elizabeth Islands.* Ottawa: Geographical Branch, Department of Mines and Technical Surveys, 1955.

Wakeham, William. *Expedition to Hudson Bay and Cumberland Gulf in the Steamship* Diana *Under the Command of William Wakeham, Marine and Fisheries Canada in the Year 1897.* Ottawa: S.E. Dawson, Printer to the Queen's Most Excellent Majesty, 1898.

Report of the Committee of the House of Commons to Enquire into the Question of the Navigation of Hudson's Bay. Printed by Order of Parliament. Ottawa: MacLean, Roger & Co., 1884. [Found in Appendices to the Journals of the House of Commons, 1884, Vol. 18.]

Report on Hydrographic Surveys, Hudson Bay. Department of Naval Service, *Sessional Paper*, No. 38, 2 George V, A. 1912.

ARCHIVAL SOURCES

Hudson's Bay Company Archives, Winnipeg
    SF Ships — "*Arctic*"

Library and Archives Canada, Ottawa

Collection Joseph-Elzéar Bernier, MG 30, B6.

Lorris Elijah Borden Papers, MG 30, C52, Vol. 2, Typescript Diary.

John D. Craig Fonds, MG 30, B57, Vol. 1, File Despatches 1874–1923.

Richard S. Finnie Fonds, MG 31, C6, Vol. 9, File: Arctic 1974–78, 1923–27.

William Harold Grant Fonds, MG 30, B129, Vol. 1.

Department of the Interior, RG 15.

Department of Marine and Fisheries, RG 42, Vol. 105 and Vol. 338, File 13205A.

House of Commons Debates

Sir Wilfrid Laurier Fonds, MG 26-G, Correspondence, microfilm reel C-754.

Nazaire Levasseur Fonds, MG 30, B21 File, Correspondence 1898–1900.

Albert Peter Low Fonds, MG 30, B33.

Edward Macdonald Fonds, MG 30, B139, R5217-0-8-E, microfiche reel M5506.

RCMP Fonds, RG 18-A, Vol. 302, File 747; Vol. 105; Vol. 293, File 25447 Comptroller Correspondence Series, 1874–1920.

John Alexander Simpson Fonds, MG 30, B48.

INDEX